COOKING
FOR ALL
OCCASIONS

Recipes by Norma MacMillan

Published by Marshall Cavendish Books Limited
58 Old Compton Street
London W1V 5PA

© Marshall Cavendish 1985

ISBN 0 86307 053 1

Printed and bound in Hong Kong by Dai Nippon Printing Co.

COOKING FOR ALL OCCASIONS

Norma McMillan

Marshall Cavendish

CONTENTS

MEAT COOKING   6
Beef and Veal — Lamb and Pork —
Poultry and Game — Quick Cooking

CASSEROLE COOKING   100
Hearty Casseroles — Braises and Hotpots —
Rice Casseroles — Classic Casseroles

COOKING ON A BUDGET   194
Soups — Main Courses — Suppers and Snacks
— Desserts — Baking

Steaks with ham

Metric/Imperial

4 × 300g/10oz steaks (fillet,
 sirloin, etc)
50g/2oz butter
4 ham slices (Parma or Westphalian
 or similar)
1 garlic clove, crushed
1 green pepper, cored, seeded
 and chopped
1 red pepper, cored, seeded
 and chopped
250g/8oz mushrooms, sliced
175ml/6fl oz red wine
175ml/6fl oz double cream

American

4 × 10oz steaks (fillet,
 sirloin, etc)
¼ cup butter
4 ham slices (Parma or Westphalian
 or similar)
1 garlic clove, crushed
1 green pepper, cored, seeded
 and chopped
1 red pepper, cored, seeded
 and chopped
½lb sliced mushrooms
¾ cup red wine
¾ cup heavy cream

Rub the steaks all over with seasoning to taste. Melt the butter in a
frying pan. Add the steaks and fry for 4 minutes on each side for
rare; double the cooking time for medium steaks. Remove from the
heat.
Arrange the ham slices on a serving plate and arrange the steaks on
top. Keep warm.
Add the garlic and peppers to the pan and fry until they have
softened. Add the mushrooms and fry for 3 minutes. Pour over the
wine and bring to the boil. Boil rapidly until the liquid has reduced
by about one-third. Reduce the heat to low and stir in the cream.
Season to taste and simmer for 1 minute.
Pour the sauce over the steaks and serve at once, with plain boiled
rice.   **SERVES 4**

Steaks with mushrooms

Metric/Imperial	American
4 rump steaks	*4 rump steaks*
30ml/2 tbs. chopped tarragon	*2 tbs. chopped tarragon*
60g/2½oz butter	*¼ cup + 1 tbs. butter*
8 large mushrooms	*8 large mushrooms*
100g/4oz mushroom purée	*1 cup mushroom purée*
30ml/2 tbs. chopped parsley	*2 tbs. chopped parsley*

Rub the steaks all over with seasoning to taste, then the tarragon, working the latter into the flesh with your fingertips.

Melt 40g/1½oz (3 tablespoons) of the butter in a large frying pan. Add the steaks and fry for 4 minutes on each side for rare; double the cooking time for medium steaks. Remove from the heat.

Add the remaining butter to the pan. Add the large mushrooms to the pan and fry until browned. Drain on paper towels. Spoon the mushroom purée into the mushroom cavities and arrange two mushrooms on each steak. Serve, sprinkled with parsley.　**SERVES 4**

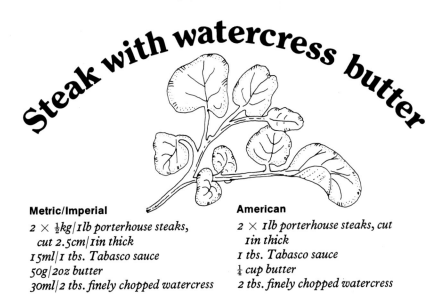

Steak with watercress butter

Metric/Imperial	American
2 × ½kg/1lb porterhouse steaks, cut 2.5cm/1in thick	2 × 1lb porterhouse steaks, cut 1in thick
15ml/1 tbs. Tabasco sauce	1 tbs. Tabasco sauce
50g/2oz butter	¼ cup butter
30ml/2 tbs. finely chopped watercress	2 tbs. finely chopped watercress

Preheat the grill (broiler) to moderately high. Cut each steak in half crossways. Rub each steak with Tabasco sauce and seasoning to taste on both sides. Place on the grill (broiler) rack and cook for about 4 minutes on each side for rare; double the cooking time for medium steaks.

Meanwhile, beat the butter and watercress together. When the steaks are cooked, transfer them to a warmed serving platter. Top each steak with a pat of watercress butter before serving. **SERVES 4**

Variation:

You can make an alternative topping for the steaks by beating together 25g/1oz (2 tablespoons) of butter, 15ml/1 tablespoon of sour cream and 75g/3oz of crumbled Roquefort or other blue cheese until smooth.

Easy roast beef

Metric/Imperial	American
1 × 5kg/10lb aitchbone of beef	1 × 10lb aitchbone of beef
10ml/2 tsp. flour	2 tsp. flour
5ml/1 tsp. butter	1 tsp. butter
30ml/2 tbs. cream	2 tbs. cream
MARINADE	**MARINADE**
4 garlic cloves, crushed	4 garlic cloves, crushed
1 large onion, chopped	1 large onion, chopped
½kg/1lb mushrooms, sliced	1lb mushrooms, sliced
250ml/8fl oz Madeira	1 cup Madeira
250ml/8fl oz red wine	1 cup red wine

Rub the beef with seasoning to taste. Put all the marinade ingredients in a roasting pan, add the beef and marinate in the refrigerator for 24 hours, or overnight, turning occasionally.

Preheat the oven to 220°C/425°F, Gas Mark 7.

Put the pan into the oven and braise for 20 minutes. Reduce the oven temperature to 180°C/350°F, Gas Mark 4 and braise for a further 2½ hours for rare beef, 3 hours for well-done. Transfer the beef to a serving dish and keep hot.

Strain the cooking juices into a saucepan and bring to the boil over high heat. Boil for 10 minutes or until they have reduced by about one-third. Mix the flour and butter to make a paste (beurre manié), and add to the sauce in small pieces. Cook, stirring, until thickened. Stir in the cream. Cut the beef into slices and serve with the sauce.

SERVES 10

Marinated pot roast

Metric/Imperial	American
1 × 3kg/6lb rump steak, rolled and tied	1 × 6lb rump steak, rolled and tied
600ml/1 pint red wine	2½ cups red wine
1 onion, sliced into rings	1 onion, sliced into rings
4 garlic cloves	4 garlic cloves
5ml/1 tsp. dried basil	1 tsp. dried basil
75g/3oz butter	6 tbs. butter
400g/14oz canned tomatoes	14oz canned tomatoes
50g/2oz black olives, stoned	½ cup pitted black olives
10ml/2 tsp. flour	2 tsp. flour
5ml/1 tsp. butter	1 tsp. butter

Put the meat in a large bowl and pour over the wine, onion, garlic and basil. Set aside to marinate at room temperature for 6 hours, turning occasionally. Remove the meat from the marinade and dry on paper towels. Reserve the marinade.

Preheat the oven to 180°C/350°F, Gas Mark 4.

Melt the butter in a large flameproof casserole. Add the meat and fry until it is browned all over. Add the reserved marinade and seasoning to taste, and bring to the boil. Transfer to the oven and cook for 2 hours. Add the drained tomatoes and cook for a further 1 hour, or until the meat is tender. Transfer the meat to a serving dish and keep hot.

Strain the cooking liquid, then return to the cleaned-out casserole. Bring to the boil, then add the olives. Reduce the heat to low. Mix the flour and butter to a paste (beurre manié) and add to the sauce. Cook, stirring, until thickened. Pour over the meat and serve, garnished with parsley. **SERVES 8-10**

Beef teriyaki

Metric/Imperial

1kg/2lb fillet steak, cut into
   5mm/¼in slices

MARINADE

2.5cm/1in root ginger, chopped
2 garlic cloves, crushed
4 spring onions, chopped
25g/1oz soft brown sugar
250ml/8fl oz soya sauce
120ml/4fl oz saké or dry sherry

American

2lb beef tenderloin, cut into
   ¼in slices

MARINADE

1in root ginger, chopped
2 garlic cloves, crushed
4 scallions, chopped
3 tbs. soft brown sugar
1 cup soy sauce
½ cup saké or dry sherry

Combine the marinade ingredients in a large shallow dish and add the steak slices. Set aside to marinate at room temperature for 2 hours. Preheat the grill (broiler) to high. Transfer the steaks to the lined grill (broiler) rack and brush generously with the marinade. Grill (broil) for 3 minutes on each side for rare; double the cooking time for medium steaks.
Serve at once.

SERVES 4

Stir-fried beef with broccoli

Metric/Imperial	American
45ml/3 tbs. soya sauce	3 tbs. soy sauce
15ml/1 tbs. dry sherry	1 tbs. dry sherry
2.5cm/1in root ginger, finely chopped	1in root ginger, finely chopped
60ml/4 tbs. oil	¼ cup oil
½kg/1lb fillet of beef, thinly sliced across the grain into 7.5 × 5cm/3 × 2in pieces	1lb beef tenderloin, thinly sliced across the grain into 3 × 2in pieces
75ml/3fl oz beef stock	⅓ cup beef stock
½kg/1lb broccoli, chopped	1lb broccoli, chopped
15ml/1 tbs. lard	1 tbs. lard
10ml/2 tsp. cornflour dissolved in 60ml/4 tbs. water	2 tsp. cornstarch dissolved in ¼ cup water

Mix together the soy sauce, sherry, ginger and 15ml/1 tablespoon of the oil in a shallow dish. Add the beef pieces and leave to marinate for 5 minutes, turning occasionally.

Heat the remaining oil in a frying pan. Add the beef mixture and stir-fry for 1½ minutes. Remove the beef strips from the pan with a slotted spoon. Add the stock to the pan and bring to the boil. Add the broccoli and cook, stirring, for 1 minute. Cover and simmer gently for 4 minutes. Transfer the broccoli to a warmed serving dish. Keep warm.

Add the lard to the pan and melt it. Return the beef pieces to the pan and stir-fry for 30 seconds. Stir in the dissolved cornflour (cornstarch) and stir-fry for a further 1 minute or until the sauce becomes glossy.

Arrange the beef pieces over the broccoli and pour over the sauce.

SERVES 6

Salt brisket of beef (corned beef)

Metric/Imperial
1 × 2½kg/5lb salt brisket of beef
2 large carrots, sliced
2 onions, sliced
1 garlic clove, crushed
2 bay leaves
6 peppercorns

American
1 × 5lb corned brisket of beef
2 large carrots, sliced
2 onions, sliced
1 garlic clove, crushed
2 bay leaves
6 peppercorns

Soak the meat in water to cover for 3 hours. Drain well and pat dry with paper towels.
Preheat the oven to 170°C/325°F, Gas Mark 3.
Put the meat in an ovenproof casserole and add the remaining ingredients. Pour in boiling water to cover. Cover the casserole and place it in the oven. Cook for 3½ to 4 hours or until the meat is tender. Drain the meat and serve carved into thin slices.   **SERVES 8-10**

Hamburgers

Metric/Imperial

1½kg/3lb minced beef
50g/2oz fresh breadcrumbs
5ml/1 tsp. dried thyme
1 egg, lightly beaten

ACCOMPANIMENTS

3 tomatoes, thinly sliced
1 large onion, sliced into rings
6 lettuce leaves
6 hamburger buns
50g/2oz butter
assorted relishes

American

3lb ground beef
½ cup fresh breadcrumbs
1 tsp. dried thyme
1 egg, lightly beaten

ACCOMPANIMENTS

3 tomatoes, thinly sliced
1 large onion, sliced into rings
6 lettuce leaves
6 hamburger buns
¼ cup butter
assorted relishes

Preheat the grill (broiler) to high and the oven to 140°C/275°F, Gas Mark 1.

Mix the beef, breadcrumbs, thyme and egg together until they are blended. Divide the mixture into six and form patties between the palms of your hands.

Arrange the tomatoes, onion and lettuce on individual serving plates and butter both halves of the hamburger buns. Toast the buns gently in the oven while you cook the hamburgers.

Put the patties on the grill (broiler) rack and cook for 2 minutes on each side. Reduce the temperature to moderate and grill (broil) for a further 5 to 7 minutes on each side, or until the hamburgers are cooked to taste. Serve between the buns, with the salad and assorted relishes.   **SERVES 6**

Veal roll

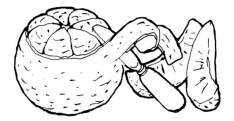

Metric/Imperial
50g/2oz fresh breadcrumbs
15ml/1 tbs. sultanas
grated rind of 1 orange
15ml/1 tbs. chopped parsley
1.25ml/¼ tsp. dried sage
1.25ml/¼ tsp. dried thyme
15ml/1 tbs. chopped onion
1kg/2lb boned breast of veal
100g/4oz butter
15ml/1 tbs. ground allspice
45ml/3 tbs. orange juice

American
1 cup fresh breadcrumbs
1 tbs. seedless white raisins
grated rind of 1 orange
1 tbs. chopped parsley
¼ tsp. dried sage
¼ tsp. dried thyme
1 tbs. chopped onion
2lb boned breast of veal
½ cup butter
1 tbs. ground allspice
3 tbs. orange juice

Preheat the oven to 180°C/350°F, Gas Mark 4.

Mix together the breadcrumbs, sultanas (raisins), orange rind, parsley, sage, thyme, onion and seasoning to taste. Lay the veal flat and spread with the stuffing. Cut 25g/1oz (2 tablespoons) of the butter into small pieces and dot over the stuffing. Roll up the veal and tie at 2.5cm/1in intervals with string.

Cream 25g/1oz (2 tablespoons) of the butter with the allspice and spread over the veal roll. Melt the remaining butter in a roasting pan and place the veal roll in the pan. Pour over the orange juice.

Roast for 1¼ hours, adding more orange juice for basting if the veal looks dry.   **SERVES 4**

Veal escalopes (scallops) with lemon

Metric/Imperial	American
4 veal escalopes	*4 veal scallops*
60ml/4 tbs. lemon juice	*¼ cup lemon juice*
50g/2oz butter	*¼ cup butter*
175ml/6fl oz dry white wine	*¾ cup dry white wine*
1 large lemon, thinly sliced	*1 large lemon, thinly sliced*
5ml/1 tsp. chopped parsley	*1 tsp. chopped parsley*

Put the veal escalopes (scallops) in a shallow dish and sprinkle them with half the lemon juice. Leave for 10 minutes, then pat dry with paper towels. Rub with salt and pepper to taste.

Melt the butter in a frying pan. Add the escalopes (scallops) and fry for 3 to 4 minutes on each side. Remove from the pan. Add the remaining lemon juice and wine to the pan and bring to the boil. Boil for 5 minutes or until well reduced.

Return the escalopes (scallops) to the pan and turn to coat with the liquid. Cook for a further 1 to 2 minutes to reheat through. Serve hot, garnished with lemon slices and parsley. **SERVES 4**

Blanquette of veal

Metric/Imperial	American
700g/1½lb pie veal, cubed	*1½lb stewing veal, cubed*
2 onions, studded with 2 cloves	*2 onions, studded with 2 cloves*
2 carrots, quartered	*2 carrots, quartered*
1 bouquet garni	*1 bouquet garni*
40g/1½oz butter	*3 tbs. butter*
40g/1½oz flour	*6 tbs. flour*
150ml/¼ pint single cream	*⅔ cup light cream*
2 egg yolks	*2 egg yolks*
4 slices of white bread, toasted	*4 slices of white bread, toasted*
and cut into triangles	*and cut into triangles*

Put the veal cubes into a saucepan and add enough water to cover. Bring to the boil, skimming off any scum from the surface of the liquid. Add the onions, carrots, bouquet garni and seasoning to taste. Cover and simmer for 1½ hours, or until the meat is tender. Strain the liquid into a bowl and reserve about 750ml/1¼ pints (3 cups). Keep the veal hot.

Melt the butter in a saucepan. Add the flour and cook, stirring, for 1 minute until smooth. Gradually add the reserved stock and, stirring, bring to the boil. Cook for 3 minutes until the sauce thickens and is smooth. Remove from the heat.

Beat the cream and egg yolks together, then carefully beat in about 45ml/3 tablespoons of the sauce mixture. Gradually whisk the cream-egg yolk mixture into the sauce over gentle heat and cook until hot but not boiling.

Transfer the veal to a serving plate and pour over the sauce. Garnish with the toast triangles before serving. **SERVES 4**

LAMB&PORK

Parsleyed roast lamb

Metric/Imperial

1 × 3kg/6lb leg of lamb
25g/1oz butter, diced
25g/1oz fresh breadcrumbs
30ml/2 tbs. chopped parsley
5ml/1 tsp. dried mint
1 garlic clove, crushed
6 watercress sprigs
1 lemon, sliced

American

1 × 6lb leg of lamb
2 tbs. butter, diced
½ cup fresh breadcrumbs
2 tbs. chopped parsley
1 tsp. dried mint
1 garlic clove, crushed
6 watercress sprigs
1 lemon, sliced

Preheat the oven to 190°C/375°F, Gas Mark 5.
Rub the lamb all over with seasoning to taste and put it into a roasting pan. Scatter over the butter dice and roast for 2 to 2½ hours, or until the juices run out faintly rosy when the meat is pierced with a skewer.
Meanwhile, mix the breadcrumbs, parsley, mint and garlic together until blended.
When the meat is cooked, remove it from the oven and spoon the breadcrumb mixture onto the lamb, pressing it in firmly with your fingers. Reduce the oven temperature to 170°C/325°F, Gas Mark 3 and return to the oven to roast for a further 10 minutes or until the breadcrumbs are golden.
Garnish with watercress and lemon slices and serve cut into thin slices. **SERVES 6-8**

Boned lamb chops with peas

Metric/Imperial	American
shortcrust pastry made with	*pie pastry made with 1 cup flour,*
100g/4oz flour and 50g/2oz fat, etc.	*¼ cup fat, etc.*
½kg/1lb fresh shelled peas	*1lb fresh shelled peas*
40g/1½oz butter	*3 tbs. butter*
8 boned lamb chops (noisettes)	*8 boned lamb chops (noisettes)*

Preheat the oven to 200°C/400°F, Gas Mark 6.
Roll out the dough to about 5mm/¼in thick. Using a 7.5cm/3in pastry cutter, cut it into circles then use to line 8 patty tins (shallow muffin pans). Line the pastry with foil and weigh with dried beans. Bake for 10 minutes. Remove the foil and beans and bake for a further 5 minutes or until golden brown. Remove from the oven and keep warm.
Cook the peas in simmering salted water for 15 to 20 minutes or until tender. Drain well, then purée in a blender, food mill or strainer. Stir 15ml/1 tablespoon of the butter into the pea purée and heat through gently. Keep warm.
Melt the remaining butter in a frying pan. Add the lamb chops and fry for 4 to 6 minutes on each side or until tender but still pink inside. Fill the pastry cases with the pea purée and arrange on a warmed serving platter. Place a lamb chop on top of each and serve. **SERVES 4**

Lamb chops reform

Metric/Imperial	American
100g/4oz cooked ham, minced	*½ cup ground cooked ham*
100g/4oz fresh breadcrumbs	*2 cups fresh breadcrumbs*
1 egg, beaten	*1 egg, beaten*
6 thick lamb chops	*6 thick lamb chops*
25g/1oz butter	*2 tbs. butter*
30ml/2 tbs. oil	*2 tbs. oil*

Preheat the oven to 180°C/350°F, Gas Mark 4.
Mix together the ham, breadcrumbs and seasoning to taste. Dip the chops first in the egg, then in the ham mixture to give a thick coating all over.
Melt the butter with the oil in a frying pan. Add the chops and brown on both sides. Transfer the chops to a baking dish and place the dish in the oven. Cook for 30 minutes, turning the chops over halfway through the cooking. **SERVES 6**

Shashlik (lamb kebabs)

Metric/Imperial

75ml/3fl oz vegetable oil
juice of 1 lemon
2 onions, sliced
1kg/2lb lean lamb, cubed
8 small tomatoes, quartered
1 large green pepper, cored, seeded
 and cut into 2.5cm/1in pieces
1 lemon, cut into wedges

American

⅓ cup vegetable oil
juice of 1 lemon
2 onions, sliced
2lb lean lamb, cubed
8 small tomatoes, quartered
1 large green pepper, cored, seeded
 and cut into 1in. pieces
1 lemon, cut into wedges

Combine the oil, lemon juice, onions and seasoning to taste in a large shallow dish. Arrange the meat cubes in the mixture, cover and marinate in the refrigerator for at least 8 hours.

Preheat the grill (broiler) to high. Thread the cubes onto eight skewers, alternating with tomato quarters and green pepper pieces. Set aside. Strain the marinade into a jug, discarding the contents of the strainer.

Coat the meat and vegetables on the skewers with the strained marinade and grill (broil) for 4 minutes, turning once. Reduce the heat to moderate and grill (broil) for a further 5 to 8 minutes, turning and basting with the marinade occasionally, until the meat is cooked to taste. Garnish with the lemon wedges before serving.   **SERVES 4-6**

Lamb saté

Metric/Imperial

3 garlic cloves, crushed
60ml/4 tbs. soya sauce
15ml/1 tbs. brown sugar
1 small onion, grated
15ml/1 tbs. lemon juice
1.25ml/¼ tsp. salt
1kg/2lb boned leg of lamb, cubed

SAUCE

150ml/¼ pint soya sauce
5ml/1 tsp. ground coriander
1 garlic clove, crushed
1 green chilli, finely chopped
45ml/3 tbs. brown sugar
30ml/2 tbs. dark treacle
15ml/1 tbs. lemon juice

American

3 garlic cloves, crushed
¼ cup soy sauce
1 tbs. brown sugar
1 small onion, grated
1 tbs. lemon juice
¼ tsp. salt
2lb boned leg of lamb, cubed

SAUCE

⅔ cup soy sauce
1 tsp. ground coriander
1 garlic clove, crushed
1 green chili pepper, finely chopped
3 tbs. brown sugar
2 tbs. molasses
1 tbs. lemon juice

Mix together the garlic, soy sauce, sugar, onion, lemon juice and salt in a shallow dish. Add the lamb cubes and turn to coat. Leave to marinate for 1 hour, turning occasionally.

Meanwhile, make the sauce. Put all the sauce ingredients in a saucepan and bring to the boil. Reduce the heat and simmer for 5 minutes.

Preheat the grill (broiler) to moderate. Remove the lamb cubes from the marinade and thread them onto skewers. Grill (broil) for about 12 to 15 minutes, turning frequently or until they are cooked through. Serve with the sauce.

SERVES 4-8

Crown roast of pork with peaches

Metric/Imperial	American
1 crown roast of pork, of 16 chops with a cavity in the centre	*1 crown roast of pork, of 16 chops, with a cavity in the centre*
STUFFING	**STUFFING**
50g/2oz butter	*¼ cup butter*
100g/4oz pickling onions, peeled and blanched	*¼lb pearl onions, peeled and blanched*
175g/6oz cucumber, diced	*1 cup diced cucumber*
1 peach, blanched, peeled, stoned and diced	*1 peach, blanched, peeled, pitted and diced*
60ml/4 tbs. dark treacle	*4 tbs. molasses*
6 peaches, blanched, peeled, stoned and halved	*6 peaches, blanched, peeled, pitted and halved*

Preheat the oven to 220°C/425°F, Gas Mark 7.

Rub the roast all over with seasoning to taste. Fill the cavity with crumpled foil and cover the ends of the bones with foil strips. Roast for 20 minutes. Reduce the oven temperature to 200°C/400°F, Gas Mark 6 and roast for a further 40 minutes.

To prepare the stuffing, melt the butter in a saucepan. Add the onions and fry until they are softened. Add the cucumber and diced peach and fry for 5 minutes. Set aside.

Remove the roast from the oven and remove the foil from the cavity. Spoon the stuffing into the cavity and brush over with the treacle (molasses). Arrange the halved peaches around the roast. Roast for 1 hour, or until the pork is cooked through. Serve hot, garnished with the peach halves. **SERVES 8**

Pork fillet in cream sauce

Metric/Imperial	American
2kg/4lb pork fillets, cubed	4lb pork tenderloin, cubed
3 medium onions, sliced	3 medium onions, sliced
4 medium carrots, sliced	4 medium carrots, sliced
3 celery stalks, chopped	3 celery stalks, chopped
juice of 1 lemon	juice of 1 lemon
300ml/½ pint dry white wine	1¼ cups dry white wine
900ml/1½ pints water	3¾ cups water
40g/1½oz butter	3 tbs. butter
40g/1½oz flour	6 tbs. flour
4 egg yolks	4 egg yolks
300ml/½ pint single cream	1¼ cups light cream

Put the pork, vegetables, lemon juice, wine, water and salt to taste into a saucepan and bring to the boil. Cover and simmer for 1¼ hours or until the pork is tender. Remove the meat and vegetables from the pan with a slotted spoon. Reserve 900ml/1½ pints (3¾ cups) of the cooking liquid.

Melt the butter in the cleaned-out saucepan. Add the flour and cook, stirring, for 1 minute. Gradually stir in the reserved cooking liquid and bring to the boil, stirring. Simmer until smooth and thickened.

Mix together the egg yolks and cream. Add 30ml/2 tablespoons of the hot sauce, then return this mixture to the remaining sauce. Stir in the pork cubes and vegetables and cook gently, stirring, for 8 minutes. Do not allow to boil or the sauce will curdle. **SERVES 8**

Sauerbrauten

Metric/Imperial	American
1 × 1¾kg/3½lb shoulder of pork, boned and rolled	*1 × 3½lb boneless pork blade Boston roast*
1.2 litres/2 pints buttermilk	*2½ pints buttermilk*
SAUCE	**SAUCE**
500ml/16fl oz water	*1 pint water*
450ml/¾ pint red wine	*1¾ cups red wine*
45ml/3 tbs. vinegar	*3 tbs. vinegar*
6 peppercorns, crushed	*6 peppercorns, crushed*
4 juniper berries	*4 juniper berries*
25g/1oz butter	*2 tbs. butter*
25g/1oz flour	*¼ cup flour*
100g/4oz lebkuchen (gingerbread), crumbled	*1 cup crumbled lebkuchen (gingerbread)*
75g/3oz raisins, soaked in 30ml/ 2 tbs. lemon juice	*½ cup raisins, soaked in 2 tbs. lemon juice*

Put the pork in a mixing bowl and pour over the buttermilk. Leave in a cool place to marinate for 2 days, turning occasionally. Drain the pork and pat dry with paper towels.

To make the sauce, put the water, wine and vinegar in a saucepan and bring to the boil. Stir in salt to taste, peppercorns and juniper berries. Put the pork in the pan and bring back to the boil. Cover and simmer for 2½ to 3 hours or until the meat is tender. Transfer the pork to a carving board and keep warm. Strain the cooking liquid and reserve 600ml/1 pint (2½ cups).

Melt the butter in a clean saucepan. Stir in the flour and cook, stirring, for 1 minute. Gradually stir in the reserved cooking liquid and bring to the boil, stirring. Simmer until smooth and thickened. Stir in the lebkuchen and raisins and cook the sauce gently for 10 minutes.

Meanwhile, carve the pork into thin slices and arrange on a warmed serving platter. Serve with the sauce. **SERVES 6**

French pork pie

Metric/Imperial

450g/1lb frozen puff pastry, thawed

1 egg yolk, lightly beaten

FILLING

1kg/2lb lean minced pork
60ml/4 tbs. brandy
40g/1½oz butter
2 spring onions, chopped
1 garlic clove, crushed
15ml/1 tbs. chopped sage
15ml/1 tbs. chopped parsley
15ml/1 tbs. cornflour dissolved
   in 15ml/1 tbs. water

American

1lb frozen puff pastry, thawed

1 egg yolk, lightly beaten

FILLING

2lb lean ground pork
¼ cup brandy
3 tbs. butter
2 scallions, chopped
1 garlic clove, crushed
1 tbs. chopped sage
1 tbs. chopped parsley
1 tbs. cornstarch dissolved
   in 1 tbs. water

First make the filling. Put the pork in a shallow dish, pour over the brandy and leave to marinate for 1 hour. Melt the butter in a frying pan. Add the onions (scallions) and garlic and fry until softened. Stir in the pork and fry, stirring, until it loses its pinkness. Add the sage, parsley and seasoning to taste. Cook for 15 minutes. Remove from the heat and stir in the cornflour (cornstarch).

Preheat the oven to 220°C/425°F, Gas Mark 7.

Divide the dough in half. Roll out one half and use to line a 23cm/9in pie plate (pan). Spoon the filling into the case and moisten the dough edges. Roll out the remaining dough and place over the pie. Seal and cut a large cross in the centre. Use any dough trimmings to make decorative shapes for the top. Brush with beaten egg yolk.

Bake for 5 minutes. Reduce the temperature to 180°C/350°F, Gas Mark 4 and continue baking for a further 30 minutes or until the pastry is deep golden brown. Serve warm or cold. **SERVES 4**

Pork stuffed artichokes

Metric/Imperial	American
4 large globe artichokes	*4 large globe artichokes*
lemon juice	*lemon juice*
STUFFING	**STUFFING**
60ml/4 tbs. oil	*¼ cup oil*
250g/8oz minced pork	*½ lb ground pork*
1 medium onion, chopped	*1 medium onion, chopped*
50g/2oz fresh breadcrumbs	*1 cup fresh breadcrumbs*
30ml/2 tbs. chopped parsley	*2 tbs. chopped parsley*
2.5ml/½ tsp. celery salt	*½ tsp. celery salt*
50g/2oz blanched almonds, chopped	*½ cup chopped blanched almonds*
1 egg, lightly beaten	*1 egg, lightly beaten*

Trim the tips of the artichoke leaves and rub the cut edges with lemon juice. Cut off the top third and pull out the leaves in the centre. Scrape out the fuzzy choke. Rub all cut surfaces with lemon juice again. Stand the artichokes in a saucepan into which they will all fit snugly. Add boiling water, a little salt and more lemon juice, then cover and simmer for 25 minutes or until the bases are tender. Drain upside down in a colander.

Preheat the oven to 180°C/350°F, Gas Mark 4.

To make the stuffing, heat 45ml/3 tablespoons of the oil in a frying pan. Add the pork and onion and fry until the pork loses its pinkness. Remove from the heat and stir in the remaining stuffing ingredients with seasoning to taste.

Arrange the artichokes in a baking dish and fill the centres with the pork stuffing. Pour a little water into the dish and brush the tops of the artichokes with the remaining oil. Cover the dish and place it in the oven. Bake for 30 to 40 minutes. **SERVES 4**

Italian style pork chops

Metric/Imperial	American
6 thick pork loin chops	6 thick pork loin chops
60ml/4 tbs. oil	¼ cup oil
7.5ml/1½ tsp. dried basil	1½ tsp. dried basil
75ml/3fl oz red wine or stock	⅓ cup red wine or stock
½kg/1lb canned tomatoes, drained and chopped	1lb canned tomatoes, drained and chopped
30ml/2 tbs. tomato purée	2 tbs. tomato paste
40g/1½oz butter	3 tbs. butter
3 green peppers, cored, seeded and finely chopped	3 green peppers, cored, seeded and finely chopped
1 onion, thinly sliced	1 onion, thinly sliced
250g/8oz button mushrooms	½lb button mushrooms
15ml/1 tbs. cornflour dissolved in 15ml/1 tbs. water	1 tbs. cornstarch dissolved in 1 tbs. water

Rub the chops with seasoning to taste. Heat the oil in a frying pan. Add the chops, three at a time, and brown on both sides. As the chops brown, remove them from the pan. Pour off almost all the oil from the pan. Stir in the basil and wine or stock and bring to the boil. Add the tomatoes and tomato purée (paste) and mix well. Return the chops to the pan and spoon over the sauce. Cover and cook for 40 minutes, turning the chops occasionally.

Ten minutes before the chops are ready, melt the butter in another frying pan. Add the peppers and onion and fry until the onion is softened. Stir in the mushrooms and cook for a further 3 minutes. Add the vegetables to the pan with the chops and mix well. Cook uncovered for a further 15 minutes.

Arrange the chops and vegetables on a warmed serving platter and keep warm. Stir the cornflour (cornstarch) into the liquid in the pan and simmer, stirring, until thickened. Pour over the chops and serve hot.

SERVES 6

Barbecued spareribs

Metric/Imperial

1½kg/3lb pork spareribs, cut into
1 or 2 rib pieces

SAUCE

30ml/2 tbs. oil
1 garlic clove, crushed
1 large onion, finely chopped
150g/5oz tomato purée
45ml/3 tbs. lemon juice
2.5ml/½ tsp. dried sage
60ml/4 tbs. brown sugar
120ml/4fl oz beef stock
60ml/4 tbs. Worcestershire sauce
10ml/2 tsp. dry mustard

American

3lb pork spareribs, cut into
1 or 2 rib pieces

SAUCE

2 tbs. oil
1 garlic clove, crushed
1 large onion, finely chopped
½ cup tomato paste
3 tbs. lemon juice
½ tsp. dried sage
¼ cup brown sugar
½ cup beef stock
¼ cup Worcestershire sauce
2 tsp. dry mustard

Preheat the oven to 200°C/400°F, Gas Mark 6.
Heat the oil in a frying pan. Add the garlic and onion and fry until softened. Stir in the remaining sauce ingredients and bring to the boil. Simmer for 10 minutes.
Arrange the spareribs on a rack in a roasting pan. Brush with some of the sauce. Place in the oven and cook for 1 to 1½ hours, basting frequently with the remaining sauce, until the ribs are brown and crisp.

SERVES 4

Ham in honey syrup

Metric/Imperial	American
1 × 1½kg/3lb middle leg of gammon, soaked in cold water overnight and drained	*1 × 3lb piece of ham*

HONEY SYRUP

30ml/2 tbs. sugar
60ml/4 tbs. water
30ml/2 tbs. clear honey
30ml/2 tbs. sherry
10ml/2 tsp. cherry brandy
10ml/2 tsp. cornflour dissolved in 45ml/3 tbs. water

HONEY SYRUP

2 tbs. sugar
¼ cup water
2 tbs. clear honey
2 tbs. sherry
2 tsp. cherry brandy
2 tsp. cornstarch dissolved in 3 tbs. water

Put the gammon (ham) in the upper part of a steamer and steam for 2¼ hours. Allow to cool, then cut into 5mm/¼in thick slices. Arrange the slices on a heatproof serving dish. Keep warm.

Mix together all the syrup ingredients in a saucepan. Bring to the boil, stirring constantly. Pour the honey syrup over the ham slices.

Place the serving dish in the top part of the steamer and return to the heat. Steam for 3 minutes. **SERVES 4-6**

Gammon (ham) baked with herbs

Metric/Imperial	American
1 × 1½kg/3lb middle leg of gammon, soaked in cold water overnight and drained	1 × 3lb piece of ham
30ml/2 tbs. chopped parsley	2 tbs. chopped parsley
5ml/1 tsp. dried basil	1 tsp. dried basil
15ml/1 tbs. chopped mint	1 tbs. chopped mint
15ml/1 tbs. chopped chives	1 tbs. chopped chives
15ml/1 tbs. grated lemon rind	1 tbs. grated lemon rind
5ml/1 tsp. grated orange rind	1 tsp. grated orange rind
50g/2oz fresh breadcrumbs	1 cup fresh breadcrumbs
1 egg, lightly beaten	1 egg, lightly beaten

Preheat the oven to 170°C/325°F, Gas Mark 3.

Wrap the gammon (ham) in foil and place on a rack in a roasting pan. Half fill the pan with water and place in the oven. Cook for 2½ hours, turning the gammon (ham) over halfway through cooking. Remove from the oven and leave to cool in the foil for 30 minutes. Do not turn off the oven.

Meanwhile, mix together the remaining ingredients with seasoning to taste. Remove the foil from the gammon (ham) and peel off the skin. Spread the herb mixture over the fat, pressing it on well with your fingertips. Return to the oven and cook for a further 10 to 15 minutes or until the herb mixture is lightly browned. Serve warm or cold.

SERVES 4-6

Chicken marengo

Metric/Imperial	American
6 chicken quarters	6 chicken quarters
75ml/3fl oz oil	⅓ cup oil
2 garlic cloves, finely chopped	2 garlic cloves, finely chopped
4 tomatoes, skinned, seeded and chopped	4 tomatoes, skinned, seeded and chopped
10ml/2 tsp. tomato purée	2 tsp. tomato paste
120ml/4fl oz brandy	½ cup brandy
25g/1oz butter	2 tbs. butter
20-24 button mushroom caps	20-24 button mushroom caps

Rub the chicken pieces with salt and pepper. Heat the oil in a frying pan. Add the chicken pieces and fry until browned on all sides. Add the garlic, cover the pan and cook gently for a further 45 minutes or until the chicken pieces are tender. Transfer the chicken to a serving dish and keep warm.

Pour off all the oil from the pan, leaving about 45ml/3 tablespoons of sediment. Add the tomatoes and tomato purée (paste) and stir well, then stir in the brandy. Cook for 2 to 3 minutes or until piping hot.

Meanwhile, melt the butter in a saucepan. Add the mushroom caps and fry for 3 minutes.

Pour the tomato sauce over the chicken pieces and top with the mushroom caps. Serve garnished with croutons and fried eggs.

SERVES 6

Chicken cacciatora

Metric/Imperial	American
20g/¾oz butter	4 tsp. butter
30ml/2 tbs. oil	2 tbs. oil
2 garlic cloves, crushed	2 garlic cloves, crushed
2 spring onions, chopped	2 scallions, chopped
175g/6oz mushrooms, sliced	1½ cups sliced mushrooms
8 chicken pieces	8 chicken pieces
175ml/6fl oz dry white wine	¾ cup dry white wine
60ml/4 tbs. chicken stock	¼ cup chicken stock
6 tomatoes, skinned, seeded and chopped	6 tomatoes, skinned, seeded and chopped
1 bay leaf	1 bay leaf
5ml/1 tsp. flour	1 tsp. flour
15ml/1 tbs. chopped parsley	1 tbs. chopped parsley

Melt 15g/½oz (1 tablespoon) of the butter with the oil in a saucepan. Add the garlic and spring onions (scallions) and fry until the onions are softened. Add the mushrooms and fry for a further 3 minutes. Remove the vegetables from the pan with a slotted spoon.

Add the chicken pieces to the pan and fry until they are golden brown on all sides. Add seasoning to taste, the wine, stock, tomatoes, bay leaf and onion and mushroom mixture. Bring to the boil, cover and simmer for 40 minutes or until the chicken is tender. Transfer the chicken to a serving dish and keep warm.

Boil the cooking liquid to reduce it slightly. Remove the bay leaf. Mix the flour with the remaining butter to make a paste (beurre manié) and add this in small pieces to the liquid. Cook, stirring, until thickened.

Pour the sauce over the chicken and garnish with the parsley.

SERVES 4-6

Cumin chicken

Metric/Imperial	American
1 × 2½kg/5lb chicken, cut into into 8 serving pieces	*1 × 5lb chicken, cut into 8 serving pieces*
juice of 2 lemons	*juice of 2 lemons*
5ml/1 tsp. salt	*1 tsp. salt*
5ml/1 tsp. cayenne	*1 tsp. cayenne*
60ml/4 tbs. flour	*4 tbs. flour*
50g/2oz butter	*¼ cup butter*
2 medium onions, sliced	*2 medium onions, sliced*
2 garlic cloves, crushed	*2 garlic cloves, crushed*
2.5cm/1in root ginger, chopped	*1in. root ginger, chopped*
10ml/2 tsp. cumin seeds	*2 tsp. cumin seeds*
300ml/10fl oz yogurt	*1¼ cups yogurt*
150ml/¼ pint double cream	*⅔ cup heavy cream*
thinly pared rind of 1 lemon, in one piece	*thinly pared rind of 1 lemon, in one piece*

Rub the chicken pieces all over with lemon juice and set aside for 20 minutes. Pat dry with paper towels.

Mix the salt, cayenne and flour together and roll the chicken pieces in the mixture.

Melt the butter in a deep frying pan. Add the chicken and brown all over. Set aside. Add the onions, garlic, ginger and cumin to the pan and fry until the onions are golden. Stir in the yogurt, cream and lemon rind and return the chicken to the pan. Bring to the boil, reduce the heat to low and cover the pan. Simmer for 1 hour or until the meat is tender. (Uncover for the last 15 minutes to thicken the sauce.)

Serve hot.

SERVES 4-6

Chicken grilled (broiled) with herbs

Metric/Imperial	American
2 × 1kg/2lb chickens, halved lengthways	*2 × 2lb chickens, halved lengthwise*
1 large garlic clove, halved	*1 large garlic clove, halved*
100g/4oz butter	*½ cup butter*
30ml/2 tbs. olive oil	*2 tbs. olive oil*
juice of ½ lemon	*juice of ½ lemon*
15ml/1 tbs. chopped parsley	*1 tbs. chopped parsley*
15ml/1 tbs. chopped basil	*1 tbs. chopped basil*

Preheat the grill (broiler).

Rub the chicken halves all over with the garlic, salt and pepper. Discard the garlic. Melt the butter with the oil in a saucepan. Remove from the heat and stir in the lemon juice, parsley and basil.

Place the chicken halves, skin side down, on the grill (broiler) rack and brush with the herb butter mixture. Cook for 15 minutes, basting frequently with the herb butter mixture, or until tender.

SERVES 4

Roasted poussins with stuffing

Metric/Imperial	American
4 poussins, boned	4 small spring chickens, boned
2.5ml/½ tsp. dried tarragon	½ tsp. dried tarragon
50g/2oz butter, melted	¼ cup butter, melted
STUFFING	**STUFFING**
4 streaky bacon rashers, chopped	4 fatty bacon slices, chopped
25g/1oz butter	2 tbs. butter
1 onion, chopped	1 onion, chopped
1 large bunch watercress, finely chopped	1 large bunch watercress, finely chopped
grated rind of 1 orange	grated rind of 1 orange
1 orange, peeled and chopped	1 orange, peeled and chopped
150g/5oz cooked rice	2 cups cooked rice

Preheat the oven to 190°C/375°F, Gas Mark 5.

To make the stuffing, fry the bacon in a large saucepan until it is crisp and has rendered its fat. Drain on paper towels. Add the butter to the bacon fat and add the onion. Fry until it is softened. Tip into a bowl and add the remaining stuffing ingredients with seasoning to taste. Stir in the bacon.

Lay the poussins (spring chickens) on large sheets of foil and season with salt and pepper and tarragon. Divide the stuffing between the birds then push out the legs so that they are square. Tuck in the wings, fold over the ends then the sides to make a neat parcel, and truss with string. Brush with melted butter and enclose in foil.

Roast for 15 to 20 minutes or until they are cooked through. Uncover the foil and return to the oven to brown for 10 minutes. Serve garnished with extra watercress. **SERVES 4**

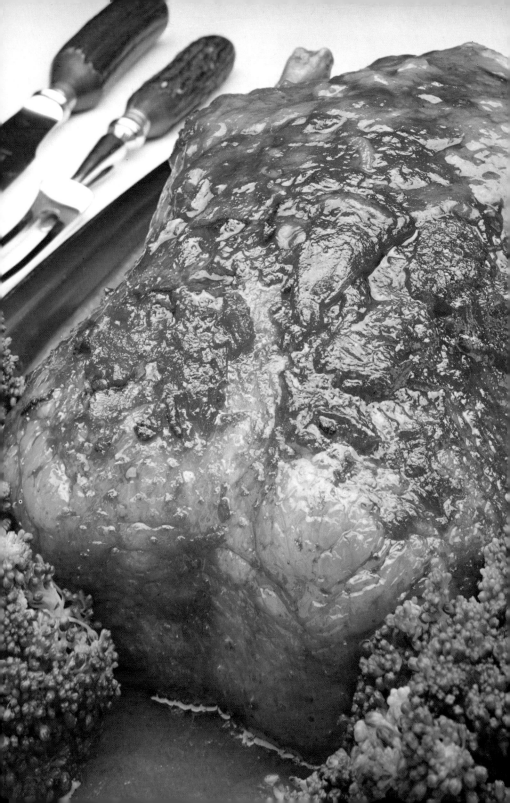

Spiced duck

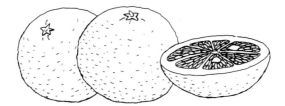

Metric/Imperial	American
1 × 2½kg/5lb duck	*1 × 5lb duck*
5ml/1 tsp. dry mustard	*1 tsp. dry mustard*
1.25ml/¼ tsp. cayenne	*¼ tsp. cayenne*
SAUCE	**SAUCE**
1 garlic clove, crushed	*1 garlic clove, crushed*
1.25ml/¼ tsp. Tabasco sauce	*¼ tsp. Tabasco sauce*
30ml/2 tbs. Worcestershire sauce	*2 tbs. Worcestershire sauce*
30ml/2 tbs. tomato purée	*2 tbs. tomato paste*
60ml/4 tbs. red wine	*¼ cup red wine*
10ml/2 tsp. paprika	*2 tsp. paprika*
grated rind and juice of 1 orange	*grated rind and juice of 1 orange*
30ml/2 tbs. lemon juice	*2 tbs. lemon juice*
5ml/1 tsp. brown sugar	*1 tsp. brown sugar*
10ml/2 tsp. arrowroot dissolved	*2 tsp. arrowroot dissolved*
in 15ml/1 tbs. water	*in 1 tbs. water*

Preheat the oven to 220°C/425°F, Gas Mark 7. Rub the duck all over with mustard and cayenne. Prick the skin and place it in a roasting pan. Roast for 20 minutes.

Mix together the ingredients for the sauce, except the arrowroot, with seasoning to taste. Pour the fat out of the pan and pour the sauce over the duck. Reduce the temperature to 180°C/350°F, Gas Mark 4 and continue roasting for 1 hour, basting every 15 minutes with the sauce in the pan.

Transfer the duck to a warmed serving platter and keep warm. Place the roasting pan on top of the stove over gentle heat and stir in the dissolved arrowroot. Cook, stirring, until thickened. Pour the sauce over the duck and serve.

SERVES 4

Goose pie

Metric/Imperial

*175g/6oz frozen puff pastry,
  thawed*

FILLING

*½kg/1lb cooked goose meat, sliced
175g/6oz goose stuffing, sliced
½kg/1lb cooking apples, peeled,
  cored and thinly sliced
60ml/4 tbs. beef stock
75ml/3fl oz brown sauce*

American

*1½ cups frozen puff pastry,
  thawed*

FILLING

*1lb cooked goose meat, sliced
⅓lb goose stuffing, sliced
1lb cooking apples, peeled,
  cored and thinly sliced
¼ cup beef stock
⅓ cup brown sauce*

Preheat the oven to 220°C/425°F, Gas Mark 7.
Lay one-third of the sliced goose over the bottom of a 1.2 litre/2 pint
(2½ pint) capacity pie dish and cover with one-third of the stuffing
slices. Put half of the apple slices on top and season to taste. Repeat
the layers, ending with stuffing. Pour over the stock and sauce.
Roll out the pastry dough to a circle about 5mm/¼in thick and place
over the pie dish. Trim off the excess dough and seal the dough to
the rim of the dish. Brush with the egg yolk.
Bake for 20 minutes, then reduce the temperature to 190°C/375°F,
Gas Mark 5. Continue baking for 10 minutes or until the pastry is
risen and golden brown. Serve warm. **SERVES 4**

Turkey with cherry stuffing

Metric/Imperial	American
1 × 5½kg/12lb turkey	*1 × 12lb turkey*
100g/4oz butter, melted	*½ cup butter, melted*
STUFFING	**STUFFING**
½kg/1lb canned Morello cherries, chopped (120ml/4fl oz of the syrup reserved)	*1lb canned Bing cherries, chopped, (½ cup of the syrup reserved)*
175g/6oz fresh breadcrumbs	*3 cups fresh breadcrumbs*
1 large egg, beaten	*1 large egg, beaten*
50g/2oz butter	*¼ cup butter*
4 spring onions, chopped	*4 scallions, chopped*
1½kg/3lb pork sausagemeat	*3lb pork sausagemeat*
grated rind and juice of 2 lemons	*grated rind and juice of 2 lemons*
2.5ml/½ tsp. ground allspice	*½ tsp. ground allspice*
5ml/1 tsp. dried basil	*1 tsp. dried basil*

Preheat the oven to 170°C/325°F, Gas Mark 3.
Rub the turkey, inside and out, with salt and pepper. To make the stuffing, mix together the cherry can syrup, breadcrumbs and egg. Leave to soak for 10 minutes. Melt the butter in a saucepan. Add the spring onions (scallions) and fry until softened. Add the sausagemeat and fry until it loses its pinkness. Remove from the heat and beat in the breadcrumb mixture, cherries, lemon rind and juice, allspice, basil and seasoning to taste.

Spoon the stuffing into the stomach cavity of the turkey and arrange in a roasting pan. Brush with some of the melted butter. Place in the oven and roast for 3¾ hours, turning the turkey over halfway through the cooking time and basting occasionally with melted butter. Turn the turkey over again breast upwards. Increase the temperature to 230°C/450°F, Gas Mark 8 and continue roasting for 30 minutes or until the turkey is cooked. **SERVES 12**

Pigeons with cherries

Metric/Imperial	American
75g/3oz butter	6 tbs. butter
4 pigeons	4 pigeons
6 shallots or spring onions, chopped	6 shallots or scallions, chopped
30ml/2 tbs. chopped blanched almonds	2 tbs. chopped blanched almonds
15ml/1 tbs. flour	1 tbs. flour
600ml/1 pint chicken stock	2½ cups chicken stock
1 bouquet garni	1 bouquet garni
½kg/1lb cherries, stoned	1lb cherries, pitted
150ml/¼ pint single cream	⅔ cup light cream

Melt 50g/2oz (¼ cup) of the butter in a saucepan. Add the pigeons and fry until browned on all sides. Remove the pigeons from the pan. Add the shallots and almonds to the pan and fry until the shallots are softened. Sprinkle over the flour and cook, stirring, for 1 minute. Gradually stir in the stock and bring to the boil. Add the bouquet garni and return the pigeons to the pan. Cover and simmer for 1 hour or until tender.

Transfer the pigeons to a warmed serving plate and keep warm. Discard the bouquet garni. Boil the sauce to reduce by one-quarter. Add the cherries, cream and remaining butter to the sauce and cook gently, stirring frequently, until piping hot. Pour the sauce over the pigeons and serve. **SERVES 4**

QUICK COOKING

Liver with bacon

Metric/Imperial

½kg/1lb lamb's or calf's liver,
  thinly sliced
30ml/2 tbs. lemon juice
50g/2oz seasoned flour
2.5ml/½ tsp. cayenne
50g/2oz butter
4-6 lean bacon rashers
chopped parsley

American

1lb lamb or calf liver,
  thinly sliced
2 tbs. lemon juice
½ cup seasoned flour
½ tsp. cayenne
¼ cup butter
4-6 lean bacon slices
chopped parsley

Sprinkle the liver slices with lemon juice and set aside for 10 minutes. Pat dry with paper towels, then coat the slices in the seasoned flour, to which you have added the cayenne.

Melt the butter in a large frying pan. Add the liver slices and cook for 2 to 3 minutes on each side, or until they are just cooked through and tender. Using a slotted spoon, transfer the slices to a warmed serving plate.

Add the bacon slices to the pan and cook them until they are browned all over and cooked through. Drain on paper towels and arrange around the liver slices. Garnish with parsley and more lemon juice if liked, before serving.   **SERVES 4-6**

Kidney & mushroom croutes

Metric/Imperial	American
4 large slices of bread, cut 2cm/¾in thick	4 large slices of bread, cut ¾in thick
1 egg	1 egg
150ml/¼ pint milk	⅔ cup milk
50g/2oz butter	¼ cup butter
4 back bacon rashers, chopped	4 Canadian bacon slices, chopped
4 lambs' kidneys, chopped	4 lamb kidneys, chopped
250g/8oz mushrooms, chopped	½lb mushrooms, chopped
15ml/1 tbs. lemon juice	1 tbs. lemon juice
60ml/4 tbs. oil	¼ cup oil
4 hot poached eggs	4 hot poached eggs

Trim the crusts from the bread and slightly hollow out the centres of the slices so that there is a 1cm/½in indentation. Beat together the egg and milk in a shallow dish. Add the bread slices and turn to coat. Leave to soak for 15 minutes.

Melt half the butter in a saucepan. Add the bacon and fry until golden brown. Add the kidney pieces and fry for a further 5 minutes. Stir in the mushrooms and fry for 3 minutes, then stir in the lemon juice and seasoning to taste. Cook gently for 2 minutes. Remove from the heat and keep warm.

Melt the remaining butter with the oil in frying pan. Add the bread slices and fry for 2 minutes on each side, or until golden brown and crisp. Drain on paper towels and arrange on a warmed serving platter. Spoon the kidney mixture into the indentations in each slice and top each with a poached egg.   **SERVES 4**

Quick beef with macaroni

Metric/Imperial

15ml/1 tbs. oil
2 onions, sliced into rings
1 garlic clove, crushed
½kg/1lb minced beef
5ml/1 tsp. dried oregano
175g/6oz quick-cooking macaroni,
  cooked and drained
400g/14oz canned tomatoes
30ml/2 tbs. tomato purée
10ml/2 tsp. paprika
75g/3oz Cheddar cheese, sliced

American

1 tbs. oil
2 onions, sliced into rings
1 garlic clove, crushed
1lb ground beef
1 tsp. dried oregano
1 cup quick-cooking macaroni,
  cooked and drained
14oz canned tomatoes
2 tbs. tomato paste
2 tsp. paprika
3oz Cheddar cheese, sliced

Preheat the oven to 180°C/350°F, Gas Mark 4.
Heat the oil in a flameproof casserole. Add the onions and garlic and fry until the onions are softened. Stir in the beef and fry until it loses its pinkness. Stir in the oregano, cooked macaroni, undrained tomatoes, tomato purée (paste) and paprika, and bring to the boil. Arrange the cheese slices on the top of the mixture and bake in the oven for 20 minutes or until the cheese has melted and become golden brown. **SERVES 4**

Noodles with ham

Metric/Imperial
½kg/1lb egg noodles
50g/2oz butter
5ml/1 tsp. dried basil
50g/2oz proscuitto, cut into
    thin strips
175g/6oz cooked ham, cut into
    thin strips
1 small garlic sausage, cut into
    thin strips
2 large tomatoes, skinned, seeded
    and cut into strips

American
1lb egg noodles
¼ cup butter
1 tsp. dried basil
2 oz. proscuitto, cut into
    thin strips
¾ cup cooked ham
    strips
1 small garlic sausage, cut into
    thin strips
2 large tomatoes, skinned, seeded
    and cut into strips

Cook the noodles in boiling salted water until they are tender. Drain well and return to the saucepan. Add the butter, seasoning to taste and the basil, and toss until the butter has melted and coats the noodles.

Stir in the remaining ingredients and cook gently for 6 to 8 minutes or until piping hot.   **SERVES 4-6**

Beef in onion & mushroom sauce

Metric/Imperial	American
50g/2oz butter	¼ cup butter
2 large onions, finely chopped	2 large onions, finely chopped
100g/4oz mushrooms, finely chopped	¼lb mushrooms, finely chopped
5ml/1 tsp. flour	1 tsp. flour
150ml/¼ pint beef stock	⅔ cup beef stock
60ml/4 tbs. white wine	¼ cup white wine
1 bay leaf	1 bay leaf
1 garlic clove, crushed	1 garlic clove, crushed
5ml/1 tsp. chopped sage	1 tsp. chopped sage
½kg/1lb cold rare roast beef, thinly sliced	1lb cold rare roast beef, thinly sliced
10ml/2 tsp. lemon juice	2 tsp. lemon juice

Melt the butter in a frying pan. Add the onions and fry until softened. Add the mushrooms and fry for a further 2 minutes. Sprinkle over the flour and stir well, then stir in the stock, wine, bay leaf, garlic, sage and seasoning to taste. Bring to the boil and simmer for 20 minutes. Add the beef and spoon the sauce over the slices. Continue cooking for 5 minutes or until the beef is piping hot.

Transfer the beef slices to a warmed serving platter and keep warm. Stir the lemon juice into the sauce and simmer for a further 3 minutes. Pour the sauce over the beef and serve with sliced boiled potatoes. **SERVES 4**

Rabbit deep-fried in breadcrumbs

Metric/Imperial

1 x 2kg/4lb rabbit, cut into serving portions
60ml/4 tbs. milk
40g/1½oz seasoned flour
1 egg, lightly beaten with 1 tbs. water
75g/3oz breadcrumbs
oil for deep-frying
parsley sprigs (to garnish)

American

1 x 4lb rabbit, cut into serving portions
4 tbs. milk
⅓ cup seasoned flour
1 egg, lightly beaten with 1 tbs. water
1 cup breadcrumbs
oil for deep-frying
parsley sprigs (to garnish)

Dip the rabbit pieces first in the milk then in the flour, shaking off the excess. Set aside for 10 minutes, to allow the coating to dry. Now dip the pieces in the egg mixture, then roll in the breadcrumbs to coat them generously. Store in the refrigerator for 15 minutes.

Fill a large saucepan about one-third full with oil and heat until it is very hot. Arrange the rabbit pieces in a deep-frying basket and carefully lower into the hot oil. Fry for about 20 minutes, or until the pieces are deeply browned and crisp.

Remove from the oil, dry on paper towels and serve at once, garnished with parsley sprigs. **SERVES 4**

Sausage & leek tart

Metric/Imperial	American
shortcrust pastry made with 175g/6oz flour, 75g/3oz fat, etc.	*pie pastry made with 1½ cups flour, 6 tbs. fat, etc.*
½kg/1lb cooked leeks, chopped	*1lb cooked leeks, chopped*
175g/6oz pork sausages, chopped	*6oz pork sausages, chopped*
4 hard-boiled eggs, sliced	*4 hard-cooked eggs, sliced*
300ml/10fl oz double cream	*1¼ cups heavy cream*
50g/2oz Cheddar cheese, grated	*½ cup grated cheese*

Preheat the oven to 200°C/400°F, Gas Mark 6.
Roll out the dough and use to line a 23cm/9in flan dish (pie plate).
Bake blind (unfilled) for about 10 minutes or until the pastry is just set. Reduce the temperature to 180°C/350°F, Gas Mark 4.
Put half the leeks in the bottom of the flan case and cover with sausage, then egg slices. Finish with the remaining leeks.
Put the cream, cheese and seasoning to taste in a small saucepan and cook over low heat until the cheese has melted. Pour the mixture over the leek mixture, then bake the tart for 30 to 35 minutes or until the top is golden and bubbling. Serve hot or cold. **SERVES 4-6**

Toad in the hole

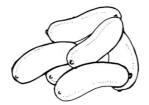

Metric/Imperial

15g/½oz lard
½kg/1lb pork sausages, skinned

BATTER

100g/4oz flour
1.25ml/¼ tsp. salt
1 egg
300ml/½ pint milk

American

1 tbs. lard
1lb pork sausages, skinned

BATTER

1 cup flour
¼ tsp. salt
1 egg
1¼ cups milk

Preheat the oven to 220°C/425°F, Gas Mark 7.

First make the batter. Sift the flour and salt into a mixing bowl. Add the egg and half the milk and beat well, then beat in enough of the remaining milk to make a pouring batter.

Put the lard in a baking dish and place the dish in the oven. When the fat has melted, arrange the sausages in the dish in one layer. Return the dish to the oven and cook for 10 to 15 minutes, turning the sausages to brown on all sides.

Pour over the batter and reduce the temperature to 180°C/350°F, Gas Mark 4. Continue cooking for 30 minutes or until the batter is puffed up and golden brown. **SERVES 4**

Southern-style frankfurters

Metric/Imperial	American
50g/2oz butter	¼ cup butter
1 large onion, chopped	1 large onion, chopped
2 celery stalks, chopped	2 celery stalks, chopped
1 green pepper, cored, seeded and chopped	1 green pepper, cored, seeded and chopped
250g/8oz canned sweetcorn	8oz. canned corn kernels
400g/14oz canned tomatoes	14oz canned tomatoes
½kg/1lb frankfurters, thickly sliced	1lb frankfurters, thickly sliced
5ml/1 tsp. dried oregano	1 tsp. dried oregano
CORN BATTER	**CORN BATTER**
160g/5½oz corn meal	1 cup corn meal
100g/4oz self-raising flour	1 cup self-rising flour
50g/2oz margarine	¼ cup margarine
250ml/8fl oz milk	1 cup milk
1 egg, beaten	1 egg, beaten

To make the batter, mix the corn meal, flour and 5ml/1 teaspoon of salt together. Cut in the margarine until the mixture resembles breadcrumbs. Beat the milk and egg together, then beat into the corn meal mixture until well blended. Set aside.

Melt the butter in a large frying pan. Add the onion, celery and pepper and fry until softened. Stir in the drained corn, undrained tomatoes, frankfurters, oregano and seasoning to taste and bring to the boil. Simmer for 15 minutes, stirring occasionally.

Preheat the oven to 220°C/425°F, Gas Mark 7.

Turn the mixture into a medium ovenproof casserole and pour over the corn bread batter. Bake for 25 to 30 minutes or until the batter is cooked through. Serve hot. **SERVES 4**

German country breakfast

Metric/Imperial	American
50g/2oz butter	¼ cup butter
4 back bacon rashers, diced	4 Canadian bacon slices, diced
1 medium onion, thinly sliced into rings	1 medium onion, thinly sliced into rings
175g/6oz German sausage, such as Fleischwurst, sliced and chopped	6oz German sausage, such as Fleischwurst, sliced and chopped
4 small cooked potatoes, sliced	4 small cooked potatoes, sliced
45ml/3 tbs. grated cheese	3 tbs. grated cheese
4 large eggs, lightly beaten	4 large eggs, lightly beaten
15ml/1 tbs. chopped chives	1 tbs. chopped chives

Melt half the butter in a frying pan. Add the bacon and fry until it is crisp. Stir in the onion, sausage and potato slices with the remaining butter and fry until the vegetables are lightly browned. Stir in seasoning to taste and the cheese, then pour over the eggs. Cook gently, stirring frequently, until the eggs are lightly scrambled. Serve hot, sprinkled with chives. **SERVES 2-3**

Swedish hash

Metric/Imperial	American
75g/3oz butter or margarine	*6 tbs. butter or margarine*
6 medium potatoes, diced	*6 medium potatoes, diced*
2 medium onions, chopped	*2 medium onions, chopped*
350g/12oz cooked beef, diced	*1½ cups diced cooked beef*
100g/4oz cooked lamb, diced	*½ cup diced cooked lamb*
15ml/1 tbs. chopped parsley	*1 tbs. chopped parsley*
4 hot fried eggs	*4 hot fried eggs*

Melt half the butter or margarine in a frying pan. Add the potatoes and fry for 15 to 20 minutes or until they are tender and golden brown. Remove from the pan with a slotted spoon and drain on paper towels.

Melt the remaining butter in the pan, then add the onions and fry until softened. Stir in the beef and lamb and fry for 5 minutes, stirring. Return the potatoes to the pan and cook for a further 5 minutes. Season to taste and sprinkle over the parsley.

Pile the hash on four warmed serving plates and top each portion with a fried egg. **SERVES 4**

CASSEROLE COOKING

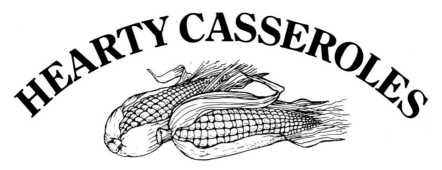

HEARTY CASSEROLES

Beef with corn & tomatoes

Metric/Imperial	American
1kg/2lb topside of beef, cubed	*2lb top round of beef, cubed*
60ml/4 tbs. paprika	*¼ cup paprika*
50g/2oz butter	*¼ cup butter*
2 medium onions, chopped	*2 medium onions, chopped*
2 garlic cloves, crushed	*2 garlic cloves, crushed*
250g/8oz canned tomatoes	*8oz canned tomatoes*
5ml/1 tsp. dried thyme	*1 tsp dried thyme*
1 bay leaf	*1 bay leaf*
2 carrots, sliced	*2 carrots, sliced*
200ml/⅓ pint white wine or stock	*1 cup white wine or stock*
½kg/1lb sweetcorn kernels	*1lb (3 cups) corn kernels*
150ml/¼ pint single cream	*⅔ cup light cream*
30ml/2 tbs. flour	*2 tbs. flour*

Preheat the oven to 180°C/350°F, Gas Mark 4.
Coat the beef cubes with the paprika. Melt the butter in a frying pan. Add the onions and garlic and fry until softened. Transfer to a casserole using a slotted spoon. Add the beef cubes to the pan, in batches, and fry until browned on all sides. Transfer the cubes to the casserole as they brown.

Add the undrained tomatoes, herbs and seasoning to taste, carrots and wine or stock to the pan and bring to the boil, stirring. Pour this mixture into the casserole and stir well. Cover the casserole and place it in the oven. Cook for 1 hour. Stir in the corn and cook for a further 20 minutes, covered.

Mix together the cream and flour. Stir into the mixture in the casserole. Re-cover and continue cooking for 20 minutes or until the beef cubes are tender. Serve hot. **SERVES 4**

Beef stew with chick peas

Metric/Imperial	American
3 bacon rashers, chopped	3 bacon slices, chopped
1½kg/3lb stewing steak, cubed	3lb chuck steak, cubed
30ml/2 tbs. oil	2 tbs. oil
2 large onions, thinly sliced	2 large onions, thinly sliced
2 garlic cloves, crushed	2 garlic cloves, crushed
15ml/1 tbs. flour	1 tbs. flour
1.2 litres/2 pints water	2½ pints water
30ml/2 tbs. tomato purée	2 tbs. tomato paste
350g/12oz tomatoes, skinned and quartered	¾lb tomatoes, skinned and quartered
5ml/1 tsp. dried basil	1 tsp. dried basil
175g/6oz canned and drained chick peas	1 cup canned and drained chick peas

Preheat the oven to 170°C/325°F, Gas Mark 3.
Fry the bacon in a frying pan until it is crisp and has rendered most of its fat. Transfer to a casserole, using a slotted spoon. Add the steak cubes to the pan, in batches, and fry until browned on all sides. Transfer the cubes to the casserole as they brown.
Add the oil to the frying pan. When it is hot, add the onions and garlic and fry until softened. Sprinkle over the flour and cook, stirring, until the flour is golden brown. Gradually stir in the water and bring to the boil, stirring. Stir in the tomato purée (paste), tomatoes, basil and seasoning to taste. Pour into the casserole, cover and place in the oven. Cook for 2 hours.
Add the chick peas, stir well and continue cooking for a further 30 minutes or until the meat is tender. Serve hot. **SERVES 6**

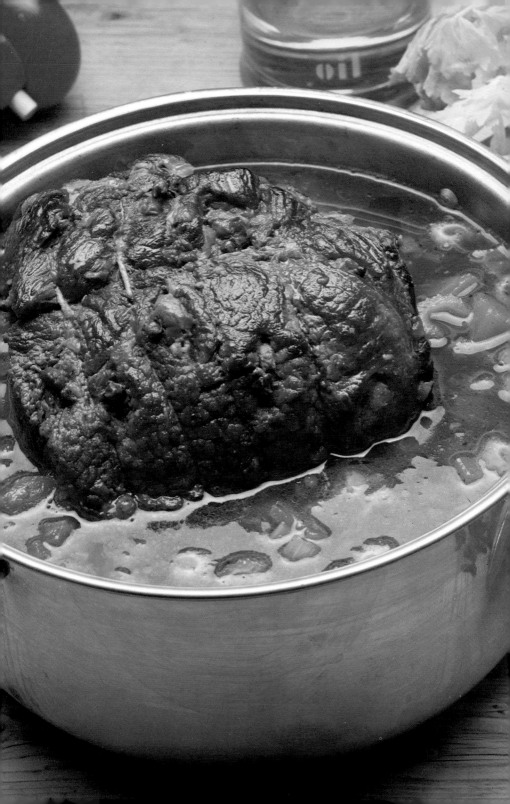

Beef & clove casserole

Metric/Imperial	American
1 garlic clove, crushed	*1 garlic clove, crushed*
5ml/1 tsp. dried marjoram	*1 tsp. dried marjoram*
25g/1oz salt pork	*1oz fatback*
1½kg/3lb lean topside of beef, in one piece	*3lb lean top round of beef, in one piece*
8 cloves	*8 cloves*
100g/4oz butter	*½ cup butter*
250ml/8fl oz red wine	*1 cup red wine*
250ml/8fl oz beef stock	*1 cup beef stock*
1 large onion, chopped	*1 large onion, chopped*
3 carrots, chopped	*3 carrots, chopped*
1 celery stalk, chopped	*1 celery stalk, chopped*

Mix together the garlic, marjoram and seasoning to taste. Cut the salt pork into thin strips and roll each strip in the garlic mixture. Make small incisions in the beef and insert the salt pork strips and the cloves.

Melt the butter in a saucepan. Add the beef and brown on all sides. Add the remaining ingredients with seasoning to taste and bring to the boil. Cover and simmer for 1¾ hours or until the beef is tender.

Transfer the beef to a warmed serving platter and remove the string used to tie it into shape. Slice and strain over some of the cooking juices. Serve hot.   **SERVES 6**

Flank steak stew with herbs

Metric/Imperial	American
40g/1½oz seasoned flour	6 tbs. seasoned flour
1½kg/3lb flank steak, cubed	3lb flank steak, cubed
75g/3oz butter	6 tbs. butter
30ml/2 tbs. oil	2 tbs. oil
2 medium onions, thinly sliced	2 medium onions, thinly sliced
1 garlic clove, crushed	1 garlic clove, crushed
1 large green pepper, cored, seeded and chopped	1 large green pepper, cored, seeded and chopped
50g/2oz walnuts, finely chopped	½ cup finely chopped walnuts
30ml/2 tbs. chopped parsley	2 tbs. chopped parsley
5ml/1 tsp. mixed herbs	1 tsp. mixed herbs
2 bay leaves	2 bay leaves
500ml/16fl oz beef stock	1 pint beef stock
30ml/2 tbs. tomato purée	2 tbs. tomato paste

Coat the beef cubes in all but 1 tablespoon of the seasoned flour. Melt half the butter with the oil in a saucepan. Add the beef cubes, in batches, and brown on all sides. Remove the cubes from the pan as they brown. Add 25g/1oz (2 tablespoons) of the remaining butter to the pan. When it has melted, add the onions, garlic and pepper and fry until the onions are softened. Stir in the walnuts, parsley, mixed herbs, bay leaves, stock, tomato purée (paste) and seasoning to taste and bring to the boil. Return the steak cubes to the pan, cover and simmer for 1½ hours or until the meat is tender.

Mix the reserved flour with the remaining butter to form a paste (beurre manié). Add this to the stew in small pieces, stirring, and simmer until thickened. Remove the bay leaves and serve hot.

SERVES 6

Beef with dumplings

Metric/Imperial	American
1kg/2lb stewing steak, cubed	*2lb chuck steak, cubed*
25g/1oz seasoned flour	*¼ cup seasoned flour*
50g/2oz butter	*4 tbs. butter*
1 large onion, finely chopped	*1 large onion, finely chopped*
1.2 litres/2 pints beef stock	*2½ pints beef stock*
1 bay leaf	*1 bay leaf*
175g/6oz button mushrooms	*6oz button mushrooms*
150ml/¼ pint soured cream	*⅔ cup sour cream*
DUMPLINGS	**DUMPLINGS**
250g/8oz fresh breadcrumbs	*4 cups fresh breadcrumbs*
60ml/4 tbs. water	*¼ cup water*
3 eggs, beaten	*3 eggs, beaten*
22.5ml/1½ tbs. chopped parsley	*1½ tbs. chopped parsley*
1 onion, finely chopped	*1 onion, finely chopped*

Preheat the oven to 170°C/325°F, Gas Mark 3.

Coat the beef cubes in the seasoned flour. Melt the butter in a flame-proof casserole. Add the beef cubes, in batches, and brown on all sides. As the cubes brown, remove them from the casserole. Add the onion to the casserole and fry until softened. Return the beef to the casserole. Stir in the stock and bay leaf. Bring to the boil, cover and transfer to the oven. Cook for 2 hours.

Meanwhile, make the dumplings. Moisten the breadcrumbs with the water, and mix in the eggs, seasoning to taste, parsley and onion. With floured hands, shape the mixture into small dumplings.

Add the dumplings to the casserole with the mushrooms. Spoon the liquid over them, re-cover the casserole and continue cooking for 30 minutes. Remove the bay leaf and spoon over the sour cream before serving. **SERVES 4**

Lamb with celery

Metric/Imperial	American
1kg/2lb lean lamb, cubed	*2lb lean lamb, cubed*
30ml/2 tbs. chopped fennel leaves	*2 tbs. chopped fennel leaves*
25g/1oz flour	*¼ cup flour*
60ml/4 tbs. oil	*¼ cup oil*
1 garlic clove, halved	*1 garlic clove, halved*
3 medium onions, thinly sliced into	*3 medium onions, thinly sliced into*
rings	*rings*
3 celery stalks, chopped	*3 celery stalks, chopped*
½kg/1lb okra, cut into 2.5cm/1in	*1lb okra, cut into 1 in*
pieces	*pieces*
45ml/3 tbs. chopped parsley	*3 tbs. chopped parsley*
250ml/8fl oz white wine or stock	*1 cup white wine or stock*
120ml/4fl oz soured cream	*½ cup sour cream*
120ml/4fl oz double cream	*½ cup heavy cream*
250ml/8fl oz tomato juice	*1 cup tomato juice*
7.5ml/1½ tsp. dried thyme	*1½ tsp. dried thyme*

Season the lamb cubes and rub with the fennel. Leave in a cool place for 1 hour. Coat the cubes with the flour.

Heat the oil with the garlic in a flameproof casserole. Discard the garlic. Add the lamb cubes, in batches, and fry until they are browned on all sides. Remove the cubes from the casserole as they brown. Add the onions to the casserole and fry until softened. Stir in the celery, okra, parsley and wine or stock and bring to the boil. Return the lamb cubes to the casserole, cover and simmer for 15 minutes.

Meanwhile, mix together the sour cream and double (heavy) cream. Stir the cream mixture into the casserole. Re-cover and cook gently for a further 20 minutes.

Preheat the oven to 170°C/325°F, Gas Mark 3.

Stir the tomato juice and thyme into the casserole. Re-cover and transfer to the oven. Cook for 30 to 45 minutes or until the lamb cubes are tender. Serve hot. **SERVES 4**

Lamb stew with vegetables

Metric/Imperial	American
2 small aubergines, cubed	*2 small eggplants, cubed*
50g/2oz seasoned flour	*½ cup seasoned flour*
1½kg/3lb boned lamb, cubed	*3lb boneless lamb, cubed*
2.5ml/½ tsp. grated nutmeg	*½ tsp. grated nutmeg*
2.5ml/½ tsp. dried mint	*½ tsp. dried mint*
2.5ml/½ tsp. turmeric	*½ tsp. turmeric*
45ml/3 tbs. oil	*3 tbs. oil*
2 onions, thinly sliced	*2 onions, thinly sliced*
4 large tomatoes, sliced	*4 large tomatoes, sliced*
250g/8oz courgettes, sliced	*½lb zucchini, sliced*
600ml/1 pint chicken stock	*2½ cups chicken stock*
2 large potatoes, peeled and cubed	*2 large potatoes, peeled and cubed*
200g/7oz canned chick peas, drained	*7oz canned chick peas, drained*

Put the aubergine (eggplant) cubes in a colander and sprinkle with salt. Leave for 30 minutes, then rinse and pat dry with paper towels. Preheat the oven to 180°C/350°F, Gas Mark 4. Coat the lamb cubes with the seasoned flour. Mix together the nutmeg, mint, turmeric and seasoning.

Heat the oil in a flameproof casserole. Add the lamb cubes, in batches, and fry until lightly browned on all sides. Remove the cubes from the pan as they brown. Add the onions to the casserole and fry until softened. Remove the casserole from the heat. Arrange the lamb, aubergines (eggplants), tomatoes and courgettes (zucchini) in the casserole in layers, sprinkling each layer with the spice mixture. Pour in the stock, cover and place the casserole in the oven. Cook for 1 hour.

Stir in the potatoes and chick peas. Return to the oven and continue to cook for 30 to 45 minutes or until tender. Serve hot.   **SERVES 6**

Lamb casserole with leeks

Metric/Imperial	American
25g/1oz butter	2 tbs. butter
25g/1oz flour	¼ cup flour
600ml/1 pint milk	2½ cups milk
8 crushed peppercorns	8 crushed peppercorns
1.25ml/¼ tsp. paprika	¼ tsp. paprika
10ml/2 tsp. Worcestershire sauce	2 tsp. Worcestershire sauce
½kg/1lb shelled fresh peas	3 cups shelled fresh peas
2 medium leeks, chopped	2 medium leeks, chopped
1 celery stalk, chopped	1 celery stalk, chopped
2.5ml/½ tsp. dried sage	½ tsp. dried sage
½kg/1lb cooked lean lamb, diced	2 cups diced lean cooked lamb
30ml/2 tbs. chopped parsley	2 tbs. chopped parsley
45ml/3 tbs. wheat germ	3 tbs. wheat germ
50g/2oz grated cheese	½ cup grated cheese

Melt the butter in a flameproof casserole. Add the flour and cook, stirring, for 2 minutes. Gradually stir in the milk off the heat. Stir in the peppercorns, paprika and Worcestershire sauce and bring to the boil. Simmer until the sauce is smooth and thickened. Stir in the vegetables and sage and cook, stirring frequently, for 5 minutes. Add the lamb and cook gently for 15 minutes. Do not allow the mixture to boil.

Preheat the grill (broiler). Stir in the parsley and half the wheat germ. Remove the casserole from the heat and sprinkle the remaining wheat germ and cheese over the top. Place the casserole under the grill (broiler) and cook until the cheese has melted and the topping is golden brown. Serve hot. **SERVES 4**

Apple & pork casserole

Metric/Imperial	American
50g/2oz butter	*¼ cup butter*
1kg/2lb boned lean pork, cubed	*2lb boneless lean pork, cubed*
2 medium onions, chopped	*2 medium onions, chopped*
2.5ml/½ tsp. dried sage	*½ tsp. dried sage*
2 cooking apples, peeled, cored and thinly sliced	*2 cooking apples, peeled, cored and thinly sliced*
45ml/3 tbs. water	*3 tbs. water*
¾kg/1½lb potatoes, peeled	*1½lb potatoes, peeled*
30ml/2 tbs hot milk	*2 tbs. hot milk*

Preheat the oven to 170°C/325°F, Gas Mark 3.

Grease a casserole with 15g/½oz (1 tablespoon) of the butter. Put about one-third of the pork cubes in the casserole. Mix together the onions, sage and seasoning to taste and sprinkle about half of this over the pork. Cover with half the apple slices. Continue making layers in this way, finishing with pork. Sprinkle over the water. Cover the casserole and place it in the oven. Cook for 2 to 2½ hours or until the pork is tender.

Thirty minutes before the casserole is ready, cook the potatoes in boiling salted water until they are tender. Drain well and mash with the milk and 25g/1oz (2 tablespoons) of the remaining butter. Spread the mashed potatoes over the pork mixture. Cut the remaining butter into small pieces and dot over the potato. Return to the oven and cook for a further 15 minutes or until the top of the potato layer is golden brown. Serve hot. **SERVES 4**

Southern sparerib (boston blade)

Metric/Imperial	American
1 x 1½kg/3lb pork spare rib joint, boned, rolled, cut into four and each piece halved lengthways	3lb boneless pork Boston blade roast, rolled, cut into four and each piece halved lengthwise
50g/2oz seasoned flour	½ cup seasoned flour
30ml/2 tbs. oil	2 tbs. oil
450ml/¾ pint dry cider	1 pint hard cider
GARNISH	**GARNISH**
30ml/2 tbs. olive oil	2 tbs. olive oil
2 garlic cloves, crushed	2 garlic cloves, crushed
1 large onion, thinly sliced	1 large onion, thinly sliced
1 large green pepper, cored, seeded and sliced	1 large green pepper, cored, seeded and sliced
250g/8oz courgettes, sliced	½lb zucchini, sliced
½kg/1lb tomatoes, skinned, seeded and chopped	1lb tomatoes, skinned, seeded and chopped
250ml/8fl oz chicken stock	1 cup chicken stock
15ml/1 tbs. tomato purée	1 tbs. tomato paste
1 bay leaf	1 bay leaf

Preheat the oven to 180°C/350°F, Gas Mark 4.
Coat the meat with the seasoned flour. Heat the oil in a flameproof casserole. Add the pork pieces and brown on all sides. Pour in the cider and bring to the boil. Cover and transfer the casserole to the oven. Cook for 1 to 1¼ hours or until the meat is tender.
Meanwhile, make the garnish. Heat the oil in a frying pan. Add the garlic and onion and fry until softened. Add the pepper and courgettes (zucchini) and cook for a further 3 minutes. Stir in the remaining ingredients and bring to the boil. Simmer for 15 to 20 minutes or until all the vegetables are tender. Remove the bay leaf.
Drain the pork pieces and arrange them in a warmed serving dish. Spoon around the garnish and serve. **SERVES 4**

White meat casserole

Metric/Imperial	American
50g/2oz butter	*¼ cup butter*
1 medium onion, finely chopped	*1 medium onion, finely chopped*
1½kg/3lb stewing veal, cubed	*3lb veal stew meat, cubed*
298g/10½oz canned condensed cream of mushroom soup	*10½oz canned condensed cream of mushroom soup*
250ml/8fl oz milk	*1 cup milk*
5ml/1 tsp. paprika	*1 tsp. paprika*
1.25ml/¼ tsp grated nutmeg	*¼ tsp. grated nutmeg*
250g/8oz button mushrooms, halved	*½lb button mushrooms, halved*

Preheat the oven to 180°C/350°F, Gas Mark 4.

Melt half the butter in a flameproof casserole. Add the onion and fry until softened. Add the veal cubes and fry until they are lightly browned on all sides. Mix the soup with the milk and add to the casserole with the paprika, nutmeg and seasoning to taste. Cover the casserole and transfer it to the oven. Cook for 2 hours.

Melt the remaining butter in a saucepan. Add the mushrooms, cover and cook until they are just tender. Add the mushrooms to the casserole and stir well. Re-cover and cook for a further 30 minutes or until the veal is tender.   **SERVES 6**

Quick cassoulet

Metric/Imperial	American
50g/2oz pork fat, finely diced	2oz pork fatback, finely diced
½kg/1lb pie veal, cubed	1lb veal stew meat, cubed
250g/8oz boned blade of pork, cubed	½lb boneless pork blade steak, cubed
350g/12oz German sausage, thickly sliced	¾lb German sausage, thickly sliced
175g/6oz garlic sausage, sliced	6oz garlic sausage, sliced
10 garlic cloves	10 garlic cloves
400g/14oz canned tomatoes	14oz canned tomatoes
15ml/1 tbs. tomato purée	1 tbs. tomato paste
1kg/2lb canned haricot beans, drained	2lb canned navy beans, drained
1 bouquet garni	1 bouquet garni
275g/10oz canned carrots, drained	10oz canned carrots, drained
5ml/1 tsp. paprika	1 tsp. paprika
175ml/6fl oz red wine or stock	¾ cup red wine or stock

Preheat the oven to 190°C/375°F, Gas Mark 5.

Fry the pork fat in a flameproof casserole until it has rendered some of its fat and the dice are crispy. Add the veal, pork and sausages and fry until browned on all sides. Stir in the garlic, undrained tomatoes, tomato purée (paste), beans and bouquet garni. Cover the casserole and transfer to the oven. Cook for 30 minutes.

Remove the bouquet garni from the casserole and add the carrots, paprika and wine or stock. Stir well, re-cover and continue cooking for 20 minutes. Serve hot. **SERVES 8**

Liver Italian-style

Metric/Imperial	American
100g/4oz butter	*½ cup butter*
2 shallots, finely chopped	*2 shallots, finely chopped*
2 garlic cloves, crushed	*2 garlic cloves, crushed*
6 spring onions, finely chopped	*6 scallions, finely chopped*
125g/4oz mushrooms, sliced	*¼lb mushrooms, sliced*
¾kg/1½lb lamb's liver, thickly sliced and cut into 7.5cm/3in pieces	*1½lb lamb liver, thickly sliced and cut into 3in pieces*
400g/14oz canned tomatoes, chopped	*14oz canned tomatoes, chopped*
30ml/2 tbs. tomato purée	*2 tbs. tomato paste*
120ml/4fl oz beef stock	*½ cup beef stock*
7.5ml/1½ tsp. wine vinegar	*1½ tsp. wine vinegar*
5ml/1 tsp. dried basil	*1 tsp. dried basil*
15ml/1 tbs. chopped parsley	*1 tbs. chopped parsley*

Preheat the oven to 180°C/350°F, Gas Mark 4.
Melt half the butter in a frying pan. Add the shallots, garlic and spring onions (scallions) and fry until softened. Add the mushrooms and fry until they are lightly browned. Transfer the mushroom mixture to a casserole. Add the remaining butter to the pan. When it has melted, add the liver in batches, and fry until browned on all sides. Transfer the pieces to the casserole as they brown.

Add the undrained tomatoes, tomato purée (paste), stock and vinegar to the frying pan and bring to the boil, stirring. Stir in seasoning to taste and the remaining ingredients. Stir this mixture into the casserole. Transfer to the oven and cook 30 to 45 minutes or until the liver is tender. Serve hot. **SERVES 4**

Chicken with beans & corn

Metric/Imperial	American
8 chicken pieces	*8 chicken pieces*
50g/2oz butter	*¼ cup butter*
175g/6oz French beans	*¾ cup green beans*
250g/8oz sweetcorn kernels	*1½ cups corn kernels*
MARINADE	**MARINADE**
250ml/8fl oz orange juice	*1 cup orange juice*
grated rind of 1 large orange	*grated rind of 1 large orange*
2 garlic cloves, crushed	*2 garlic cloves, crushed*
2 shallots, finely chopped	*2 shallots, finely chopped*
2.5ml/½ tsp ground cumin	*½ tsp. ground cumin*
1.25ml/¼ tsp. ground allspice	*¼ tsp. ground allspice*
1.25ml/¼ tsp. mild chilli powder	*¼ tsp. mild chili powder*

Mix together the ingredients for the marinade with seasoning to taste. Add the chicken pieces and leave to marinate for 8 hours, stirring occasionally. Remove the chicken pieces from the marinade and pat dry with paper towels. Reserve the marinade.

Preheat the oven to 180°C/350°F, Gas Mark 4.

Melt the butter in a flameproof casserole. Add the chicken pieces, in batches, and brown on all sides. Return all the chicken pieces to the pot and add the beans, corn and reserved marinade. Bring to the boil, then cover and transfer to the oven. Cook for 1 hour or until the chicken pieces are tender. Serve hot.   **SERVES 4**

Hare stew

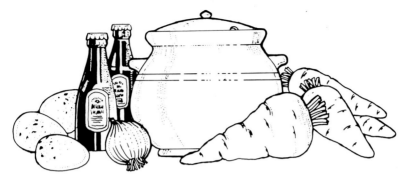

Metric/Imperial

1 x 2½kg/5lb hare, cut into
  serving pieces
50g/2oz seasoned flour
60ml/4 tbs. oil
175g/6oz pickling onions
2 garlic cloves, halved
1 parsnip, quartered
6 small turnips
250g/8oz red cabbage, shredded
300ml/½ pint chicken stock

MARINADE

1 bottle dry white wine
1 large onion, sliced
15ml/1 tbs. peppercorns
5ml/1 tsp. paprika
30ml/2 tbs. olive oil

American

1 x 5lb hare, cut up into
  serving pieces
½ cup seasoned flour
¼ cup oil
6oz pearl onions
2 garlic cloves, halved
1 parsnip, quartered
6 small turnips
½lb red cabbage, shredded
1¼ cups chicken stock

MARINADE

1 bottle dry white wine
1 large onion, sliced
1 tbs. peppercorns
1 tsp. paprika
2 tbs. olive oil

Mix together the marinade ingredients. Add the hare pieces and leave to marinate for 24 hours, turning occasionally. Remove the hare pieces from the marinade and pat dry with paper towels. Strain the marinade and reserve. Coat the hare pieces with the seasoned flour.

Heat the oil in a saucepan. Add the hare pieces, in batches, and brown on all sides. Return the hare pieces to the pan and add the onions, garlic, parsnip, turnips, cabbage, stock and reserved marinade. Bring to the boil, cover and simmer for 3 to 4 hours or until the hare pieces are very tender. Serve hot. **SERVES 8**

Sausage & lentil casserole

Metric/Imperial	American
½kg/1lb lentils	2 cups lentils
1.2 litres/2 pints beef stock	2½ pints beef stock
1 large onion, halved	1 large onion, halved
1 bouquet garni	1 bouquet garni
25g/1oz butter	2 tbs. butter
6 bacon rashers, chopped	6 bacon slices, chopped
2 garlic cloves, chopped	2 garlic cloves, chopped
6 large sausages (such as knackwurst), sliced	6 large sausages (such as knackwurst), sliced
100g/4oz Cheddar cheese, grated	1 cup grated Cheddar cheese

Put the lentils in a saucepan and pour over the stock. Add the onion, bouquet garni and 5ml/1 teaspoon salt. Bring to the boil, then simmer for 1 hour or until the lentils are tender. Drain the lentils, reserving the liquid. Discard the onion and bouquet garni.

Preheat the oven to 180°C/350°F, Gas Mark 4.

Melt the butter in a frying pan. Add the bacon and garlic and fry until the bacon is crisp. Add the sausages and fry for a further 5 minutes, stirring occasionally. Remove from the heat.

Make a layer of half the lentils in a casserole. Cover with the sausages and bacon mixture and sprinkle with pepper. Top with the remaining lentils and pour in the lentil cooking liquid. Sprinkle the cheese over the top and place in the oven. Cook for 1 hour or until the ingredients are piping hot and the cheese is golden brown. Serve hot. **SERVES 6**

Kidney bean & bacon casserole

Metric/Imperial	American
250g/8oz bacon, diced	½lb bacon, diced
1 large onion, finely chopped	1 large onion, finely chopped
2 garlic cloves, crushed	2 garlic cloves, crushed
1 large red pepper, cored, seeded and thinly sliced	1 large red pepper, cored, seeded and thinly sliced
4 celery stalks, cut into 5cm/2 in pieces	4 celery stalks, cut into 2 in pieces
250g/8oz tomatoes, skinned, seeded and chopped	½lb tomatoes, skinned, seeded and chopped
1 bouquet garni	1 bouquet garni
400g/14oz canned red kidney beans, drained	14oz canned red kidney beans, drained
30ml/2 tbs. chopped parsley	2 tbs. chopped parsley
30ml/2 tbs. chopped chives	2 tbs. chopped chives
50g/2oz Parmesan cheese, grated	½ cup grated Parmesan cheese

Fry the bacon in a saucepan until it is crisp and has rendered most of its fat. Add the onion, garlic, pepper and celery and fry until the onion is softened. Stir in the tomatoes, bouquet garni and seasoning to taste. Cover and cook for 30 minutes. Stir in the beans, parsley and chives and cook, covered, for a further 15 minutes. Serve hot, sprinkled with the Parmesan. **SERVES 4**

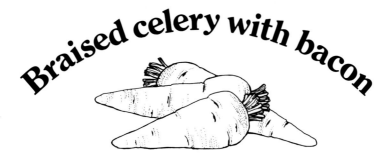

Braised celery with bacon

Metric/Imperial	American
2 small bunches of celery	2 small heads of celery
100g/4oz bacon rashers	¼lb bacon slices
1 small carrot, sliced	1 small carrot, sliced
1 onion, sliced	1 onion, sliced
1 bouquet garni	1 bouquet garni
900ml/1½ pints boiling chicken stock	3¾ cups boiling chicken stock

Preheat the oven to 180°C/350°F, Gas Mark 4.
Blanch the celery stalks in boiling water for 1 minute. Drain. Lay the bacon on the bottom of a casserole. Put in the sliced carrot and onion and place the celery on top. Add the bouquet garni and seasoning to taste and pour in the stock. Cover the casserole and place it in the oven. Cook for 1½ hours. Uncover the casserole and continue cooking for 30 minutes at 200°C/400°F, Gas Mark 6.
Remove the celery from the casserole. Halve the stalks and arrange them in a warmed serving dish. Keep warm. Strain the cooking liquid into a saucepan and boil to reduce. If necessary, thicken the liquid with a little beurre manié (made with 1 tablespoon each of flour and butter mixed to a paste). Pour the liquid over the celery and serve. **SERVES 4**

Barley & mushroom casserole

Metric/Imperial	American
30ml/2 tbs. oil	2 tbs. oil
3 large onions, thinly sliced	3 large onions, thinly sliced
350g/12oz mushrooms, sliced	¾lb mushrooms, sliced
350g/12oz pearl barley	1⅔ cups pearl barley
900g/1lb 14 oz canned tomatoes	1lb 14oz canned tomatoes
175ml/6fl oz chicken stock	¾ cup chicken stock
2 green peppers, cored, seeded and sliced	2 green peppers, cored, seeded and sliced
10ml/2 tsp. chopped thyme	2 tsp. chopped thyme
30ml/2 tbs. chopped parsley	2 tbs. chopped parsley

Preheat the oven to 180°C/350°F, Gas Mark 4.
Heat the oil in a frying pan. Add the onions and fry until softened.
Add the mushrooms and fry for a further 2 minutes.
Put the barley in a casserole and stir in the onions and mushrooms.
Stir in the undrained tomatoes, stock, peppers, thyme and seasoning
to taste. Cover and place in the oven. Cook for 1 hour or until the
barley is tender and most of the liquid has been absorbed. Serve
hot, sprinkled with parsley. **SERVES 6**

Oven-braised beef

Metric/Imperial	American
1½kg/3lb stewing beef, cubed	3lb chuck steak, cubed
75g/3oz seasoned flour	¾ cup seasoned flour
75g/3oz butter	6 tbs. butter
6 medium onions, thinly sliced	6 medium onions, thinly sliced
6 carrots, chopped	6 carrots, chopped
350ml/12fl oz red wine	1½ cups red wine
5ml/1 tsp. grated lemon rind	1 tsp. grated lemon rind
5ml/1 tsp. dried oregano	1 tsp. dried oregano

Preheat the oven to 170°C/325°F, Gas Mark 3.

Coat the beef cubes with the seasoned flour.

Melt 50g/2oz (¼ cup) of the butter in a flameproof casserole. Add the beef cubes, in batches, and fry until they are browned on all sides. Remove the cubes from the pan as they brown. Add the remaining butter to the casserole. When it has melted, add the onions and fry until softened. Add the carrots and fry until they are lightly browned. Stir in the remaining ingredients with seasoning to taste and bring to the boil.

Return the beef cubes to the casserole. Cover and transfer to the oven. Cook for 2 to 2½ hours or until the beef cubes are tender. Serve hot.   **SERVES 6**

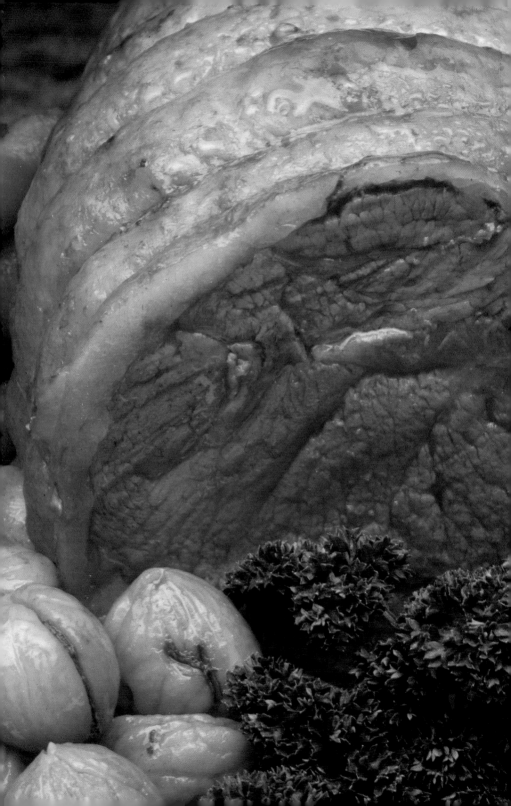

Braised beef with sausages

Metric/Imperial	American
22.5ml/1½ tbs. oil	1½ tbs. oil
1 x 1¾-2kg/3½-4lb boned and rolled sirloin of beef	1 x 3½-4lb beef tenderloin tip roast
1 carrot, sliced	1 carrot, sliced
1 small onion, sliced	1 small onion, sliced
1 bay leaf	1 bay leaf
½kg/1lb chipolata sausages	1lb pork link sausages
½kg/1lb pickling onions	1lb pearl onions
22.5ml/1½ tbs. butter	1½ tbs. butter
5ml/1 tsp. sugar	1 tsp. sugar
300ml/½ pint beef stock	1¼ cups beef stock
7.5ml/1½ tsp. flour	1½ tsp. flour

Preheat the oven to 190°C/375°F, Gas Mark 5.
Heat the oil in a flameproof casserole. Put in the beef and brown lightly on all sides. Remove the beef from the casserole. Add the vegetables to the casserole and fry until lightly browned. Add the bay leaf and seasoning to taste. Put the beef on top of the vegetables, cover and transfer to the oven. Cook for 50 minutes for rare beef. Turn and baste the meat at least twice during cooking.
Meanwhile grill (broil) or fry the sausages. Drain and keep warm.
Parboil the onions for 1 minute, then drain. Return the cleaned-out pan to the heat and add 15ml/1 tablespoon of the butter. When it has melted stir in the sugar, seasoning to taste and onions. Cook gently for 10 minutes or until the onions are tender and glazed.
Transfer the beef to a carving board. Skim the fat from the cooking juices and strain into a saucepan. Stir in the stock and bring to the boil. Boil for 4 minutes. Mix the remaining butter with the flour to make a paste (beurre manié). Add this in small pieces to the cooking liquid, stirring, and simmer until thickened.
Carve the beef in thick slices and garnish with the sausages and onions. Serve with the sauce. **SERVES 6-8**

Braised beef with brandy & wine

Metric/Imperial	American
60ml/4 tbs. oil	*¼ cup oil*
1 x 2.5kg/5lb topside of beef, rolled and tied	*1 x 5lb top round of beef, rolled and tied*
2 large onions, sliced	*2 large onions, sliced*
2 carrots, sliced	*2 carrots, sliced*
2 garlic cloves, crushed	*2 garlic cloves, crushed*
120ml/4fl oz brandy	*½ cup brandy*
300ml/½ pint dry red wine	*1¼ cups dry red wine*
4 bacon rashers, chopped	*4 bacon slices, chopped*
1 bouquet garni	*1 bouquet garni*
3 tomatoes, halved	*3 tomatoes, halved*

Preheat the oven to 150°C/300°F, Gas Mark 2.
Heat the oil in a flameproof casserole. Put in the beef and brown on all sides. Add the onions, carrots and garlic and cook for a further 5 minutes. Stir in the brandy, wine, bacon, bouquet garni and seasoning to taste and bring to the boil. Cover the casserole and transfer it to the oven. Cook for 4 hours or until the meat is very tender.
Transfer the beef to a warmed serving platter. Strain the cooking liquid and skim off all the fat. Serve the beef garnished with the tomatoes and the cooking liquid as a sauce. **SERVES 8**

Country-style lamb

Metric/Imperial	American
1 x 1kg/2lb best end of lamb, chine bone removed	*1 x 2lb lamb rib roast, chine bone removed*
25g/1oz butter	*2 tbs. butter*
45ml/3 tbs. oil	*3 tbs. oil*
1 cooking apple, peeled, cored and chopped	*1 cooking apple, peeled, cored and chopped*
3 medium potatoes, sliced	*3 medium potatoes, sliced*
1 medium onion, thinly sliced	*1 medium onion, thinly sliced*
175ml/6fl oz beef stock	*¾ cup beef stock*
10ml/2 tsp. tomato purée	*2 tsp. tomato paste*
2.5ml/½ tsp. dried marjoram	*½ tsp. dried marjoram*

Preheat the oven to 190°C/375°F, Gas Mark 5.

Cut the flap of bones from the lamb (or have the butcher do this for you) and remove the strips of meat from between the bones. Melt the butter with 15ml/1 tablespoon of the oil in a roasting pan. Put the meat, including the strips of meat, and apple into the pan and place in the oven. Roast for 30 minutes, turning occasionally.

Meanwhile, heat the remaining oil in a frying pan. Add the potato and onion slices and fry for 10 minutes or until the potatoes are lightly browned. Remove from the heat.

Remove the meat from the oven and cut between the bones into chops. Make a layer of about a third of the potato and onion slices in a casserole. Put half the chops on top. Cover with another third of the potato and onion slices and put the remaining chops, meat strips and apple on top. Pour over the juices from the roasting pan and cover with the remaining potato and onion slices.

Mix together the stock, tomato purée (paste), marjoram and seasoning to taste and pour into the casserole. Cover and place in the oven. Cook for 15 minutes. **SERVES 3-4**

Italian braised lamb

Metric/Imperial

1kg/2lb boned shoulder of lamb,
  trimmed and cubed
25g/1oz seasoned flour
2 bacon rashers, diced
30ml/2 tbs. oil
1 onion, finely chopped
1 garlic clove, crushed
250g/8oz canned tomatoes
600ml/1 pint beef stock
1 bay leaf
5ml/1 tsp. dried oregano
3 egg yolks
30ml/2 tbs. lemon juice

American

2lb boned shoulder of lamb, trimmed
  and cubed
¼ cup seasoned flour
2 bacon slices, diced
2 tbs. oil
1 onion, finely chopped
1 garlic clove, crushed
8oz canned tomatoes
2½ cups beef stock
1 bay leaf
1 tsp. dried oregano
3 egg yolks
2 tbs. lemon juice

Preheat the oven to 180°C/350°F, Gas Mark 4.
Coat the lamb cubes with the seasoned flour. Put the bacon in a frying pan and fry until it is crisp and has rendered most of its fat. Remove from the pan with a slotted spoon and place in a casserole. Add the oil to the pan. When it is hot, add the lamb, in batches, and fry until it is browned on all sides. As the cubes brown, transfer them to the casserole. Add the onion and garlic to the pan and fry until softened. Stir in the undrained tomatoes, stock, bay leaf, oregano and seasoning to taste and bring to the boil. Stir into the casserole, cover and place in the oven. Cook for 1¾ hours or until the meat is tender.
Transfer the lamb cubes to a warmed serving dish, using a slotted spoon. Keep warm. Strain the cooking liquid into a saucepan. Skim any fat from the surface.
Mix together the egg yolks and lemon juice and stir in about 45ml/3 tablespoons of the cooking liquid. Whisk this egg mixture into the remaining cooking liquid. Cook gently, stirring, until the sauce thickens enough to coat the back of the spoon. Do not let the sauce boil or it will curdle. Pour the sauce over the lamb and serve hot.

SERVES 4

Cabbage & lamb hotpot

Metric/Imperial

15g/½oz butter
4 large lamb chops
1 medium green cabbage, shredded
2.5ml/½ tsp. dried rosemary
150g/5oz tomato purée
60ml/4 tbs. water

American

1 tbs. butter
4 large lamb chops
1 medium green cabbage, shredded
½ tsp. dried rosemary
½ cup tomato paste
¼ cup water

Preheat the oven to 180°C/350°F, Gas Mark 4.
Melt the butter in a flameproof casserole. Add the chops and brown on both sides. Remove the chops from the casserole.
Add the remaining ingredients to the casserole with seasoning to taste and mix well. Return the chops to the casserole and bury them in the cabbage mixture. Cover the casserole and transfer it to the oven. Cook for 45 minutes or until the meat is tender. Serve hot.   **SERVES 4**

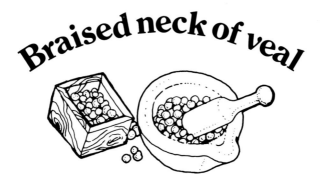

Braised neck of veal

Metric/Imperial	American
1 x 2kg/4lb best end of neck of veal, chine bone removed	*1 x 4lb veal rib roast, chine bone bone removed*
1.25ml/¼ tsp. ground cloves	*¼ tsp. ground cloves*
1.25ml/¼ tsp. ground mace	*¼ tsp. ground mace*
4 bacon rashers	*4 bacon slices*
1 medium onion, finely chopped	*1 medium onion, finely chopped*
1 large carrot, sliced	*1 large carrot, sliced*
2 celery stalks, chopped	*2 celery stalks, chopped*
1 bouquet garni	*1 bouquet garni*
6 black peppercorns	*6 black peppercorns*
350ml/12fl oz chicken stock	*1½ cups chicken stock*
15ml/1 tbs. lemon juice	*1 tbs. lemon juice*

Preheat the oven to 180°C/350°F, Gas Mark 4.

Cut off the short pieces of rib bone from the flap on the veal, or have your butcher do this for you. Rub the meat all over with seasoning, the cloves and mace.

Fry the bacon in a flameproof casserole until it is crisp and has rendered its fat. Discard the bacon. Add the vegetables to the casserole and fry until the onion is softened. Stir in the bouquet garni, peppercorns, stock and lemon juice. Put the veal on top and bring to the boil. Cover and transfer the casserole to the oven. Cook for 2 hours or until the veal is tender. Uncover and continue cooking for a further 20 minutes.

Transfer the veal to a warmed serving dish. Skim the fat from the cooking liquid and strain over the meat.   **SERVES 4-6**

Braised oxtail with celery

Metric/Imperial	American
2 oxtails, cut into pieces	2 oxtails, cut into pieces
50g/2oz seasoned flour	½ cup seasoned flour
75ml/5 tbs. olive oil	5 tbs. olive oil
1 large onion, finely chopped	1 large onion, finely chopped
2 garlic cloves, finely chopped	2 garlic cloves, finely chopped
450ml/15fl oz beef stock	2 cups beef stock
400g/14oz canned tomatoes, drained and chopped	14oz canned tomatoes, drained and chopped
30ml/2 tbs. tomato purée	2 tbs. tomato paste
1 bouquet garni	1 bouquet garni
1 bunch of celery, chopped	1 head of celery, chopped
10ml/2 tsp. cornflour	2 tsp. cornstarch
15ml/1 tbs. cold water	1 tbs. cold water

Preheat the oven to 170°C/325°F, Gas Mark 3.
Coat the oxtail pieces with the seasoned flour. Heat half the oil in a frying pan. Add the oxtail pieces, in batches, and brown on all sides. Remove the oxtail pieces as they brown and place them in a flame-proof casserole. Add the remaining oil to the frying pan. When it is hot, add the onion and garlic and fry until softened. Stir in the stock and return to the boil. Boil until reduced by a quarter. Pour over the oxtail pieces, then mix in the tomatoes, tomato purée (paste) and bouquet garni. Cover and place in the oven. Cook for 3½ hours.
Blanch the celery in boiling water for 5 minutes. Drain well and add to the casserole. Re-cover and continue cooking for 30 minutes. Skim any fat from the surface of the oxtail mixture. Discard the bouquet garni. Dissolve the cornflour in the water and add to the casserole. Stir well and simmer on top of the stove until the liquid thickens slightly. Serve hot. **SERVES 6**

RICE CASSEROLES

Mexican pork & rice

Metric/Imperial	American
30ml/2 tbs. oil	*2 tbs. oil*
1 medium onion, chopped	*1 medium onion, chopped*
¾kg/1½lb minced pork	*1½lb ground pork*
2 celery stalks, chopped	*2 celery stalks, chopped*
1 small green pepper, cored, seeded and cut into rings	*1 small green pepper, cored, seeded and cut into rings*
75g/3oz sultanas	*½ cup seedless white raisins*
1 garlic clove, crushed	*1 garlic clove, crushed*
1.25ml/¼ tsp. ground cumin	*¼ tsp. ground cumin*
2.5ml/½ tsp. hot chilli powder	*½ tsp. hot chilli powder*
15ml/1 tbs. chopped parsley	*1 tbs. chopped parsley*
175g/6oz long-grain rice	*1 cup long-grain rice*
400g/14oz canned tomatoes	*14oz canned tomatoes*
120ml/4fl oz water	*½ cup water*
30ml/2 tbs. tomato purée	*2 tbs. tomato paste*
juice of ½ lemon	*juice of ½ lemon*
45ml/3 tbs. pine nuts	*3 tbs. pine nuts*

Preheat the oven to 180°C/350°F, Gas Mark 4.
Heat the oil in a flameproof casserole. Add the onion and fry until softened. Add the pork and fry until the meat loses its pinkness. Stir in the celery, pepper, sultanas (raisins), garlic, cumin, chilli powder, parsley, seasoning to taste and rice. Fry for 5 minutes, stirring, until the rice has changed colour. Stir in the undrained tomatoes, water and tomato purée (paste). Bring to the boil, cover and simmer for 15 minutes. Transfer to the oven and cook for 25 minutes.
Uncover and sprinkle over the lemon juice and pine nuts. Return the casserole to the oven and cook for a further 10 minutes. **SERVES 4**

Beef stew with rice & tomatoes

Metric/Imperial	American
30ml/2 tbs. olive oil	2 tbs. olive oil
2 bacon rashers, diced	2 bacon slices, diced
1½kg/3lb stewing steak, cubed	3lb chuck steak, cubed
2 medium onions, sliced	2 medium onions, sliced
250g/8oz long-grain rice	1⅓ cups long-grain rice
300ml/½ pint dry white wine	1¼ cups dry white wine
450ml/¾ pint beef stock	1 pint beef stock
2 garlic cloves, crushed	2 garlic cloves, crushed
2.5ml/½ tsp. dried thyme	½ tsp. dried thyme
pinch of powdered saffron	pinch of powdered saffron
½kg/1lb ripe tomatoes, skinned, seeded and chopped	1lb ripe tomatoes, skinned, seeded and chopped
100g/4oz grated cheese	1 cup grated cheese

Preheat the oven to 170°C/325°F, Gas Mark 3.

Heat the oil in a frying pan and fry the bacon until it is browned. Transfer to a casserole, using a slotted spoon. Add the beef cubes to the frying pan, in batches, and brown on all sides. As the cubes of beef brown, transfer them to the casserole. Add the onions to the pan and fry until softened. Transfer to the casserole. Add the rice to the pan and cook, stirring, until it looks milky. Transfer the rice to a bowl.

Add the wine to the frying pan and stir well to mix with the sediment in the pan, then stir in the stock, seasoning to taste, garlic, thyme and saffron. Bring to the boil and pour into the casserole. Stir, cover and place in the oven. Cook for 1 hour. Stir in the tomatoes, re-cover and continue cooking for 2 hours or until the meat is tender.

Increase the oven temperature to 190°C/375°F, Gas Mark 5. Stir the rice into the casserole, re-cover and continue to cook for 20 minutes or until the rice is tender and the liquid absorbed. Adjust the seasoning, stir in the cheese and serve hot.   **SERVES 6-8**

Veal & rice casserole

Metric/Imperial	American
50g/2oz butter	*¼ cup butter*
1kg/2lb pie veal, cubed	*2lb veal stew meat, cubed*
2 medium onions, finely chopped	*2 medium onions, finely chopped*
30ml/2 tbs. paprika	*2 tbs. paprika*
600ml/1 pint chicken stock	*2½ cups chicken stock*
5ml/1 tsp. dried thyme	*1 tsp. dried thyme*
300g/10oz long-grain rice	*1⅔ cups long-grain rice*

Melt the butter in a saucepan. Add the veal cubes and onions and fry until the veal cubes are lightly browned on all sides and the onions are softened. Stir in the paprika, then stir in the stock, seasoning to taste and thyme. Bring to the boil, cover and simmer for 1¼ hours. Stir in the rice. Re-cover the pan and simmer for a further 20 to 25 minutes or until the rice is cooked and has absorbed all the liquid. Serve hot. **SERVES 4**

Chicken with rice

Metric/Imperial

8 chicken pieces
25g/1oz seasoned flour
6 bacon rashers, diced
2 onions, chopped
1 garlic clove, crushed
400g/14oz canned tomatoes
75g/3oz canned pimientos, drained
10ml/2 tsp. paprika
1.25ml/¼ tsp. powdered saffron
600ml/1 pint water
250g/8oz long-grain rice
175g/6oz frozen peas
30ml/2 tbs. chopped parsley

American

8 chicken pieces
¼ cup seasoned flour
6 bacon slices, diced
2 onions, chopped
1 garlic clove, crushed
14oz canned tomatoes
3oz canned pimientos, drained
2 tsp. paprika
¼ tsp. powdered saffron
2½ cups water
1½ cups long-grain rice
1 cup frozen peas
2 tbs. chopped parsley

Preheat the oven to 180°C/350°F, Gas Mark 4.
Coat the chicken pieces with the seasoned flour. Fry the bacon in a flameproof casserole until it is crisp and has rendered its fat. Add the chicken pieces and brown on all sides in the bacon fat. Remove the chicken pieces from the casserole. Add the onions and garlic to the casserole and fry until softened. Return the chicken pieces and add the undrained tomatoes, pimientos, paprika, saffron, seasoning to taste and water. Bring to the boil, then stir in the rice.
Cover the casserole and transfer it to the oven. Cook for 30 minutes. Add the peas and cook for a further 10 minutes or until the chicken is tender. Serve sprinkled with the parsley. **SERVES 4**

Chicken liver risotto

Metric/Imperial	American
50g/2oz butter	¼ cup butter
1 onion, finely chopped	1 onion, finely chopped
100g/4oz mushrooms, sliced	¼lb mushrooms, sliced
300g/10oz long-grain rice	1⅔ cups long-grain rice
600ml/1 pint boiling chicken stock	2½ cups boiling chicken stock
8 chicken livers, chopped	8 chicken livers, chopped
30ml/2 tbs. chopped parsley	2 tbs. chopped parsley
50g/2oz Parmesan cheese, grated	½ cup grated Parmesan cheese

Melt three-quarters of the butter in a saucepan. Add the onion and fry until softened. Stir in the mushrooms and fry for a further 3 minutes. Stir in the rice and cook, stirring, for 2 minutes, then stir in the stock. Cover and simmer gently for 20 minutes or until the rice is tender and has absorbed all the stock.

Meanwhile, melt the remaining butter in another pan. Add the chicken livers and fry for 10 minutes, stirring occasionally.

Stir the chicken livers into the rice mixture with the parsley. Serve hot, sprinkled with the Parmesan.   **SERVES 4**

Long Island seafood pilau

Metric/Imperial	American
50g/2oz butter	¼ cup butter
1 large onion, chopped	1 large onion, chopped
1 garlic clove, crushed	1 garlic clove, crushed
1 green pepper, cored, seeded and chopped	1 green pepper, cored, seeded and chopped
1 red pepper, cored, seeded and chopped	1 red pepper, cored, seeded and chopped
4 medium tomatoes, skinned, seeded and chopped	4 medium tomatoes, skinned, seeded and chopped
2.5ml/½ tsp. cayenne	½ tsp. cayenne
250g/8oz peeled shrimps	½lb shelled shrimp
24 oysters, removed from their shells and chopped	24 oysters, shucked and chopped
24 clams, steamed, removed from their shells and chopped	24 clams, steamed, removed from their shells and chopped
350g/12oz sweetcorn kernels	2¼ cups corn kernels
350g/12oz long-grain rice, cooked	2 cups long-grain rice, cooked

Melt the butter in a saucepan. Add the onion, garlic and peppers and fry until the onion is golden brown. Stir in the tomatoes, seasoning to taste, cayenne, shrimps, oysters, clams and sweetcorn and cook for 5 minutes, stirring frequently.

Stir in the rice, cover and cook gently for 10 minutes. Serve hot.

SERVES 6-8

Beef bourguignonne

Metric/Imperial	American
45ml/3 tbs. oil	3 tbs. oil
1½kg/3lb stewing steak, cubed	3lb chuck steak, cubed
1 carrot, sliced	1 carrot, sliced
1 onion, sliced	1 onion, sliced
25g/1oz flour	¼ cup flour
750ml/1¼ pints red wine	1½ pints red wine
450ml/¾ pint beef stock	1 pint beef stock
3 garlic cloves, crushed	3 garlic cloves, crushed
30ml/2 tbs. chopped parsley	2 tbs. chopped parsley
18 pickling onions	18 pearl onions
½kg/1lb mushrooms, quartered	1lb mushrooms, quartered

Preheat the oven to 230°C/450°F, Gas Mark 8.
Heat the oil in a flameproof casserole. Add the beef cubes, in batches, and fry until browned on all sides. Remove the beef cubes from the casserole as they brown. Add the carrot and onion to the casserole and fry until softened. Return the beef cubes, stir in seasoning to taste and sprinkle over the flour, turning over the cubes to coat. Transfer to the oven and cook for 10 minutes. Remove from the oven and reduce the temperature to 170°C/325°F, Gas Mark 3.
Stir in the wine, stock, garlic and parsley and bring to the boil. Cover and return the casserole to the oven. Cook for 2 hours or until the meat is nearly tender. Stir in the onions and cook for a further 30 to 40 minutes. Ten minutes before serving, stir in the mushrooms. Remove the casserole from the oven and transfer the meat and vegetables to a warmed serving platter with a slotted spoon. Put the cooking juices over a high heat and boil rapidly to reduce and thicken them slightly. Strain over the meat and vegetables and serve hot. **SERVES 6-8**

Beef carbonnade

Metric/Imperial

1kg/2lb braising steak, cubed
25g/1oz seasoned flour
60ml/4 tbs. oil
6 onions, thinly sliced
2 garlic cloves, crushed
600ml/1 pint dark beer
15ml/1 tbs. brown sugar

American

2lb chuck steak, cubed
¼ cup seasoned flour
¼ cup oil
6 onions, thinly sliced
2 garlic cloves, crushed
2½ cups dark beer
1 tbs. brown sugar

Coat the steak cubes with the seasoned flour. Heat the oil in a saucepan. Add the steak cubes, in batches, and brown on all sides. Remove the steak cubes from the pan as they brown. Add the onions and garlic to the pan and fry gently until softened. Add more oil if necessary. Return the steak cubes to the pan and stir in the beer and sugar. Bring to the boil, then cover and simmer for 1½ hours. Remove the lid and continue simmering for 30 minutes or until the steak cubes are tender. Serve hot. **SERVES 4**

Chinese beef in fruit sauce

Metric/Imperial	American
30ml/2 tbs. oil	*2 tbs. oil*
1 medium onion, thinly sliced	*1 medium onion, thinly sliced*
2 garlic cloves, crushed	*2 garlic cloves, crushed*
2.5cm/1in chopped fresh ginger	*1in piece chopped fresh ginger*
1¼-1½kg/2½-3lb boned leg of beef, cubed	*2½-3lb boneless beef heel of round, cubed*
juice of 1 lemon	*juice of 1 lemon*
juice of 2 oranges	*juice of 2 oranges*
60ml/4 tbs. soy sauce	*¼ cup soy sauce*
300ml/½ pint dry red wine	*1¼ cups dry red wine*
600ml/1 pint water	*2½ cups water*

Preheat the oven to 150°C/300°F, Gas Mark 2.

Heat the oil in a flameproof casserole. Add the onion, garlic and ginger and stir-fry for 1 minute. Add the beef and fry, stirring, for 3 minutes. Stir in the remaining ingredients with seasoning to taste and bring to the boil.

Cover the casserole and place it in the oven. Cook for 4 hours, stirring occasionally. **SERVES 4-6**

Daube de boeuf à la Provençale

Metric/Imperial	American
1½kg/3lb stewing steak, cubed	3lb chuck steak, cubed
250g/8oz bacon rashers, cut into strips	½lb bacon slices, cut into strips
250g/8oz mushrooms, sliced	½lb mushrooms, sliced
¾kg/1½lb tomatoes, skinned, seeded and chopped	1½lb tomatoes, skinned, seeded and chopped
3 garlic cloves, crushed	3 garlic cloves, crushed
5ml/1 tsp. grated orange rind	1 tsp. grated orange rind
15ml/1 tbs. chopped parsley	1 tbs. chopped parsley
1 bouquet garni	1 bouquet garni
175ml/6fl oz beef stock	¾ cup beef stock
10 black olives, halved and stoned	10 black olives, halved and pitted
MARINADE	**MARINADE**
300ml/½ pint dry white wine	1¼ cups dry white wine
2.5ml/½ tsp. dried thyme	½ tsp. dried thyme
1 bay leaf	1 bay leaf
2 garlic cloves, crushed	2 garlic cloves, crushed
4 medium onions, sliced	4 medium onions, sliced
4 medium carrots, sliced	4 medium carrots, sliced

Mix all the marinade ingredients together. Add the steak cubes and stir well. Cover and leave to marinate for at least 12 hours, basting occasionally. Remove the beef cubes from the marinade and pat dry with paper towels. Strain the marinade and reserve both the liquid and the vegetables. Discard the bay leaf.

Preheat the oven to 170°C/325°F, Gas Mark 3.

Place two or three bacon strips on the bottom of a flameproof casserole. Spoon a few marinated vegetables, mushrooms and tomatoes on top and cover with a layer of beef cubes. Sprinkle with a little garlic, orange rind and parsley. Add the bouquet garni. Continue making layers in this way, ending with a layer of bacon. Pour in the stock and reserved marinating liquid and scatter over the olives. Bring the liquid to the boil, then transfer to the oven. Cook for 4 hours or until the beef is tender. **SERVES 6-8**

Jamaican casserole

Metric/Imperial	American
1½kg/3lb stewing steak, cubed	*3lb chuck steak, cubed*
50g/2oz seasoned flour	*½ cup seasoned flour*
75g/3oz butter	*6 tbs. butter*
2 onions, sliced	*2 onions, sliced*
1 green chilli, seeded and chopped	*1 green chili, seeded and chopped*
1 garlic clove, chopped	*1 garlic clove, chopped*
5ml/1 tsp. ground ginger	*1 tsp. ground ginger*
400g/14oz canned tomatoes, chopped	*14oz canned tomatoes, chopped*
2.5ml/½ tsp. dried thyme	*½ tsp. dried thyme*

Coat the beef cubes with the seasoned flour. Melt the butter in a large saucepan. Add the beef cubes, in batches, and brown on all sides. Remove the cubes with a slotted spoon. Add the onions, chilli, garlic and ginger to the pan and fry until they are softened. Return the beef to the pan and add the undrained tomatoes and thyme. Bring to the boil. Cover and simmer the mixture for 3 hours or until the beef cubes are tender. Serve hot.   **SERVES 6-8**

Pork vindaloo

Metric/Imperial	American
5cm/2in piece chopped fresh ginger	2in piece of chopped fresh ginger
4 garlic cloves, chopped	4 garlic cloves, chopped
7.5ml/1½ tsp. chilli powder	1½ tsp. chili powder
10ml/2 tsp. turmeric	2 tsp. turmeric
6 cloves	6 cloves
2.5ml/½ tsp. ground cardamon	½ tsp. ground cardamon
30ml/2 tbs. coriander seeds	2 tbs. coriander seeds
15ml/1 tbs. cumin seeds	1 tbs. cumin seeds
150ml/5fl oz vinegar	⅔ cup vinegar
1kg/2lb pork fillet, cubed	2lb pork tenderloin, cubed
60ml/4 tbs. oil	4 tbs oil
5ml/1 tsp. mustard seeds	1 tsp. mustard seeds
150ml/5fl oz water	⅔ cup water

Put all the spices and vinegar into a blender and blend to a smooth purée. Add more vinegar if necessary until the mixture forms a liquid paste. Put the pork into a large bowl and mix in the spice paste to coat. Cover and leave to marinate for 1 hour. Transfer to the refrigerator and marinate for 24 hours or overnight, turning occasionally.

Heat the oil in a large saucepan. Add the mustard seeds, cover the pan and cook until they stop spattering. Add the pork, marinade and water and bring to the boil, stirring. Reduce the heat to low and simmer for 40 minutes. Uncover and simmer for a further 30 minutes or until the meat is tender. Serve hot. **SERVES 4-6**

Veal sauté marengo

Metric/Imperial	American
1½kg/3lb lean veal, cubed	3lb lean veal, cubed
100g/4oz butter	½ cup butter
2 medium onions, sliced	2 medium onions, sliced
2 garlic cloves, crushed	2 garlic cloves, crushed
250ml/8fl oz veal or chicken stock	1 cup veal or chicken stock
1 bouquet garni	1 bouquet garni
250g/8oz canned tomatoes, chopped	8oz canned tomatoes, chopped
65g/2½oz tomato purée	¼ cup tomato paste
5ml/1 tsp. paprika	1 tsp. paprika
12 pickling onions	12 pearl onions
350g/12oz button mushrooms, sliced	¾lb button mushrooms, sliced
7.5ml/1½ tsp. flour	1½ tsp. flour

Preheat the oven to 170°C/325°F, Gas Mark 3.
Rub the veal cubes with salt and pepper. Melt half the butter in a flameproof casserole. Add the onions and garlic and fry until softened. Add the veal cubes, in batches, and brown on all sides. Return the veal cubes to the casserole and stir in the stock, bouquet garni, undrained tomatoes, tomato purée (paste) and paprika. Bring to the boil, cover and transfer to the oven. Cook for 1½ hours. Stir in the pickling (pearl) onions, re-cover and cook for a further 30 minutes or until the meat is tender.
Meanwhile, melt 25g/1oz of the remaining butter in a frying pan. Add the mushrooms and fry for 3 minutes, stirring frequently. Transfer the mushrooms to a warmed serving dish.
When the veal is cooked, transfer the veal cubes and pickling (pearl) onions to the serving dish. Keep warm. Strain the cooking liquid into a saucepan and skim off any fat from the surface. Boil until reduced by about one-third. Mix together the remaining butter and the flour to a paste (beurre manié). Add this in small pieces to the liquid and simmer, stirring, until thickened. Pour over the meat and vegetables and serve. **SERVES 6**

Osso buco

Metric/Imperial	American
1½kg/3lb veal knuckle, sawn into	*3lb veal shank, sawn into 3 inch*
7.5cm/3 inch pieces	*pieces*
75g/3oz seasoned flour	*¾ cup seasoned flour*
100g/4oz butter	*½ cup butter*
1 large onion, sliced	*1 large onion, sliced*
400g/14oz canned tomatoes	*14oz canned tomatoes*
30ml/2 tbs. tomato purée	*2 tbs. tomato paste*
175ml/6fl oz dry white wine	*¾ cup dry white wine*
5ml/1 tsp. sugar	*1 tsp. sugar*
15ml/1 tbs. grated lemon rind	*1 tbs. grated lemon rind*
2 garlic cloves, crushed	*2 garlic cloves, crushed*
22.5ml/1½ tbs. chopped parsley	*1½ tbs. chopped parsley*

Coat the veal pieces with the seasoned flour. Melt the butter in a saucepan. Add the veal pieces, in batches, and fry until browned on all sides. Remove the veal from the pan as it browns. Add the onion to the pan and fry until softened. Stir in the undrained tomatoes, tomato purée (paste), wine, seasoning to taste and sugar and bring to the boil. Return the veal pieces to the pan and mix well. Cover and simmer for 1½ to 2 hours or until the meat is so tender it is almost dropping off the bones.

Meanwhile, mix together the remaining ingredients. Stir into the veal mixture and serve. **SERVES 6**

Chicken casserole bonne femme

Metric/Imperial	American
1 x 2kg/4lb chicken	*1 x 4lb chicken*
50g/2oz butter	*¼ cup butter*
¾kg/1½lb pickling onions	*1½lb pearl onions*
¾kg/1½lb small new potatoes	*1½lb small new potatoes*
6 back bacon rashers, diced	*6 Canadian bacon slices, diced*
1 bouquet garni	*1 bouquet garni*

Preheat the oven to 180°C/350°F, Gas Mark 4.
Rub the chicken inside and out with salt and pepper. Melt the butter in a flameproof casserole. Add the chicken and brown lightly on all sides. Remove the chicken from the casserole.
Put the onions, potatoes and bacon in the casserole and cook for 10 minutes, stirring frequently. Return the chicken to the casserole and add the bouquet garni. Cover the casserole and transfer it to the oven. Cook for 45 minutes to 1 hour or until the chicken is tender. Discard the bouquet garni and serve the chicken with the bacon and vegetables.   **SERVES 4**

Chicken paprikash

Metric/Imperial	American
6 chicken quarters	6 chicken quarters
25g/1oz butter	2 tbs. butter
2 large onions, chopped	2 large onions, chopped
1 garlic clove, crushed	1 garlic clove, crushed
22.5ml/1½ tbs. paprika	1½ tbs. paprika
300ml/½ pint chicken stock	1¼ cups chicken stock
2 green peppers, cored, seeded and sliced	2 green peppers, cored, seeded and sliced
4 tomatoes, skinned and chopped	4 tomatoes, skinned and chopped
22.5ml/1½ tbs. flour	1½ tbs. flour
150ml/¼ pint soured cream	⅔ cup sour cream

Rub the chicken pieces with salt and pepper. Melt the butter in a saucepan. Add the onions and garlic and fry until golden brown. Stir in the paprika and cook for a further 2 minutes, then stir in the stock. Add the chicken pieces, peppers and tomatoes to the pan. Cover and simmer for 1 hour or until the chicken is tender. Mix the flour with the sour cream and add to the pan. Cook gently for 2 to 3 minutes, stirring or until the liquid is thickened. **SERVES 6**

Spanish fish stew

Metric/Imperial

150ml/¼ pint olive oil
1 large onion, thinly sliced
250g/8oz squid, cut into rings
6 tomatoes, skinned and chopped
10ml/2 tsp. chopped basil
450ml/¾ pint fish stock
350g/12oz eel, cut into pieces
24 clams, steamed and removed from
  their shells
200g/7oz canned tuna fish, drained
  and flaked
250g/8oz sole fillets, skinned and cut
  into pieces
50g/2oz ground almonds
2.5ml/½ tsp. powdered saffron
2 garlic cloves, crushed
2 slices white bread, fried and
  quartered
8 cooked prawns, unpeeled

American

⅔ cup olive oil
1 large onion, thinly sliced
½lb squid, cut into rings
6 tomatoes, skinned and chopped
2 tsp. chopped basil
2 cups fish stock
¾lb eel, cut into pieces
24 clams, steamed and removed from
  their shells
7oz canned tuna fish, drained and
  flaked
½lb sole fillets, skinned and cut into
  pieces
½ cup ground almonds
½ tsp. powdered saffron
2 garlic cloves, crushed
2 slices white bread, fried and
  quartered
8 cooked jumbo shrimp, unshelled

Heat the oil in a frying pan. Add the onion and fry until it is golden brown. Stir in the squid, tomatoes, basil and quarter of the stock and cook for 3 minutes. Add the eel, clams, seasoning to taste and remaining stock and simmer for 10 minutes. Add the tuna and sole and simmer for a further 10 minutes.

Meanwhile, put the almonds, saffron, garlic, the remaining olive oil and one piece of the fried bread in a mortar. Add 15ml/1 tablespoon of the liquid from the fish mixture and pound together with a pestle to form a paste. Spread the paste on the bottom of a warmed serving dish. Pour the fish mixture into the dish and garnish with the remaining fried bread and the prawns (jumbo shrimp). **SERVES 4-6**

Mediterranean seafood casserole

Metric/Imperial	American
½kg/1lb cod fillets, skinned and cut into 5cm/2in pieces	1lb cod fillets, skinned and cut into 2in pieces
25g/1oz seasoned flour	¼ cup seasoned flour
100g/4oz butter	½ cup butter
2 medium onions, thinly sliced	2 medium onions, thinly sliced
2 garlic cloves, crushed	2 garlic cloves, crushed
200g/7oz canned tuna fish, drained and flaked	7oz canned tuna fish, drained and flaked
100g/4oz mushrooms, sliced	¼lb mushrooms, sliced
1 green pepper, cored, seeded and thinly sliced	1 green pepper, cored, seeded and thinly sliced
400g/14oz canned tomatoes	14oz canned tomatoes
250g/8oz prawns, peeled	½lb shrimp, shelled
250g/8oz frozen scallops, thawed, drained and chopped	½lb frozen scallops, thawed, drained and chopped
250ml/8fl oz dry white wine	1 cup dry white wine
1.25ml/¼ tsp. red pepper flakes	¼ tsp. red pepper flakes
1.25ml/¼ tsp. powdered saffron	¼ tsp. powdered saffron
36 stuffed olives, halved	36 stuffed olives, halved

Preheat the oven to 180°C/350°F, Gas Mark 4.
Coat the fish pieces with the seasoned flour. Melt half the butter in a frying pan. Add the fish pieces, in batches, and brown on all sides. As the fish pieces brown transfer them to a casserole. Add the remaining butter to the pan. When it has melted, add the onions and garlic and fry until softened. Stir in the tuna, mushrooms, pepper, un-drained tomatoes, prawns (shrimp) and scallops. Cook for 3 minutes, then stir in the wine, seasoning to taste, red pepper flakes and saffron. Bring to the boil. Stir in the olives and pour over the fish.
Place the casserole in the oven and cook for 20 minutes or until the fish flakes easily.

SERVES 6

Boston baked beans

Metric/Imperial	American
1kg/2lb dried haricot beans	*2lb (2¼ cups) dried navy beans*
1 large onion	*1 large onion*
250g/8oz fat salt pork, cubed	*½lb fatback, cubed*
75g/3oz brown sugar	*½ cup brown sugar*
90ml/6 tbs. black treacle	*6 tbs. molasses*
15ml/1 tbs. dry mustard	*1 tbs. dry mustard*

Put the beans in a saucepan with 5ml/1 teaspoon salt and cover with water. Bring to the boil and boil for 2 minutes. Remove from the heat and leave to soak for 1 hour. Return to the heat and bring back to the boil. Half cover the pan and simmer for 30 minutes. Drain the beans.

Preheat the oven to 130°C/250°F, Gas Mark ½.

Put the onion in a casserole. Make a layer of half the beans in the casserole and arrange a layer of half the salt pork chunks on top. Add another layer of beans and finish with the salt pork. Mix together the sugar, treacle (molasses), mustard and seasoning to taste and spoon over the salt pork layer. Pour in enough boiling water to cover. Cover the casserole and place it in the oven. Cook for 5 hours, adding more boiling water when necessary to keep the beans covered. Remove the lid and bake uncovered for a further 45 minutes.

SERVES 6-8

COOKING ON A BUDGET

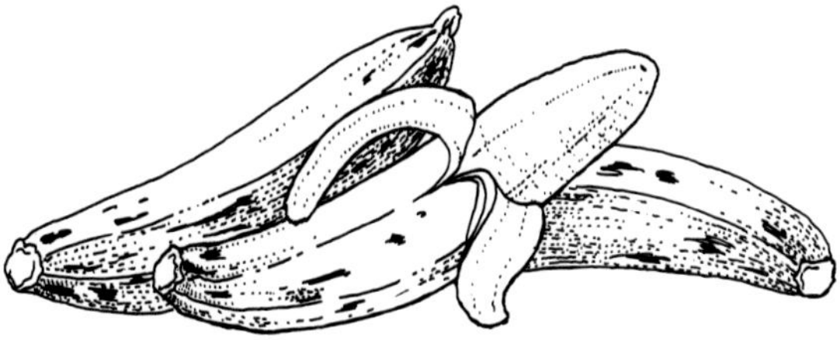

SOUPS

Scotch broth

Metric/Imperial	American
1½kg/3lb neck of mutton or lamb, chined, excess fat removed and cut into 4 or 5 pieces	3lb lamb neck slices, excess fat removed
1.8 litres/3 pints water	7½ cups water
50g/2oz pearl barley	¼ cup pearl barley
50g/2oz dried green split peas, soaked overnight and drained	¼ cup dried green split peas, soaked overnight and drained
1 large carrot, chopped	1 large carrot, chopped
1 large onion, chopped	1 large onion, chopped
2 leeks, chopped	2 leeks, chopped
2 celery stalks, chopped	2 celery stalks, chopped
1 large turnip, chopped	1 large turnip, chopped
chopped parsley	chopped parsley

Put the meat in a saucepan with the water and bring to the boil. Skim any scum from the surface, then add the barley and peas with seasoning to taste. Cover and simmer for 1½ hours. Add the vegetables and stir well. Re-cover and continue to simmer for 1 hour or until the vegetables are tender.

Remove the meat from the pan. Discard the bones and cut the meat into shreds. Return to the soup and reheat for 5 minutes. Serve sprinkled with parsley. **SERVES 4-6**

Oxtail soup

Metric/Imperial	American
1 oxtail, cut into pieces	*1 oxtail, cut into pieces*
45ml/3 tbs. oil	*3 tbs. oil*
1 turnip, chopped	*1 turnip, chopped*
1 parsnip, chopped	*1 parsnip, chopped*
2 celery stalks, chopped	*2 celery stalks, chopped*
2 carrots, sliced	*2 carrots, sliced*
2 onions, sliced	*2 onions, sliced*
2.25 litres/4 pints water	*5 pints water*
½kg/1lb tomatoes, skinned	*1lb tomatoes, skinned*
2.5ml/½ tsp. dried basil	*½ tsp. dried basil*
pinch of cayenne	*pinch of cayenne*
30ml/2 tbs. flour	*2 tbs. flour*

Rub the oxtail pieces with salt and pepper. Heat the oil in a saucepan and add the oxtail pieces. Fry until browned on all sides, then remove from the pan. Add the turnip, parsnip, celery, carrots and onions to the pan and fry until beginning to brown. Stir in the water and return the oxtail pieces. Bring to the boil, skimming any scum from the surface. Cover and simmer for 4 hours or until the oxtail meat is falling from the bones.

Add the tomatoes, basil and cayenne and cook for a further 10 minutes. Dissolve the flour in a little of the soup liquid and add to the remaining soup. Simmer for 10 minutes longer.

Cool the soup, then chill overnight. The next day, remove the layer of fat on the surface. Bring the soup to the boil and simmer for 5 minutes. **SERVES 4**

Bean & bacon soup

Metric/Imperial	American
350g/12oz dried butter beans, soaked	*1½ cups dried lima beans, soaked*
overnight and drained	*overnight and drained*
1kg/2lb bacon hock with bone	*2lb ham hock*
1 large onion, quartered	*1 large onion, quartered*
1 large garlic clove, crushed	*1 large garlic clove, crushed*
2 litres/3½ pints water	*2 quarts water*
1 bouquet garni	*1 bouquet garni*
20 black olives, halved	*20 black olives, halved*
chopped parsley	*chopped parsley*

Put the beans, bacon (ham) hock, onion, garlic and water in a saucepan and bring to the boil. Add the bouquet garni and pepper to taste and simmer for 1½ to 2 hours or until the beans are tender.
Remove the bacon (ham) hock and cut the meat into small pieces. Discard the bouquet garni. Purée some of the beans and return to the soup with the bacon (ham) pieces and olives. Reheat gently and serve hot, sprinkled with parsley. **SERVES 6**

Chicken soup with dumplings

Metric/Imperial	American
2 litres/3½ pints water	2 quarts water
2 onions, quartered	2 onions, quartered
6 carrots, 3 chopped and 3 cut into matchsticks	6 carrots, 3 chopped and 3 cut into matchsticks
4 celery stalks, chopped	4 celery stalks, chopped
6 peppercorns	6 peppercorns
2 bay leaves	2 bay leaves
1 x 1¾kg/3½lb chicken with giblets (not liver)	1 x 3½lb chicken with giblets (not liver)

DUMPLINGS

140g/4½oz flour	1 cup + 2 tbs. flour
5ml/1 tsp. baking powder	1 tsp. baking powder
½ egg, beaten	½ egg, beaten
60ml/4 tbs. milk	¼ cup milk

Put the water in a saucepan and bring to the boil. Add the onions, chopped carrots, celery, peppercorns, bay leaves and salt to taste. Place the chicken and giblets in the pan, cover and simmer for 2 hours or until cooked. Remove the chicken from the pan. Discard the skin and bones and cut the meat into bite-size pieces. Strain the stock into another saucepan and bring to the boil. Add the carrot matchsticks and simmer for 10 minutes.

To make the dumplings, sift the flour, baking powder and 2.5ml/½ teaspoon salt into a bowl. Add the egg and milk and mix to a firm dough. Shape into walnut-size balls.

Add the chicken meat to the stock, then drop in the dumplings. Simmer for 4 to 5 minutes, or until the dumplings are fluffy and have risen to the top. Serve hot. **SERVES 4**

Cock-a-leekie

Metric/Imperial	American
1 x 2kg/4lb chicken	*1 x 4lb chicken*
7 leeks, sliced	*7 leeks, sliced*
2 celery stalks, chopped	*2 celery stalks, chopped*
50g/2oz pearl barley	*¼ cup pearl barley*
1 bouquet garni	*1 bouquet garni*
chopped parsley	*chopped parsley*

Put the chicken in a saucepan and cover with water. Bring to the boil. Add the leeks, celery, barley, bouquet garni and salt to taste. Half cover the pan and simmer for 1½ to 2 hours or until cooked.

Remove the chicken from the pan. Discard the skin and bones and shred the meat. Return the shredded meat to the pan and discard the bouquet garni. Reheat gently and serve sprinkled with chopped parsley. **SERVES 6**

Manhattan clam chowder

Metric/Imperial	American
125g/4 oz salt pork, diced	¼lb fatback, diced
1 medium onion, chopped	1 medium onion, chopped
4 large tomatoes, skinned, seeded and chopped	4 large tomatoes, skinned, seeded and chopped
3 medium potatoes, diced	3 medium potatoes, diced
2.5ml/½ tsp. dried thyme	½ tsp. dried thyme
150ml/¼ pint tomato juice	⅔ cup tomato juice
600ml/1 pint water	2½ cups water
150ml/¼ pint clam cooking liquid (if available)	⅔ cup clam cooking liquid (if available)
24 small clams, steamed, removed from their shells and chopped	24 small clams, steamed, removed from their shells and chopped

Fry the salt pork (fatback) in a saucepan until it is golden brown and has rendered most of its fat. Remove from the pan with a slotted spoon. Add the onion to the pan and fry until softened. Stir in the tomatoes, potatoes, thyme and seasoning to taste, then add the tomato juice, water and clam cooking liquid.

Return the salt pork (fatback) to the pan and bring to the boil. Cover and simmer for 12 to 15 minutes or until the potatoes are tender. Add the clams and cook for a further 5 minutes. Taste and adjust the seasoning before serving. **SERVES 6**

Vegetable soup

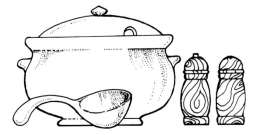

Metric/Imperial

1 x 1½kg/3lb veal bone
2.25 litres/4 pints water
1 bouquet garni
1 large onion, quartered
1 head of celery, sliced
4 large carrots, sliced
15ml/1 tbs. cornflour
  dissolved in 30ml/2 tbs. water
100g/4oz button mushrooms
120ml/4fl oz single cream
chopped parsley

American

1 x 3lb veal bone
5 pints water
1 bouquet garni
1 large onion, quartered
1 bunch of celery, sliced
4 large carrots, sliced
1 tbs. cornstarch
  dissolved in 2 tbs. water
¼lb button mushrooms
½ cup light cream
chopped parsley

Put the veal bone in a saucepan with the water, bouquet garni, onion and seasoning to taste. Bring to the boil, skimming off the scum that rises to the surface. Simmer for 2 hours.

Discard the veal bone and strain the stock into a clean saucepan. Add the celery and carrots and simmer for 10 minutes. Stir in the dissolved cornflour (cornstarch) and simmer, stirring, until thickened. Add the mushrooms and cream and cook gently for a further 5 minutes. Serve hot, sprinkled with chopped parsley. **SERVES 6-8**

Lentil & vegetable soup

Metric/Imperial	American
2.25 litres/4 pints water	*5 pints water*
½kg/1lb lentils, soaked overnight and drained	*2 cups lentils, soaked overnight and drained*
1 bacon bone (optional)	*1 ham bone (optional)*
250g/8oz bacon, in one piece	*½lb slab bacon*
1 leek, chopped	*1 leek, chopped*
2 large carrots, chopped	*2 large carrots, chopped*
1 parsnip, chopped	*1 parsnip, chopped*
2 celery stalks, chopped	*2 celery stalks, chopped*
30ml/2 tbs. oil	*2 tbs. oil*
2 medium onions, chopped	*2 medium onions, chopped*
30ml/2 tbs. flour	*2 tbs. flour*
22.5ml/1½ tbs. cider vinegar	*1½ tbs. cider vinegar*
250g/8oz garlic sausage, diced	*½lb garlic sausage, diced*
1.25ml/¼ tsp. dried thyme	*¼ tsp. dried thyme*

Put the water in a saucepan and bring to the boil. Add the lentils, bacon (ham) bone, bacon, leek, carrots, parsnip, celery and salt to taste. Return to the boil, then simmer for 45 minutes.

Meanwhile, heat the oil in another pan. Add the onions and fry until softened. Sprinkle over the flour and cook, stirring, until golden brown. Stir in a little of the soup liquid and the vinegar, then add this mixture to the remaining soup. Cover and simmer for 1 hour or until the lentils are tender.

Discard the bacon (ham) bone. Cut the meat into small pieces and return to the soup with the sausage, thyme and seasoning to taste. Simmer for a further 5 minutes or until piping hot. **SERVES 6**

Spinach soup

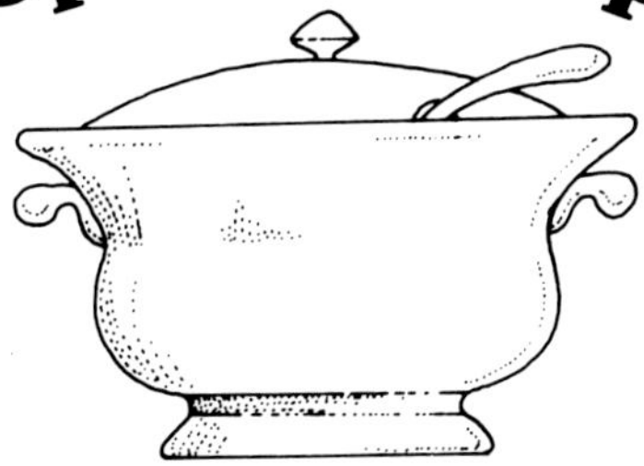

Metric/Imperial

25g/1oz butter
1 large onion, chopped
30ml/2 tbs. flour
1.2 litres/2 pints chicken stock
2.5ml/½ tsp. paprika
2.5ml/½ tsp. grated nutmeg
30ml/2 tbs. lemon juice
¾kg/1½lb spinach, chopped
75ml/3fl oz double cream, whipped
6 back bacon rashers, cooked
  until crisp and crumbled

American

2 tbs. butter
1 large onion, chopped
2 tbs. flour
2½ pints chicken stock
½ tsp. paprika
½ tsp. grated nutmeg
2 tbs. lemon juice
1½lb spinach, chopped
⅓ cup heavy cream, whipped
6 Canadian bacon slices, cooked
  until crisp and crumbled

Melt the butter in a saucepan. Add the onion and fry until softened. Sprinkle over the flour and cook, stirring, for 2 minutes. Gradually stir in the stock, then add the paprika, nutmeg, lemon juice, spinach and seasoning to taste. Bring to the boil, then cover and simmer for 20 to 25 minutes or until the spinach is very tender.

Blend the soup to a smooth purée and return to the pan. Reheat gently. Serve topped with the whipped cream and crumbled bacon.

SERVES 6

MAIN COURSES

Yale chilli

Metric/Imperial

45ml/3 tbs. oil
1 large onion, chopped
2 celery stalks, chopped
1 green pepper, cored, seeded and
  chopped
2 garlic cloves, crushed
1 kg/2lb minced beef
400g/14oz canned tomatoes
150g/5oz tomato purée
5ml/1 tsp. hot chilli powder
400g/14oz canned red kidney beans,
  drained
2 medium cooking apples, peeled,
  cored and chopped
50g/2oz dried stoned prunes,
  chopped
30ml/2 tbs. silvered almonds
100g/4oz frozen French beans,
  chopped
2.5ml/½ tsp. grated nutmeg

American

3 tbs. oil
1 large onion, chopped
2 celery stalks, chopped
1 green pepper, cored, seeded and
  chopped
2 garlic cloves, crushed
2lb ground beef
14oz canned tomatoes
½ cup tomato paste
1 tsp. hot chilli powder
14oz canned red kidney beans,
  drained
2 medium cooking apples, peeled,
  cored and chopped
⅓ cup chopped dried pitted
  prunes
2 tbs. slivered almonds
½ cup chopped frozen green
  beans
½ tsp. grated nutmeg

Heat the oil in a saucepan. Add the onion, celery, pepper and garlic and fry until the onion is softened. Stir in the beef and fry until it loses its pinkness.

Stir in the remaining ingredients with salt to taste and bring to the boil. Cover and simmer for 30 minutes. Uncover the pan and simmer for a further 10 minutes. Serve hot. **SERVES 4**

Steak & kidney pudding

Metric/Imperial	American
450g/1lb self-raising flour	4 cups self-rising flour
250g/8oz shredded suet	1 cup shredded suet
300ml/½ pint water	1¼ cups water
FILLING	**FILLING**
¾kg/1½lb braising steak, cubed	1½lb chuck steak, cubed
250g/8oz ox kidney, chopped	½lb beef kidney, chopped
30ml/2 tbs. flour	2 tbs. flour
10ml/2 tsp. dried mixed herbs	2 tsp. dried mixed herbs

Sift the flour and 1.25ml/¼ teaspoon salt into a bowl. Rub in the suet, then bind to a soft dough with the water. Roll out the dough to a circle about 1cm/½in thick and cut a triangle (about one-third the diameter) from it. Use the larger piece to line a 1.5-1.8 litre/2½-3 pint (6½-7 cup) pudding basin (steaming mold).

Mix together the filling ingredients with seasoning to taste. Spoon into the dough-lined basin (mold) and add enough water to fill it to two-thirds full. Use the reserved triangle of dough to shape into a lid. Dampen the edges and place over the filling. Press the edges to seal. Cover the basin (mold) with foil and steam for 3 hours. **SERVES 4-6**

Boiled beef & horseradish sauce

Metric/Imperial

1 x 2kg/4lb boned brisket of beef,
  rolled
2 leeks, chopped
4 carrots, quartered
2 large onions, stuck with 4 cloves
1 bouquet garni

SAUCE

40g/1½oz butter
30ml/2 tbs. flour
300ml/½ pint canned consommé
15ml/1 tbs. fresh breadcrumbs
45ml/3 tbs. prepared horseradish
1.25ml/¼ tsp. sugar

American

1 x 4lb boned brisket of beef,
  rolled
2 leeks, chopped
4 carrots, quartered
2 large onions, stuck with 4 cloves
1 bouquet garni

SAUCE

3 tbs. butter
2 tbs. flour
1¼ cups canned consommé
1 tbs. fresh breadcrumbs
3 tbs. prepared horseradish
¼ tsp. sugar

Put the beef in a saucepan and cover with water. Bring to the boil, skimming the scum that rises to the surface. Add the leeks, carrots, onions, bouquet garni and seasoning to taste, cover and simmer for 3 hours or until the meat is tender. Drain the meat and place on a carving board. Remove the string and carve into thick slices. Arrange on a warmed serving platter and keep hot.

To make the sauce, melt the butter in a saucepan. Add the flour and cook, stirring, for 1 minute. Gradually stir in the consommé and bring to the boil. Simmer, stirring, until thickened. Stir in the remaining sauce ingredients with seasoning to taste. Heat through, then serve with the meat. **SERVES 6-8**

Lamb hotpot

Metric/Imperial	American
1½kg/3lb middle neck of lamb, cut into chops	3lb lamb shoulder chops
3 garlic cloves, crushed	3 garlic cloves, crushed
5ml/1 tsp. sugar	1 tsp. sugar
45ml/3 tbs. chopped basil	3 tbs. chopped basil
1¼kg/2½lb potatoes, peeled and sliced	2½lb potatoes, peeled and sliced
100g/4oz butter, melted	½ cup butter, melted
30ml/2 tbs. chopped parsley	2 tbs. chopped parsley

Preheat the oven to 150°C/300°F, Gas Mark 2.
Rub the lamb with the garlic, sugar, basil and seasoning to taste.
Make a layer of potato slices in a greased casserole. Cover with a layer of lamb chops. Continue making layers in this way, ending with a layer of potato slices. Pour over the melted butter.
Cover the casserole and place it in the oven. Cook for 4 hours.
Uncover the casserole and sprinkle with parsley before serving.

SERVES 4-6

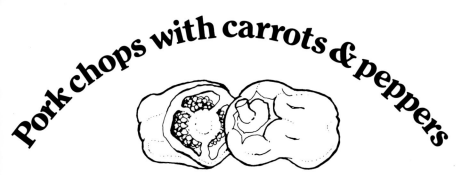

Pork chops with carrots & peppers

Metric/Imperial	American
6 loin pork chops	6 loin pork chops
1 garlic clove, halved	1 garlic clove, halved
60ml/4 tbs. oil	¼ cup oil
1 large onion, sliced	1 large onion, sliced
2 carrots, sliced	2 carrots, sliced
2 celery stalks, sliced	2 celery stalks, sliced
1 red pepper, cored, seeded and cut into strips	1 red pepper, cored, seeded and cut into strips
300ml/½ pint orange juice	1¼ cups orange juice
5ml/1 tsp. dried rosemary	1 tsp. dried rosemary
5ml/1 tsp. grated orange rind	1 tsp. grated orange rind
1.25ml/¼ tsp. cayenne	¼ tsp. cayenne

Rub the chops with the garlic and seasoning to taste. Discard the garlic. Heat the oil in a frying pan. Add the chops and brown on both sides. Remove the chops from the pan. Add the onion, carrots, celery and pepper to the pan and fry until the onion is softened. Stir in the orange juice, rosemary, orange rind and cayenne and bring to the boil. Return the chops to the pan and spoon the orange mixture over them. Cover and simmer for 45 minutes to 1 hour or until the chops are cooked through.

Transfer the chops and vegetables to a warmed serving dish. Boil the liquid until reduced and pour over the chops. Serve hot. **SERVES 6**

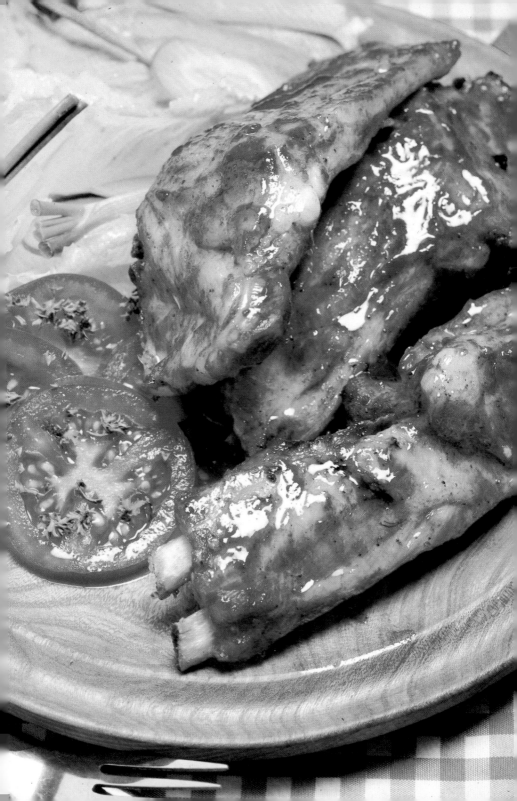

Maple sparerib casserole

Metric/Imperial

2kg/4lb pork spareribs, cut into
  2-rib serving pieces
150ml/¼ pint maple syrup
1.25ml/¼ tsp. cayenne
2 garlic cloves, crushed
30ml/2 tbs. tomato purée
15ml/1 tbs. mild mustard
30ml/2 tbs. lemon juice

American

4lb pork spareribs, cut into 2-rib
  serving pieces
⅔ cup maple syrup
¼ tsp. cayenne
2 garlic cloves, crushed
2 tbs. tomato paste
1 tbs. mild mustard
2 tbs. lemon juice

Preheat the oven to 200°C/400°F, Gas Mark 6.

Put the spareribs in a roasting pan in one layer and roast for 30 minutes.

Remove the ribs from the pan and pour off the fat. Put the ribs back into the pan. Mix together the remaining ingredients with seasoning to taste and pour over the ribs. Return to the oven and reduce the temperature to 180°C/350°F, Gas Mark 4. Continue cooking for 45 minutes, basting frequently with the maple syrup mixture in the pan, or until the ribs are browned and glazed. Serve hot. **SERVES 4**

Braised oxtail

Metric/Imperial	American
1 oxtail, cut into pieces	*1 oxtail, cut into pieces*
1.25ml/¼ tsp. mixed spice	*¼ tsp. apple pie spice*
25g/1oz butter	*2 tbs. butter*
2 medium onions, chopped	*2 medium onions, chopped*
2 medium carrots, chopped	*2 medium carrots, chopped*
1 bouquet garni	*1 bouquet garni*
175ml/6fl oz brown stock	*¾ cup brown stock*
175ml/6 fl oz red wine or more stock	*¾ cup red wine or more stock*
30ml/2 tbs. tomato purée	*2 tbs. tomato paste*

Rub the oxtail pieces with the spice and seasoning to taste. Leave for 20 minutes.

Melt the butter in a saucepan. Add the oxtail pieces and fry until evenly browned. Remove from the pan. Add the onions and carrots to the pan and fry until the onions are softened. Return the oxtail pieces to the pan and add the remaining ingredients. Bring to the boil, then cover and simmer for 4 hours or until the oxtail meat is almost falling off the bones.

Cool, then chill overnight. The next day, remove the layer of fat on the surface. Bring to the boil and simmer for 10 minutes. Transfer the oxtail pieces to a warmed serving dish and keep hot. Boil the cooking liquid to reduce, then pour a little of it over the oxtail pieces and the remainder into a sauceboat. **SERVES 4**

Red cabbage & bacon casserole

Metric/Imperial	American
6 streaky bacon rashers, chopped	6 bacon slices, chopped
1 large onion, sliced	1 large onion, sliced
1 large cooking apple, peeled, cored and sliced	1 large cooking apple, peeled, cored and sliced
2 large potatoes, sliced	2 large potatoes, sliced
1 medium red cabbage, shredded	1 medium red cabbage, shredded
7.5ml/1½ tsp. caraway seeds	1½ tsp. caraway seeds
30ml/2 tbs. lemon juice	2 tbs. lemon juice
15ml/1 tbs. wine vinegar	1 tbs. wine vinegar
300ml/½ pint chicken stock	1¼ cups chicken stock
15ml/1 tbs. brown sugar	1 tbs. brown sugar

Preheat the oven to 180°C/350°F, Gas Mark 4.
Fry the bacon and onion together in a flameproof casserole until the onion is softened. Stir in the remaining ingredients with seasoning to taste and bring to the boil. Cover the casserole and transfer to the oven. Cook for 2 hours or until the cabbage is very tender. **SERVES 4**

Stuffed roast chicken

Metric/Imperial	American
75g/3oz butter	*6 tbs. butter*
1 large onion, chopped	*1 large onion, chopped*
1 x 2½kg/5lb chicken with giblets	*1 x 5lb chicken with giblets*
4 chicken livers, chopped	*4 chicken livers, chopped*
5ml/1 tsp. dried mixed herbs	*1 tsp. dried mixed herbs*
100g/4oz cream cheese	*½ cup cream cheese*
50g/2oz dry breadcrumbs	*⅔ cup dry breadcrumbs*
300ml/½ pint chicken stock	*1¼ cups chicken stock*
150ml/¼ pint single cream	*⅔ cup light cream*

Preheat the oven to 220°C/425°F, Gas Mark 7.
Melt 25g/1oz (2 tablespoons) of the butter in a frying pan. Add the onion and fry until softened. Chop the chicken giblets and add to the pan with the livers and herbs. Fry for a further 3 minutes, remove from the heat and stir in the cream cheese, breadcrumbs and seasoning to taste. Use to stuff the chicken.
Place the chicken in a roasting pan and rub with the remaining butter. Roast for 15 minutes, then reduce the temperature to 180°C/350°F, Gas Mark 4 and continue roasting for 1 hour.
Mix together the chicken stock, cream and seasoning to taste and pour over the chicken. Return to the oven and roast for a further 30 minutes or until the chicken is cooked.
Transfer the chicken to a warmed serving platter. Skim the fat from the surface of the cooking juices in the pan and pour into a sauceboat.

SERVES 6

Turkey & walnut pie

Metric/Imperial	American
25g/1oz butter	2 tbs. butter
250g/8oz mushrooms, sliced	½lb mushrooms, sliced
25g/1oz flour	¼ cup flour
1.25ml/¼ tsp. cayenne	¼ tsp. cayenne
300ml/½ pint double cream	1¼ cups heavy cream
150ml/¼ pint soured cream	⅔ cup sour cream
2.5ml/½ tsp. dried thyme	½ tsp. dried thyme
2.5ml/½ tsp. dried sage	½ tsp. dried sage
1 bay leaf	1 bay leaf
¾kg/1½lb cooked turkey meat, diced	3 cups diced cooked turkey meat
100g/4oz walnuts, chopped	1 cup chopped walnuts
350g/12oz frozen puff pastry, thawed	¾lb frozen puff pastry, thawed
beaten egg yolk	beaten egg yolk

Preheat the oven to 220°C/425°F, Gas Mark 7.
Melt the butter in a saucepan. Add the mushrooms and fry for 3 minutes. Remove the mushrooms from the pan with a slotted spoon. Add the flour, cayenne and seasoning to taste to the pan and cook, stirring, for 2 minutes. Gradually stir in the double (heavy) and sour cream, then stir in the herbs and cook gently for 10 minutes, stirring frequently.
Remove from the heat and discard the bay leaf. Stir in the mushrooms, turkey and walnuts. Spoon into a deep pie dish. Roll out the dough and use to cover the pie. Make a slit in the centre and brush with the beaten egg yolk. Bake for 50 minutes, then reduce the temperature to 190°C/375°F, Gas Mark 5 and continue baking for 35 minutes or until golden brown. **SERVES 4-6**

Rabbit casserole

Metric/Imperial	American
2 x 2kg/4lb rabbits, cut into serving pieces	*2 x 4lb rabbits, cut into serving pieces*
30ml/2 tbs. malt vinegar	*2 tbs. malt vinegar*
75g/3oz butter	*6 tbs. butter*
900ml/1½ pints light beer	*3¾ cups light beer*
15ml/1 tbs. mustard	*1 tbs. mustard*
2 egg yolks	*2 egg yolks*
250g/8oz shallots or spring onions	*½lb shallots or scallions*
2 carrots, sliced	*2 carrots, sliced*
2 parsnips, sliced	*2 parsnips, sliced*
15g/½oz flour	*2 tbs. flour*
chopped parsley	*chopped parsley*

Put the rabbit pieces in a mixing bowl and sprinkle over the vinegar. Cover with water, then leave to marinate overnight.

Preheat the oven to 180°C/350°F, Gas Mark 4.

Drain the rabbit pieces and pat dry with paper towels. Rub the rabbit pieces with salt and pepper. Melt 50g/2oz (¼ cup) of the butter in a flameproof casserole. Add the rabbit and brown on all sides. Pour in the beer, then stir in the mustard and egg yolks. Heat gently, stirring, until just simmering. Remove from the heat and stir in the vegetables. Cover the casserole and transfer to the oven. Cook for 1 to 1¾ hours or until the rabbit is tender.

Place the casserole on top of the stove again. Mix the flour with the remaining butter to make a paste (beurre manié) and add in small pieces to the casserole, stirring. Simmer until thickened. Adjust the seasoning and serve sprinkled with parsley. **SERVES 6-8**

Whiting au gratin

Metric/Imperial	American
4 whiting fillets, skinned	*4 whiting fillets, skinned*
75g/3oz butter	*6 tbs. butter*
25g/1oz flour	*¼ cup flour*
250ml/8fl oz milk	*1 cup milk*
150ml/¼ pint single cream	*⅔ cup light cream*
175g/6oz Cheddar cheese, grated	*1½ cups grated Cheddar cheese*
50g/2oz dry breadcrumbs	*⅔ cup dry breadcrumbs*

Rub the fish with salt and pepper. Melt 50g/2oz (¼ cup) of the butter in a frying pan. Add the fish and fry for 5 minutes on each side or until cooked. Transfer to a warmed flameproof serving dish and keep hot.

Preheat the grill (broiler) to moderate.

Melt the remaining butter in a saucepan. Add the flour and cook, stirring, for 1 minute. Gradually stir in the milk and cream and bring to the boil. Simmer, stirring, until thickened. Pour the sauce over the fish and sprinkle with the cheese and breadcrumbs. Grill (broil) for 3 to 5 minutes or until the top is golden brown and bubbling. **SERVES 4**

Swedish herring

Metric/Imperial	American
6 large potatoes, thinly sliced	*6 large potatoes, thinly sliced*
6 salted herrings, soaked in water overnight, drained, boned and chopped	*6 salted herrings, soaked in water overnight, drained, boned and chopped*
6 medium onions, sliced	*6 medium onions, sliced*
300ml/½ pint single cream	*1¼ cups light cream*
25g/1oz butter	*2 tbs. butter*

Preheat the oven to 180°C/350°F, Gas Mark 4.
Cover the bottom of a greased baking dish with half the potato slices. Arrange the herrings on top and cover with the onions. Cover with the remaining potato slices and pour over half the cream. Dot the butter over the surface.
Bake for 40 minutes, then pour over the remaining cream. Bake for a further 25 to 30 minutes or until the potatoes are tender. **SERVES 6**

Ham & celery rolls

Metric/Imperial	American
40g/1½oz butter	3 tbs. butter
15ml/1 tbs. flour	1 tbs. flour
300ml/½ pint milk	1¼ cups milk
pinch of grated nutmeg	pinch of grated nutmeg
100g/4oz Cheddar cheese, grated	1 cup grated Cheddar cheese
4 canned celery hearts, drained	4 canned celery hearts, drained
and halved	and halved
8 slices ham	8 slices ham
30ml/2 tbs. toasted breadcrumbs	2 tbs. toasted breadcrumbs

Preheat the oven to 180°C/350°F, Gas Mark 4.

Melt 25g/1oz (2 tablespoons) of the butter in a saucepan. Add the flour and cook, stirring, for 1 minute. Gradually stir in the milk and bring to the boil. Simmer, stirring, until thickened. Add the nutmeg, all but 15ml/1 tablespoon of the cheese and seasoning to taste.

Wrap each celery heart in a slice of ham and arrange in an ovenproof serving dish. Pour over the sauce and sprinkle with the remaining cheese and the breadcrumbs. Dot the top with the remaining butter. Bake for 20 to 25 minutes or until the top is golden brown. **SERVES 4**

Stuffed peppers

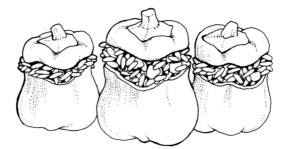

Metric/Imperial

4 large red or green peppers
15ml/1 tbs. oil
1 small onion, chopped
1 garlic clove, crushed
250g/8oz minced lamb
400g/14oz canned tomatoes
5ml/1 tsp. ground coriander
150g/5oz cooked long-grain rice
5ml/1 tsp. chopped mint

American

4 large red or green peppers
1 tbs. oil
1 small onion, chopped
1 garlic clove, crushed
½lb ground lamb
14oz canned tomatoes
1 tsp. ground coriander
2 cups cooked long-grain rice
1 tsp. chopped mint

Cut the stalk end from each pepper and carefully remove the seeds and white pith.

Heat the oil in a saucepan. Add the onion and garlic and fry until softened. Stir in the lamb and fry until browned. Add the undrained tomatoes, coriander and seasoning to taste and simmer, covered, for 30 minutes. Stir in the rice and mint and cook for a further 5 minutes. Preheat the oven to 190°C/375°F, Gas Mark 5.

Fill the peppers with the lamb and rice mixture. Stand them upright in a greased baking dish and bake for 40 minutes. **SERVES 4**

Bacon & apple flan

Metric/Imperial	American
shortcrust pastry made with 175g/6oz flour, 75g/3oz fat, etc.	pie pastry made with 1½ cups flour, 6 tbs. fat, etc.
15g/½oz butter	1 tbs. butter
6 back bacon rashers, chopped	6 Canadian bacon slices, chopped
2 large cooking apples, peeled, cored and chopped	2 large cooking apples, peeled, cored and chopped
450ml/¾ pint hot white sauce	1 pint hot white sauce
175g/6oz Cheddar cheese, grated	1½ cups grated Cheddar cheese
chopped parsley	chopped parsley

Preheat the oven to 200°C/400°F, Gas Mark 6.

Roll out the dough and use to line a 23cm/9 inch loose-bottomed flan tin (tart pan). Bake blind for 15 minutes or until golden brown. Allow to cool.

Melt the butter in a frying pan. Add the bacon and fry until it is golden brown and crisp. Remove from the pan with a slotted spoon and drain on paper towels. Add the apples to the pan and cook for 5 minutes or until just tender. Remove from the heat and stir in the bacon, white sauce, half the cheese and seasoning to taste. Stir until the cheese has melted, then pour into the pastry case.

Preheat the grill (broiler) to moderate.

Sprinkle the remaining cheese over the top of the flan (tart) and grill (broil) until the cheese is golden brown. Sprinkle with parsley and serve hot. **SERVES 4**

Walnut cauliflower

Metric/Imperial	American
25g/1oz butter	*2 tbs. butter*
25g/1oz flour	*¼ cup flour*
350ml/12fl oz milk	*1½ cups milk*
175ml/6fl oz single cream	*¾ cup light cream*
1 egg, lightly beaten	*1 egg, lightly beaten*
60ml/4 tbs. cider vinegar	*¼ cup cider vinegar*
30ml/2 tbs. dark brown sugar	*2 tbs. dark brown sugar*
30ml/2 tbs. French mustard	*2 tbs. French mustard*
100g/4oz walnuts, chopped and toasted	*1 cup chopped walnuts, toasted*
1 large cauliflower, cooked and kept hot	*1 large cauliflower, cooked and kept hot*

Melt the butter in a saucepan. Add the flour and cook, stirring, for 1 minute. Gradually stir in the milk and cream and bring to the boil, stirring. Simmer, until thickened. Add the egg, vinegar, sugar and mustard and cook gently for 2 to 3 minutes. Do not boil or the egg will curdle. Stir in the walnuts and cook for a further 2 minutes. Place the cauliflower in a warmed serving dish and pour over the walnut sauce. Serve hot. **SERVES 2-3**

Olive Pizza

Metric/Imperial

PASTRY
250g/8oz self-raising flour
5ml/1 tsp. baking powder
1.25ml/¼ tsp. dried basil
1.25ml/¼ tsp. dried oregano
25g/1oz butter
50g/2oz Cheddar cheese, grated
150ml/¼ pint milk

TOPPING
200g/7½oz canned tuna, drained
  and flaked
400g/14oz canned tomatoes,
  drained and sliced
2.5ml/½ tsp. dried oregano
250g/8oz Cheddar cheese, grated
10 stuffed olives, halved

American

PASTRY
2 cups self-rising flour
1 tsp. baking powder
¼ tsp. dried basil
¼ tsp. dried oregano
2 tbs. butter
½ cup grated Cheddar cheese
⅔ cup milk

TOPPING
7½oz canned tuna, drained and
  flaked
14oz canned tomatoes, drained
  and sliced
½ tsp. dried oregano
2 cups grated Cheddar cheese
10 stuffed olives, halved

Preheat the oven to 220°C/425°F, Gas Mark 7.
Sift the flour, baking powder, herbs and seasoning to taste into a mixing bowl. Rub in the butter until the mixture resembles breadcrumbs, then stir in the cheese. Bind together with the milk to make a soft dough. Roll out the dough to make a 25-30cm/10-12in circle and place on a greased baking sheet.
Cover the centre of the dough circle with the tuna. Arrange the tomato slices around the edge and sprinkle with the oregano and seasoning to taste. Cover all with the cheese and arrange the olives on top.
Bake for 30 to 35 minutes or until the pastry is cooked.   **SERVES 3**

Omelets

Metric/Imperial	American
6 eggs	*6 eggs*
30ml/2 tbs. water	*2 tbs. water*
15g/½oz butter	*1 tbs. butter*

Mix together the eggs, water and seasoning to taste. Melt the butter in a large omelet pan. Pour in the egg mixture, stir, then leave to cook gently until the bottom sets. Lift the set edges of the omelet to allow the liquid egg mixture to run onto the pan. When the omelet begins to set again, spoon over one of the following hot fillings:

250g/8oz cooked spinach, chopped and mixed with 15g/½oz butter, 30ml/2 tbs cream and seasoning;

1 chopped onion, 3 diced back bacon rashers (Canadian bacon slices) and 8 sliced mushrooms fried together in butter;

2 chopped potatoes, fried in butter and seasoned;

1 chopped onion, 2 crushed garlic cloves and 2 skinned and chopped tomatoes fried together in butter and seasoned.   **SERVES 2-3**

Baked bean rarebit

Metric/Imperial

25g/1oz butter
1 medium onion, chopped
1 green pepper, cored, seeded and
   finely chopped
400g/14oz canned kidney beans,
   drained
400g/14oz canned baked beans
60ml/4 tbs. tomato ketchup
15ml/1 tbs. Worcestershire sauce
10ml/2 tsp. mild chilli powder
175g/6oz Cheddar cheese, grated
4 large slices hot buttered toast

American

2 tbs. butter
1 medium onion, chopped
1 green pepper, cored, seeded and
   finely chopped
14oz canned kidney beans,
   drained
14oz canned baked beans
¼ cup tomato catsup
1 tbs. Worcestershire sauce
2 tsp. mild chilli powder
1½ cups grated Cheddar cheese
4 large slices hot buttered toast

Melt the butter in a saucepan. Add the onion and pepper and fry until softened. Stir in the beans, ketchup (catsup), Worcestershire sauce, chilli powder and seasoning to taste and cook for 5 minutes. Stir in the cheese and cook for a further 3 minutes or until the cheese has melted.

Spoon the bean mixture over the toast and serve hot. **SERVES 4**

Russian salad

Metric/Imperial	American
3 large potatoes, cooked and diced	*3 large potatoes, cooked and diced*
4 carrots, cooked and diced	*4 carrots, cooked and diced*
100g/4oz French beans, cooked and halved	*¼lb green beans, cooked and halved*
1 small onion, finely chopped	*1 small onion, finely chopped*
100g/4oz cooked peas	*¾ cup cooked peas*
50g/2oz cooked tongue, diced	*¼ cup diced cooked tongue*
100g/4oz cooked chicken, diced	*½ cup diced cooked chicken*
50g/2oz garlic sausage, diced	*¼ cup diced garlic sausage*
250ml/8fl oz mayonnaise	*1 cup mayonnaise*
1.25ml/¼ tsp. cayenne	*¼ tsp. cayenne*
2 hard-boiled eggs, sliced	*2 hard cooked eggs, sliced*
1 beetroot, cooked and thinly sliced	*1 beet, cooked and thinly sliced*
2 gherkins, thinly sliced	*2 cocktail dill pickles, thinly sliced*

Mix together the potatoes, carrots, beans, onion, peas, tongue, chicken, sausage, mayonnaise and cayenne. Spoon into a serving dish and garnish with the eggs, beetroot (beet) and gherkins (pickles). Chill for 15 to 20 minutes before serving. **SERVES 4-8**

DESSERTS

Raspberry fool

Metric/Imperial	American
½kg/1lb fresh raspberries	1lb fresh raspberries
250g/8oz caster sugar	1 cup super fine sugar
350ml/12fl oz double cream	1½ cups heavy cream

Sprinkle the raspberries with the sugar and leave for 2 hours, then mash to form a pulp. Add the cream and beat until well mixed. Pour into a glass serving dish and chill for 1 hour before serving.

SERVES 2-3

Upside down apple tart

Metric/Imperial	American
75g/3oz butter	6 tbs. butter
100g/4oz caster sugar	½ cup superfine sugar
¾kg/1½lb tart apples, peeled, cored and thinly sliced	1½lb tart apples, peeled, cored and thinly sliced
2.5ml/½ tsp. grated nutmeg	½ tsp. grated nutmeg
2.5ml/½ tsp. ground cinnamon	½ tsp. ground cinnamon
juice of 1 lemon	juice of 1 lemon
15ml/1 tbs. orange juice	1 tbs. orange juice
shortcrust pastry made with 175g/6oz flour, 75g/3oz fat, 1 egg yolk, sugar to taste, etc.	pie pastry made with 1½ cups flour, 6 tbs. fat, 1 egg yolk, sugar to taste, etc.

Preheat the oven to 190°C/375°F, Gas Mark 5.

Generously grease a shallow 20cm/8in round baking dish with 50g/2oz (¼ cup) of the butter. Sprinkle over the sugar, then arrange the apple slices in the dish and sprinkle them with the spices and fruit juices.

Roll out the dough to a 25cm/10in circle and place over the dish, letting the dough fall over the sides of the dish so as to make a case when the tart is turned out. Prick all over and bake for 30 to 40 minutes or until golden brown.

Leave for 5 minutes before turning out, upside down, onto a plate.

SERVES 4-6

Pineapple cheesecake

Metric/Imperial	American
250g/8oz shortbread, crushed	2 cups crushed shortbread
100g/4oz butter, melted	½ cup butter, melted
30ml/2tbs. sugar	2 tbs. sugar
2.5ml/½ tsp. ground allspice	½ tsp. ground allspice
FILLING	**FILLING**
1¼kg/2½lb ricotta or cottage cheese	2½lb (5 cups) ricotta or cottage cheese
50g/2oz caster sugar	¼ cup superfine sugar
30ml/2 tbs. flour	2 tbs. flour
2.5ml/½ tsp. vanilla essence	½ tsp. vanilla extract
finely grated rind of 2 lemons	finely grated rind of 2 lemons
pinch of ground allspice	pinch of ground allspice
3 egg yolks	3 egg yolks
1 large pineapple, peeled, cored and finely chopped	1 large pineapple, peeled, cored and finely chopped
6 walnut halves	6 walnut halves

Mix together the shortbread, butter, sugar and allspice and use to line the bottom of a greased 23cm/9in loose-bottomed deep cake pan (springform pan). Chill until set.

Preheat the oven to 180°C/350°F, Gas Mark 4.

Rub the cheese through a strainer, then beat in the sugar, flour, vanilla, lemon rind and allspice. Beat in the egg yolks. Spread half the ricotta mixture over the crumb base and cover with the pineapple. Spoon over the remaining ricotta mixture and smooth the top. Bake for 20 minutes. Arrange the walnuts halves on top and bake for a further 10 to 15 minutes or until the filling is firm. Allow to cool, then remove from the pan and chill well.   **SERVES 6-8**

Deep fruit tart

Metric/Imperial

shortcrust pastry made with 250g/
8oz flour, 100g/4oz butter, etc.
15g/½oz powdered gelatine
30ml/2 tbs. water
300ml/½ pint orange juice
2 apples, peeled, cored and sliced
2 oranges, peeled and segmented
2 peaches, peeled, stoned and sliced
10 plums, stoned and sliced
2 bananas, sliced
2 tangerines, peeled and segmented

American

pie pastry made with 2 cups flour,
½ cup butter, etc.
2 envelopes unflavoured gelatin
2 tbs. water
1¼ cups orange juice
2 apples, peeled, cored and sliced
2 oranges, peeled and segmented
2 peaches, peeled, pitted and sliced
10 plums, pitted and sliced
2 bananas, sliced
2 tangerines, peeled and segmented

Preheat the oven to 200°C/400°F, Gas Mark 6.
Roll out the dough and use to line a 20cm/8in round deep cake pan with a removable base (springform pan). Bake blind for 15 minutes or until the pastry is golden brown. Allow to cool completely, then remove the pastry case from the pan.
Dissolve the gelatine in the water, then stir into the orange juice. Spread one-third of this mixture over the bottom of the pastry case and chill until set.
Arrange the fruit decoratively in the pastry case and spoon the remaining liquid gelatine mixture over the top. Chill until set.

SERVES 4-6

Pavlova

Metric/Imperial	American
5 egg whites	*5 egg whites*
300g/10oz plus 15ml/1 tbs.	*1¼ cups plus 1 tbs. superfine*
caster sugar	*sugar*
10ml/2 tsp. cornflour	*2 tsp. cornstarch*
2.5ml/½ tsp. vanilla essence	*½ tsp. vanilla extract*
5ml/1 tsp. malt vinegar	*1 tsp. malt vinegar*
300ml/½ pint double cream, whipped	*1¼ cups heavy cream, whipped*
½kg/1lb fresh or canned fruit,	*1lb fresh or canned fruit,*
such as pineapple, passion	*such as pineapple, passion*
fruit, strawberries, etc.	*fruit, strawberries, etc.*

Preheat the oven to 150°C/300°F, Gas Mark 2. Line a baking sheet with non-stick (parchment) paper and draw a 23cm/9in circle on the paper.

Beat the egg whites until stiff, then gradually beat in 100g/4oz (½ cup) of the sugar. Continue beating until stiff again. Fold in all but 15ml/1 tablespoon of the remaining sugar, the cornflour (cornstarch), vanilla and vinegar. Spoon about one-third of the meringue mixture into the circle to make a base about 5mm/¼in thick. Pipe the remaining meringue around the edge in decorative swirls to form a case. Bake for 1 hour, then turn off the oven but leave the meringue inside for another 30 minutes.

Peel off the paper and place the meringue case on a serving plate. Fold the remaining sugar into the cream and use to fill the case. Pile the fruit on top and serve. **SERVES 6-8**

Steamed layer pudding

Metric/Imperial	American
SUET PASTRY	**SUET PASTRY**
175g/6oz flour	*1½ cups flour*
2.5ml/½ tsp. sugar	*½ tsp. sugar*
75g/3oz shredded suet	*⅓ cup shredded suet*
60-90ml/4-6 tbs. water	*4-6 tbs. water*
FILLING	**FILLING**
2 large cooking apples, peeled, cored and chopped	*2 large cooking apples, peeled, cored and chopped*
juice of ½ lemon	*juice of ½ lemon*
100g/4oz raisins	*⅔ cup raisins*
15ml/1 tbs. chopped mixed candied peel	*1 tbs. chopped mixed candied peel*
5ml/1 tsp. mixed spice	*1 tsp. apple pie spice*
30ml/2 tbs. brown sugar	*2 tbs. brown sugar*
15ml/1 tbs. golden syrup	*1 tbs. light corn syrup*

To make the pastry, sift the flour, sugar and a pinch of salt into a bowl. Rub in the suet, then add enough water to bind to a stiff dough. Chill for 10 minutes.

Mix together all the ingredients for the filling.

Roll out the dough to about 5mm/¼in thick and cut out four circles of graduating sizes, the first just to fit the bottom of a greased 1.2 litre/2 pint (2½ pint) pudding basin (steaming mold). Cover this first dough circle with about one-third of the filling, then add another dough circle. Continue in this way, ending with the last dough circle. The basin (mold) should not be completely full. Cover with greaseproof (waxed) paper and foil, making a pleat to allow for expansion and steam for 4 hours. **SERVES 4-6**

Treacle tart

Metric/Imperial

*shortcrust pastry made with
175g/6oz flour, 75g/3oz fat,
1 egg yolk, etc.*
6 tbs. dark treacle or molasses
60ml/4 tbs. golden syrup
*grated rind and juice of 1 large
lemon*
100g/4oz fresh breadcrumbs

American

*pie pastry made with 1½ cups
flour, 6 tbs. fat, 1 egg yolk,
etc.*
6 tbs. dark treacle or molasses
¼ cup light corn syrup
*grated rind and juice of 1 large
lemon*
2 cups fresh breadcrumbs

Preheat the oven to 190°C/375°F, Gas Mark 6.
Roll out the dough and use to line a 23cm/9in flan tin (tart pan).
Reserve the dough trimmings.
Put the treacle or molasses, syrup and lemon rind and juice into a
saucepan and heat, stirring, until the mixture has thinned. Sprinkle
the breadcrumbs over the pastry base and pour over the treacle.
mixture.
Roll out the dough trimmings and cut into strips about 1cm/½in wide.
Arrange over the filling in a lattice pattern. Bake for 25 to 30 minutes
or until the pastry is golden brown. Serve hot or cold.   **SERVES 6-8**

BAKING

Dried fruit scones

Metric/Imperial	American
250g/8oz flour	*2 cups flour*
10ml/2 tsp. baking powder	*2 tsp. baking powder*
5ml/1 tsp. bicarbonate of soda	*1 tsp. baking soda*
40g/1½oz vegetable fat	*3 tbs. vegetable fat*
50g/2oz caster sugar	*¼ cup superfine sugar*
50g/2oz raisins	*⅓ cup raisins*
30ml/2 tbs. currants	*2 tbs. currants*
1 large egg	*1 egg*
75ml/3fl oz milk	*6 tbs. milk*

Preheat the oven to 230°C/450°F, Gas Mark 8.
Sift the flour, baking powder, soda and 1.25ml/¼ teaspoon salt into a mixing bowl. Rub in the fat until the mixture resembles breadcrumbs. Stir in the sugar, raisins and currants. Mix together the egg and milk and add to the dry ingredients. Knead to form a soft dough.
Roll out the dough on a floured surface to 1cm/½in thick. Cut out about twelve 5cm/2in circles and place them on a greased baking sheet. Bake for 10 to 15 minutes or until risen and golden brown.
Serve hot or cold. **MAKES ABOUT 12**

New England soda bread

Metric/Imperial	American
100g/4oz stale crustless bread	*¼lb stale crustless bread (about 4 large slices)*
500ml/16fl oz water	*1 pint water*
120ml/4fl oz dark treacle	*½ cup molasses*
150g/5oz cornmeal	*1 cup cornmeal*
150g/5oz rye flour	*1¼ cups rye flour*
150g/5oz wholemeal flour	*1¼ cups wholewheat flour*
10ml/2 tsp. bicarbonate of soda	*2 tsp. baking soda*

Soak the bread in 350ml/12fl oz (1½ cups) of the water overnight. The next day, rub the bread through a strainer to make a purée. Stir in the treacle (molasses).

Mix together the cornmeal, rye and wholemeal (wholewheat) flours and soda in another bowl. Make a well in the centre and add the bread mixture and remaining water. Mix well.

Divide between two greased 900ml/1½ pint (2 pint) pudding basins (steaming molds) and cover with foil. Steam for 3 to 3½ hours.

Preheat the oven to 150°C/300°F, Gas Mark 2.

Remove the foil covers and place the basins (molds) in the oven. Bake for 15 minutes to remove all excess moisture from the bread. Cool on a wire rack.   **MAKES 2 LOAVES**

Angel cake

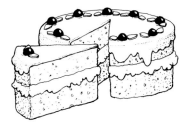

Metric/Imperial	American
100g/4oz flour	*1 cup flour*
300g/12oz caster sugar	*1½ cups superfine sugar*
12 egg whites	*12 egg whites*
6.25ml/1¼ tsp. cream of tartar	*1¼ tsp. cream of tartar*
1.25ml/¼ tsp. salt	*¼ tsp. salt*
5ml/1 tsp. vanilla essence	*1 tsp. vanilla extract*

Preheat the oven to 170°C/325°F, Gas Mark 3.
Sift the flour with one-third of the sugar three times. Beat the egg whites until frothy. Add the cream of tartar and salt and continue beating until the mixture forms soft peaks. Gradually beat in the remaining sugar and vanilla and continue beating until stiff but not dry. Fold in the flour mixture and spoon into a 25cm/10in angel cake pan or ring mould (tube pan). Bake for 45 minutes or until firm.
Cool, upside down, over a wire rack, then remove from the pan. Serve sprinkled with icing (confectioners') sugar, if liked. **SERVES 8**

Orange walnut cake

Metric/Imperial	American
300g/10oz self-raising flour	*2½ cups self-rising flour*
250g/8oz sugar	*1 cup sugar*
250g/8oz butter	*1 cup butter*
5 eggs	*5 eggs*
60ml/4 tbs. marmalade	*¼ cup marmalade*
75g/3oz walnuts, chopped	*¾ cup chopped walnuts*
15ml/1 tbs. orange juice	*1 tbs. orange juice*
7.5ml/1½ tsp. lemon juice	*1½ tsp. lemon juice*

Preheat the oven to 180°C/350°F, Gas Mark 4.

Sift the flour with 5ml/1 teaspoon salt. Cream the sugar and butter together until the mixture is pale and fluffy. Beat in the eggs one at a time, following each with 15ml/1 tablespoon of flour. Fold in the remaining flour with the remaining ingredients. Add a little more orange juice if necessary to give the batter a dropping consistency.

Pour into a greased 20cm/8in round deep cake pan and bake for 1 to 1¼ hours or until a skewer inserted into the centre of the cake comes out clean. Cool in the pan for 10 minutes, then turn out onto a wire rack and cool completely.

Cover the cake with plain icing (frosting) of your choice. If you like, shred the rind from two oranges, blanch in boiling water for 2 minutes, drain well and use to decorate the top of the cake.

MAKES A 20CM/8IN CAKE

Dundee cake

Metric/Imperial	American
300g/10oz flour	2½ cups flour
2.5ml/½ tsp. baking powder	½ tsp. baking powder
5ml/1 tsp. mixed spice	1 tsp. apple pie spice
250g/8oz butter	1 cup butter
250g/8oz caster sugar	1 cup superfine sugar
5 eggs	5 eggs
100g/4oz each raisins, currants and sultanas	⅔ cup currants 1⅓ cups raisins
50g/2oz chopped mixed candied fruit	⅓ cup chopped mixed candied fruit
50g/2oz glacé cherries	⅓ cup candied cherries
grated rind of 1 orange	grated rind of 1 orange
grated rind of 1 lemon	grated rind of 1 lemon
50g/2oz blanched almonds, halved	½ cup halved blanched almonds

Preheat the oven to 170°C/325°F, Gas Mark 3.
Sift together the flour, baking powder and spice. Cream the butter and sugar together until the mixture is pale and fluffy. Beat in the eggs one at a time, following each with 15ml/1 tablespoon of the flour mixture. Fold in the remaining flour mixture with the dried and candied fruits and rind. Spoon into a greased and lined 20cm/8in round deep cake pan. Level the top and arrange the almond halves over the surface in concentric circles.
Bake for 2 hours or until a skewer inserted into the centre comes out clean. Cover the cake if it browns too quickly. **MAKES A 20CM/8IN CAKE**

Profiteroles

Metric/Imperial

300ml/½ pint water
75g/3oz butter, cut into pieces
pinch of grated nutmeg
300g/10oz flour, sifted
5 large eggs

FILLING

300ml/½ pint double cream
100g/4oz plain or milk chocolate,
  melted

American

1¼ cups water
6 tbs. butter, cut into pieces
pinch of grated nutmeg
2½ cups flour, sifted
5 eggs

FILLING

1¼ cups whipping cream
4 squares plain or milk chocolate
  melted

For the pastry, put the water in a saucepan and bring to the boil. Add the butter, nutmeg and 5ml/1 teaspoon salt. When the butter has melted, remove from the heat and add the flour. Beat until the mixture pulls away from the sides of the pan. Beat in the eggs one at a time until the mixture is thick and somewhat glossy. (You may not need all the eggs.)

Preheat the oven to 220°C/425°F, Gas Mark 7.

Pipe or spoon the pastry in 16 mounds on two greased baking sheets. Bake for 10 minutes, then reduce the tempeature to 190°C/375°F, Gas Mark 5, and continue baking for 15 to 20 minutes or until puffed up and golden brown. Remove from the oven and make a slit in the side of each puff to allow steam to escape. Allow to cool.

Whip the cream and use to fill the puffs. Pile them up on a serving plate and pour over the melted chocolate.   **SERVES 4**

Fruit tartlets

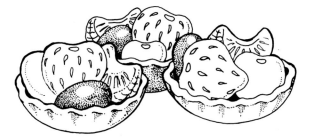

Metric/Imperial	American
shortcrust pastry made with 450g/1lb flour, 250g/8oz fat, etc.	*pie pastry made with 4 cups flour, 1 cup fat, etc.*
16 green grapes, peeled, seeded and halved	*16 green grapes, peeled, seeded and halved*
16 black grapes, peeled, seeded and halved	*16 black grapes, peeled, seeded and halved*
16 strawberries, halved	*16 strawberries, halved*
75g/3oz canned mandarin oranges, drained	*3oz canned mandarin oranges, drained*
75g/3oz canned black cherries, drained and stoned	*3oz canned black cherries, drained and pitted*
apricot jam or redcurrant jelly	*apricot jam or redcurrant jelly*

Preheat the oven to 200°C/400°F, Gas Mark 6.
Roll out the dough and use to line 16 greased patty tins (shallow muffin tins). Bake blind for 20 minutes or until golden brown. Allow to cool.
Mix together the fruit and divide between the pastry cases. Brush with a little melted apricot jam or redcurrant jelly and allow to set before serving. **MAKES 16**

Gingerbread

Metric/Imperial	American
250g/8oz flour	*2 cups flour*
2.5ml/½ tsp. bicarbonate of soda	*½ tsp. baking soda*
7.5ml/1½ tsp. ground ginger	*1½ tsp. ground ginger*
1.25ml/¼ tsp. ground cloves	*¼ tsp. ground cloves*
2.5ml/½ tsp. ground cinnamon	*½ tsp. ground cinnamon*
75g/3oz butter	*6 tbs. butter*
100g/4oz sugar	*½ cup sugar*
1 egg	*1 egg*
175ml/6fl oz treacle	*¾ cup molasses*
250ml/8fl oz soured cream	*1 cup sour cream*
50g/2oz raisins	*⅓ cup raisins*

Preheat the oven to 180°C/350°F, Gas Mark 4.

Sift the flour, soda and spices together. Cream the butter and sugar together until the mixture is pale and fluffy. Add the egg and treacle (molasses) and beat until smooth, then mix in the sour cream. Fold in the flour mixture followed by the raisins.

Spoon into a greased 1kg/2lb loaf pan and bake for 1¼ hours or until a skewer inserted into the centre of the gingerbread comes out clean. Allow to cool in the pan. **MAKES A 1KG/2 LB LOAF**

Metric/Imperial	American
90g/3½oz soft brown sugar	*½ cup + 2½ tbs. brown sugar*
75g/3oz desiccated coconut	*¾ cup shredded coconut*
75g/3oz rolled oats	*1 cup rolled oats*
90ml/6 tbs. cornflakes	*6 tbs. cornflakes*
100g/4oz butter	*½ cup butter*
15ml/1 tbs. clear honey	*1 tbs. clear honey*

Preheat the oven to 170°C/325°F, Gas Mark 3.
Mix together the sugar, coconut, oats and cornflakes. Melt the butter with the honey, then stir into the dry ingredients. Spoon into a greased shallow rectangular cake pan, spreading well into the corners. Bake for 30 minutes or until golden brown
Cut into 5cm/2in squares and allow to cool in the pan.   **MAKES 18**

Cockle soup

Metric/Imperial	American
48 cockles, cooked and cooking broth reserved	48 cockles, cooked and cooking broth reserved
50g/2oz butter	¼ cup butter
15g/½oz flour	2 tbs. flour
600ml/1 pint milk	2½ cups milk
30ml/2 tbs. chopped parsley	2 tbs. chopped parsley
2 celery stalks, chopped	2 celery stalks, chopped
15ml/1 tbs. lemon juice	1 tbs. lemon juice
60ml/4 tbs. double cream	¼ cup heavy cream

Remove the cockles from their shells. Melt the butter in a saucepan. Add the flour and cook, stirring, for 1 minute. Gradually stir in the milk and strained cockle broth and bring to the boil, stirring. Add the parsley, celery, lemon juice and seasoning to taste and cook for 10 minutes.

Add the cockles and cream and cook gently for a further 2 to 3 minutes or until the cockles are heated through. **SERVES 6**

Fish soup

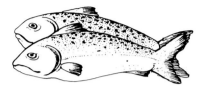

Metric/Imperial	American
75ml/3floz olive oil	⅓ cup olive oil
2 large onions, chopped	2 large onions, chopped
4 garlic cloves, crushed	4 garlic cloves, crushed
3 leeks, chopped	3 leeks, chopped
6 spring onions, chopped	6 scallions, chopped
½kg/1lb tomatoes, skinned, seeded and chopped	1lb tomatoes, skinned, seeded and chopped
15ml/1 tbs. tomato purée	1 tbs. tomato paste
5ml/1 tsp. fennel seeds	1 tsp. fennel seeds
1 bouquet garni	1 bouquet garni
1¼kg/2½lb prepared fish (mullet, bass, whiting and Dublin bay prawns), chopped	2½lb prepared fish (mullet, bass, whiting and jumbo shrimp), chopped
600ml/1 pint water	2½ cups water
250g/8oz crabmeat, flaked	½lb crabmeat, flaked

Heat the oil in a saucepan. Add the onions, garlic, leeks and spring onions (scallions) and fry until softened. Stir in the tomatoes, tomato purée (paste), fennel seeds, bouquet garni and seasoning to taste. Simmer for 5 minutes.
Add the fish and water and bring to the boil. Simmer for 15 minutes, stirring occasionally. Add the crabmeat and simmer for a further 5 minutes or until all the fish is tender. **SERVES 4-6**

Asparagus cream soup

Metric/Imperial	American
1kg/2lb asparagus	*2lb asparagus*
1 small onion, sliced	*1 small onion, sliced*
900ml/1½ pints light stock	*2 pints light stock*
25g/1oz butter	*2 tbs. butter*
25g/1oz flour	*¼ cup flour*
2 egg yolks	*2 egg yolks*
150ml/¼ pint single cream	*⅔ cup light cream*

Cut off the asparagus tips and reserve. Cut the stalks into 5cm/2in pieces. Put the stalk pieces, onion and stock in a saucepan and bring to the boil. Cover and simmer for 30 minutes.

Meanwhile, cook the asparagus tips gently in simmering salted water for 5 minutes or until they are tender. Drain.

Purée the asparagus stalk mixture and return to the saucepan. Season to taste and reheat. Mix the butter and flour together to make a paste (beurre manié) and add to the soup in small pieces, stirring. Simmer until thickened.

Mix together the egg yolks and cream. Add a little of the hot soup, then return to the pan. Heat through gently. Do not boil. Add the asparagus tips and serve hot. **SERVES 4**

Petite marmite

Metric/Imperial	American
1 chicken carcass	*1 chicken carcass*
½kg/1lb topside of beef, cut into 1cm/½in pieces	*1lb top round of beef, cut into ½in pieces*
1.8 litres/3 pints beef consommé	*4 pints beef consommé*
2 carrots, shredded	*2 carrots, shredded*
1 turnip, shredded	*1 turnip, shredded*
2 leeks, shredded	*2 leeks, shredded*
1 onion, finely chopped	*1 onion, finely chopped*
2 celery stalks, shredded	*2 celery stalks, shredded*
½ small white cabbage, cored and shredded	*½ small white cabbage, cored and shredded*
175g/6oz cooked chicken breast meat, shredded	*1 cup shredded cooked chicken breast meat*

Put the chicken carcass and beef in a marmite (earthenware pot) or saucepan and pour over the consommé. Bring to the boil and boil for 5 minutes, skimming any scum that rises to the surface. Add all the vegetables. Cover and simmer for 2 to 2½ hours or until the beef is tender.

Remove and discard the chicken carcass. Stir the chicken meat into the soup and heat through gently.   **SERVES 4-6**

Gazpacho

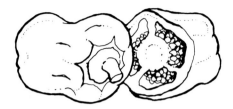

Metric/Imperial	American
3 slices of brown bread, cubed	*3 slices of brown bread, cubed*
300ml/½ pint tomato juice	*1¼ cups tomato juice*
2 garlic cloves, minced	*2 garlic cloves, minced*
½ cucumber, peeled and finely chopped	*½ cucumber, peeled and finely chopped*
1 green pepper, cored, seeded and finely chopped	*1 green pepper, cored, seeded and finely chopped*
1 red pepper, cored, seeded and finely chopped	*1 red pepper, cored, seeded and finely chopped*
1 large onion, finely chopped	*1 large onion, finely chopped*
¾kg/1½lb tomatoes, skinned, seeded and chopped	*1½lb tomatoes, skinned, seeded and chopped*
75ml/3floz olive oil	*⅓ cup olive oil*
30ml/2 tbs. wine vinegar	*2 tbs. wine vinegar*
1.25ml/¼ tsp. dried marjoram	*¼ tsp. dried marjoram*
1.25ml/¼ tsp. dried basil	*¼ tsp. dried basil*

Soak the bread cubes in the tomato juice for 5 minutes. Squeeze them to remove excess liquid and transfer to another bowl. Reserve the tomato juice.

Add the garlic, cucumber, peppers, onion and tomatoes to the bread. Purée in a blender, or pound to a paste with a pestle and mortar, or rub through a strainer or food mill. Stir in the reserved tomato juice, oil, vinegar, herbs and seasoning to taste. The soup should be the consistency of single (light) cream, so if necessary add more tomato juice. Chill well.

Drop a few ice cubes into the soup and serve with croutons and chopped cucumber, hard-boiled (hard-cooked) egg and olives.

SERVES 4

Chicken liver pâté

Metric/Imperial	American
1 celery stalk	*1 celery stalk*
3 parsley sprigs	*3 parsley sprigs*
8 peppercorns	*8 peppercorns*
½kg/1lb chicken livers	*1lb chicken livers*
2.5ml/½ tsp. Tabasco sauce	*½ tsp. Tabasco sauce*
250g/8oz butter	*1 cup butter*
1.25ml/¼ tsp. grated nutmeg	*¼ tsp. grated nutmeg*
10ml/2 tsp. dry mustard	*2 tsp. dry mustard*
1.25ml/¼ tsp. ground cloves	*¼ tsp. ground cloves*
1 medium onion, minced	*1 medium onion, minced*
1 garlic clove, minced	*1 garlic clove, minced*
30ml/2 tbs. brandy	*2 tbs. brandy*
50g/2oz stuffed olives, sliced	*½ cup sliced stuffed olives*

Half fill a saucepan with water and bring to the boil. Add the celery, parsley and peppercorns and simmer for 10 minutes. Add the chicken livers, cover and simmer for a further 10 minutes. Drain the livers and mince (grind) them. Add the Tabasco, butter, nutmeg, mustard, cloves, onion, garlic, brandy and salt to taste to the livers and mix together thoroughly.

Press the liver mixture into a serving dish and decorate the top with the olive slices. Chill for at least 6 hours before serving. **SERVES 8**

Cheese pâté

Metric/Imperial

750ml/1¼ pints milk
1 large onion, chopped
1 large carrot, chopped
2 celery stalks, chopped
1 bouquet garni
75g/3oz butter
75g/3oz flour
45ml/3 tbs. mayonnaise
10ml/2 tsp. lemon juice
3 garlic cloves, crushed
10 stuffed olives, finely chopped
pinch of cayenne
350g/12oz Stilton or other blue
    cheese, rind removed, crumbled

American

1½ pints milk
1 large onion, chopped
1 large carrot, chopped
2 celery stalks, chopped
1 bouquet garni
6 tbs. butter
¾ cup flour
3 tbs. mayonnaise
2 tsp. lemon juice
3 garlic cloves, crushed
10 stuffed olives, finely chopped
pinch of cayenne
¾lb Stilton or other blue cheese,
    rind, removed, crumbled

Scald the milk, then add the onion, carrot, celery and bouquet garni. Cover and simmer for 15 minutes. Remove from the heat and allow to cool, then strain the milk.

Melt the butter in the cleaned-out saucepan. Add the flour and cook, stirring, for 2 minutes. Gradually stir in the milk and bring to the boil, stirring. Simmer until thickened. Remove from the heat and cool.

When the sauce is cool, beat in the mayonnaise, lemon juice, garlic, olives, cayenne and seasoning to taste. Rub the cheese through a strainer, then beat it into the sauce mixture.

Spoon the paté into a serving dish. Chill until set.   **SERVES 8-10**

Spinach ring

Metric/Imperial	American
$\frac{3}{4}$kg/1$\frac{1}{2}$lb spinach, cooked, drained and chopped	1$\frac{1}{2}$lb spinach, cooked, drained and chopped
$\frac{1}{2}$ cucumber, finely chopped	$\frac{1}{2}$ cucumber, finely chopped
6 spring onions, chopped	6 scallions, chopped
2.5ml/$\frac{1}{2}$ tsp. dried marjoram	$\frac{1}{2}$ tsp. dried marjoram
1.25ml/$\frac{1}{4}$ tsp. dry mustard	$\frac{1}{4}$ tsp. dry mustard
15g/$\frac{1}{2}$oz gelatine	2 envelopes unflavored gelatin
45ml/3 tbs. hot water	3 tbs. hot water
425ml/14floz chicken stock	1$\frac{3}{4}$ cups chicken stock
30ml/2 tbs. cider vinegar	2 tbs. cider vinegar

Mix together the spinach, cucumber, spring onions (scallions), marjoram, mustard and seasoning to taste. Dissolve the gelatine in the water and mix with the stock and vinegar. Stir into the spinach mixture. Pour into a dampened 1.2 litre/2 pint (2$\frac{1}{2}$ pint) capacity ring mould. Chill until set.

Turn out of the mould to serve. If liked, fill the centre with a prawn (shrimp) cocktail mixture. **SERVES 4-6**

Grapefruit & orange appetizer

Metric/Imperial	American
2 medium grapefruit, peeled and segmented	2 medium grapefruit, peeled and segmented
1 large orange, peeled and segmented	1 large orange, peeled and segmented
½ cucumber, halved and sliced	½ cucumber, halved and sliced
mint sprig	mint sprig
DRESSING	**DRESSING**
45ml/3 tbs. corn oil	3 tbs. corn oil
2.5ml/½ tsp. lemon juice	½ tsp. lemon juice
5ml/1 tsp. sugar	1 tsp. sugar

Mix together the grapefruit and orange segments in a salad bowl. Arrange the cucumber slices decoratively around the fruit.

Mix together the dressing ingredients with seasoning to taste and pour over the fruit. Chill for 30 minutes. Serve garnished with a mint sprig.

SERVES 4

CANAPES

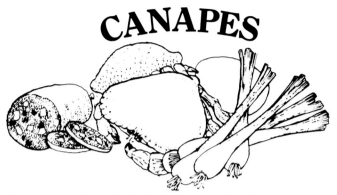

Crab canapés: fry a little finely chopped onion in butter until soit, then stir in 15ml/1 tbs. flour followed by 175ml/6floz (¾ cup) cream. Cook, stirring, until thickened. Add 250g/8oz flaked crabmeat, a dash of Tabasco sauce, 5ml/1 tsp. lemon juice and seasoning to taste. Spread this mixture over 18 toast fingers. Beat together 15ml/1 tbs. cream cheese, 25g/1oz (2 tbs.) butter and 2.5ml/½ tsp. paprika. Put a dot of this on each toast finger and grill (broil) for 1 minute. Serve hot garnished with capers.

Salami canapés: place thin slices of salami on buttered circles of toast. Garnish with gherkin (pickle) fans.

Sardine canapés: mash together 1 can of sardines (drained of oil), 2.5ml/½ tsp. lemon juice, 10ml/2 tsp. chopped parsley and pepper to taste. Spread on 4 buttered slices of white bread (crusts removed) and cut each into 4 squares. Garnish each with a slice of hard-boiled (hard-cooked) egg and a rolled anchovy fillet.

Shrimp canapés: melt 50g/2oz (¼ cup) butter in a saucepan and add 75g/3½oz canned shrimps (drained), 1.25ml/¼ tsp. mild curry powder, pinch each of cayenne and chilli pepper, juice of ¼ lemon and salt to taste. Cook for 4 minutes. Spread on 12 small fried bread ovals. Garnish with chopped parsley.

Spinach canapés: cook ¾kg/1½lb spinach, then drain and chop it finely. Mix in 25g/1oz (2 tbs.) butter, 50g/2oz grated cheese and seasoning to taste. Spread on triangles of fried bread and sprinkle over more grated cheese and dry breadcrumbs. Grill (broil) for 2 to 3 minutes.

Tomato canapés: put slices of tomato on crisp savoury biscuits (crackers) and pipe a star of cream cheese mixed with garlic and parsley on top.

Paté canapés: arrange small squares of paté on buttered rectangles of brown bread and garnish with olive slices.

Smoked salmon canapés: put slices of smoked salmon on buttered diamonds of brown bread and garnish with lemon and parsley.

FISH

Salmon steaks florentine

Metric/Imperial
*4 salmon steaks, about 2.5cm/
  1in thick*
250g/8oz butter, melted
1kg/2lb spinach
60ml/4 tbs. double cream
juice of ½ lemon
pinch of cayenne
4 lemon slices

American
*4 salmon steaks, about 1in
  thick*
1 cup butter, melted
2lb spinach
¼ cup heavy cream
juice of ½ lemon
pinch of cayenne
4 lemon slices

Preheat the grill (broiler).
Season the salmon steaks and grill (broil) for 8 to 10 minutes on each side or until cooked through. Baste them with 50g/2oz (¼ cup) of the butter while they are cooking.
Meanwhile, cook the spinach. Drain it well and return to the pan. Stir in the cream and seasoning to taste. Keep hot.
Mix the lemon juice and cayenne into the remaining butter. Season to taste.
Spread the spinach on a warmed serving platter. Place the salmon steaks on top and pour over the butter sauce. Garnish with lemon twists. **SERVES 4**

Trout with almonds

Metric/Imperial	American
6 medium trout	6 medium trout
30ml/2 tbs. lemon juice	2 tbs. lemon juice
100g/4oz flour	1 cup flour
5ml/1 tsp. grated nutmeg	1 tsp. grated nutmeg
1.25ml/¼ tsp. dried thyme	¼ tsp. dried thyme
175ml/6floz milk	¾ cup milk
150g/5oz butter	⅔ cup butter
100g/4oz slivered almonds	1 cup slivered almonds
parsley sprigs	parsley sprigs
lemon wedges	lemon wedges

Rub the fish with 15ml/1 tablespoon of the lemon juice and salt and pepper. Mix the flour with the nutmeg and thyme. Dip each fish first in the milk and then in the flour mixture to coat on all sides.

Melt 75g/3oz (6 tablespoons) of the butter in a frying pan. Add the fish and fry for 4 to 6 minutes on each side or until cooked through. Transfer them to a warmed serving platter and keep hot.

Add the remaining butter to the pan. When it has melted, stir in the almonds. Fry, stirring, for 3 to 4 minutes or until they are lightly browned. Pour them over the trout and garnish with parsley sprigs and lemon wedges.   **SERVES 6**

Mullets with tomatoes & peppers

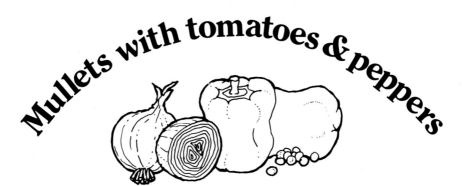

Metric/Imperial	American
6 medium mullets	6 medium mullets
juice of 1 lemon	juice of 1 lemon
75g/3oz ground pine nuts	½ cup ground pine nuts
2 garlic cloves, crushed	2 garlic cloves, crushed
1 small onion, chopped	1 small onion, chopped
60ml/4 tbs. chopped parsley	¼ cup chopped parsley
45ml/3 tbs. olive oil	3 tbs. olive oil
1 medium green pepper, cored, seeded and sliced	1 medium green pepper, cored, seeded and sliced
6 tomatoes, skinned, seeded and sliced	6 tomatoes, skinned, seeded and sliced
25g/1oz butter	2 tbs. butter
6 black olives	6 black olives

Sprinkle the fish with the lemon juice and leave to marinate for 15 minutes.

Preheat the oven to 180°C/350°F, Gas Mark 4.

Mix together the pine nuts, garlic, onion, parsley and seasoning to taste. Gradually beat in the olive oil.

Remove the fish from the lemon juice and pat dry. Arrange in a baking dish in one layer and spread over the pine nut mixture. Arrange the green pepper slices on top and cover with the tomatoes. Dot with the butter.

Place the dish in the oven and cook for 25 minutes or until the fish is tender. Transfer to a warmed serving platter. Put an olive in the uppermost empty eye socket of each fish. **SERVES 6**

Sole bonne femme

Metric/Imperial	American
¾kg/1½lb sole fillets, skinned	1½lb sole fillets, skinned
100g/4oz button mushrooms, chopped	¼lb button mushrooms, chopped
2 shallots or spring onions,	2 shallots or scallions,
finely chopped	finely chopped
120ml/4floz dry white wine	½ cup dry white wine
120ml/4floz fish stock	½ cup fish stock
15ml/1 tbs. lemon juice	1 tbs. lemon juice
1 bouquet garni	1 bouquet garni
25g/1oz butter	2 tbs. butter
15g/½oz flour	2 tbs. flour
30ml/2 tbs. double cream	2 tbs. heavy cream
12 mushroom caps, sautéed in	12 mushroom caps, sautéed in
25g/1oz butter	2 tbs. butter

Preheat the oven to 180°C/350°F, Gas Mark 4.
Rub the sole fillets with seasoning to taste. Arrange the chopped mushrooms and shallots on the bottom of a greased casserole. Place the sole fillets on top, folding them in half if necessary. Pour in half the wine, the stock and lemon juice and add the bouquet garni. Cover and put the casserole into the oven. Cook for 15 to 20 minutes or until the fish flakes easily. Transfer the fish to a warmed serving dish. Keep warm. Strain the cooking liquid into a jug.
Melt the butter in a saucepan. Add the flour and cook, stirring, for 1 minute. Gradually stir in the strained cooking liquid and the remaining wine and bring to the boil, stirring. Simmer until smooth and thickened. Stir in the cream and adjust the seasoning.
Pour the sauce over the fish and garnish with the mushroom caps.

SERVES 6

Cod with shrimp sauce

Metric/Imperial	American
25g/1oz butter	2 tbs. butter
1 onion, finely chopped	1 onion, finely chopped
100g/4oz mushrooms, sliced	¼lb mushrooms, sliced
4 tomatoes, skinned and chopped	4 tomatoes, skinned and chopped
¾-1kg/1½-2lb cod fillets, skinned	1½-2lb cod fillets, skinned
175ml/6floz dry white wine or fish stock	¾ cup dry white wine or fish stock
2 egg yolks	2 egg yolks
120ml/4floz double cream	½ cup heavy cream
15ml/1 tbs. lemon juice	1 tbs. lemon juice
100g/4oz shelled shrimps	¼lb shelled shrimp

Melt the butter in a frying pan. Add the onion and fry until softened. Stir in the mushrooms, tomatoes and seasoning to taste. Lay the fish fillets on top of the vegetables and pour over the wine or stock. Bring to the boil, then cover and simmer for 10 minutes or until the fish is cooked.

Transfer the fish to a warmed serving platter and keep hot. Boil the liquid in the frying pan until it has reduced by half. Beat the egg yolks and cream together. Stir in a little of the hot liquid, then stir into the liquid in the pan with the lemon juice. Cook gently for 3 to 4 minutes, stirring. Add the shrimps and cook for a further 2 to 3 minutes to heat through.

Pour the sauce over the fish and serve garnished with lemon slices and chopped parsley. **SERVES 6**

Halibut with tomatoes

Metric/Imperial	American
25g/1oz butter	2 tbs. butter
1 onion, sliced into rings	1 onion, sliced into rings
400g/14oz canned tomatoes, chopped	14oz canned tomatoes, chopped
5ml/1 tsp. dried marjoram	1 tsp. dried marjoram
4 halibut steaks	4 halibut steaks
250g/8oz small button mushrooms, halved	½lb small button mushrooms, halved
150ml/¼ pint double cream	⅔ cup heavy cream

Melt the butter in a saucepan. Add the onion and fry until softened. Stir in the undrained tomatoes, marjoram and seasoning to taste. Bring to the boil, then add the halibut steaks. Cover and cook for 10 minutes, or until the fish is tender.

Stir in the mushrooms and cream and cook gently for a further 2 to 3 minutes to heat through.   **SERVES 4**

Lobster salad

Metric/Imperial	American
meat from 2 x ¾kg/1½lb lobsters, cubed	meat from 2 x 1½lb lobsters, cubed
250g/8oz shelled shrimps	½lb shelled shrimp
1 small pineapple, peeled, cored and chopped	1 small pineapple, peeled, cored and chopped
1 medium green pepper, cored, seeded and shredded	1 medium green pepper, cored, seeded and shredded
300g/10oz cooked long-grain rice	4 cups cooked long-grain rice
6 large radishes, sliced	6 large radishes, sliced
250ml/8floz mayonnaise	1 cup mayonnaise
dash of Tabasco sauce	dash of Tabasco sauce
10ml/2 tsp. paprika	2 tsp. paprika
75ml/3floz double cream, whipped	⅓ cup heavy cream, whipped
lettuce leaves	lettuce leaves
4 hard-boiled eggs, sliced	4 hard-cooked eggs, sliced
4 tomatoes, sliced	4 tomatoes, sliced
chopped chives	chopped chives

Mix together the lobster, shrimps, pineapple, pepper, rice and radishes. In another bowl combine the mayonnaise, Tabasco, paprika, seasoning to taste and cream. Add to the lobster mixture and toss well.

Line a serving platter with lettuce leaves. Pile the lobster mixture on top. Make a border of alternating egg and tomato slices around the edge of the lobster salad and sprinkle the chives on top. Chill for 1 hour before serving. **SERVES 6**

Prawns (shrimp) creole

Metric/Imperial

25g/1oz butter
1 small onion, finely chopped
1 small green pepper, cored,
  seeded and finely chopped
30ml/2 tbs. flour
700g/1lb 7oz canned tomatoes,
  chopped
5ml/1 tsp. dried rosemary
5ml/1 tsp. dried thyme
5ml/1 tsp. dried oregano
5ml/1 tsp. sugar
250g/8oz peeled prawns

American

2 tbs. butter
1 small onion, finely chopped
1 small green pepper, cored, seeded
  and finely chopped
2 tbs. flour
1lb 7oz canned tomatoes,
  chopped
1 tsp. dried rosemary
1 tsp. dried thyme
1 tsp. dried oregano
1 tsp. sugar
½lb shelled shrimp

Melt the butter in a saucepan. Add the onion and pepper and fry until softened. Sprinkle over the flour and cook, stirring, for 1 minute. Gradually stir in the undrained tomatoes, the herbs, seasoning to taste and sugar. Stir well and simmer gently for 15 minutes or until thickened.

Add the prawns (shrimp) and cook for a further 5 minutes. Serve hot, with boiled rice. **SERVES 4**

Italian seafood stew

Metric/Imperial	American
120ml/4floz olive oil	½ cup olive oil
2 garlic cloves, chopped	2 garlic cloves, chopped
1 red chilli, seeded and chopped	1 red chili pepper, seeded and chopped
250g/8oz shrimps, shelled and chopped	½lb shrimp, shelled and chopped
250g/8oz squid, chopped	½lb squid, chopped
120ml/4floz dry white wine	½ cup dry white wine
45ml/3 tbs. tomato purée	3 tbs. tomato paste
500ml/16floz water	1 pint water
250g/8oz cod fillet, chopped	½lb cod fillet, chopped
250g/8oz haddock fillet, chopped	½lb haddock fillet, chopped
4 slices of toast	4 slices of toast
1 garlic clove, halved	1 garlic clove, halved
30ml/2 tbs. chopped canned pimiento	2 tbs. chopped canned pimiento

Heat the oil in a saucepan. Add the chopped garlic and chilli (chili pepper) and fry for 5 minutes. Add the shrimps and squid, cover and cook gently for 30 minutes.

Stir in the wine and continue cooking, uncovered, for 15 minutes. Add the tomato purée (paste), water, cod, haddock and salt to taste and mix well. Cover and cook for a further 15 minutes or until the fish is tender.

Meanwhile, rub the toast with the cut sides of the garlic. Place a slice in each serving bowl and ladle over the soup. Garnish with the pimiento.   **SERVES 4**

MEAT

Beef stroganoff

Metric/Imperial	American
¾-1kg/1½-2lb beef fillet or rump steak	1½-2lb boneless beef sirloin steak
75g/3oz butter	6 tbs. butter
2 onions, thinly sliced	2 onions, thinly sliced
250g/8oz mushrooms, sliced	½lb mushrooms, sliced
250ml/8floz soured cream	1 cup sour cream
10ml/2 tsp. French mustard	2 tsp. French mustard

Cut the steak into strips 5cm/2in long and 5mm/¼in wide.
Melt 50g/2oz (¼ cup) of the butter in a frying pan. Add the onions and fry until softened. Add the mushrooms and cook for a further 3 minutes.
Push the onions and mushrooms to one side and add the steak strips to the pan. Fry, turning, until they are browned on all sides. Mix in the vegetables and add seasoning to taste.
Mix together the sour cream and mustard and stir into the beef mixture. Cook for 1 minute longer, but do not boil. **SERVES 4-6**

Beef & mussel pie

Metric/Imperial	American
50g/2oz butter	¼ cup butter
1kg/2lb lean braising steak, cut into 2.5cm/1in cubes	2lb lean chuck steak, cut into 1in cubes
1 onion, finely chopped	1 onion, finely chopped
2 medium potatoes, diced	2 medium potatoes, diced
250g/8oz mushrooms, sliced	½lb mushrooms, sliced
250ml/8floz dark beer	1 cup dark beer
2.5ml/½ tsp. dried thyme	½ tsp. dried thyme
1 litre/1 quart mussels, steamed and removed from their shells	1 quart mussels, steamed and removed from their shells
250g/8oz frozen puff pastry, thawed	½lb frozen puff pastry, thawed
beaten egg	beaten egg

Preheat the oven to 200°C/400°F, Gas Mark 6.

Melt the butter in a frying pan. Add the steak cubes, in batches, and brown deeply on all sides. Remove the cubes from the pan as they brown.

Add the onion and potatoes to the pan (with more butter if necessary) and fry until the onion is softened. Stir in the mushrooms and fry for a further 3 minutes. Return the steak cubes to the pan and stir in the beer, thyme and seasoning to taste. Bring to the boil, then simmer for 1 hour.

Stir in the mussels and pour the mixture into a 23cm/9in oval or round deep pie dish. Roll out the dough and use to cover the pie. Make a slit in the centre and brush all over with beaten egg. Bake for 50 minutes to 1 hour or until the pastry is risen and golden brown.

SERVES 6

Beef roulade

Metric/Imperial	American
1½kg/3lb braising steak, in one piece	3lb chuck steak, in one piece
175ml/6floz wine vinegar	¾ cup wine vinegar
2 bay leaves	2 bay leaves
6 black peppercorns	6 black peppercorns
3 sage leaves	3 sage leaves
25g/1oz butter	2 tbs. butter
30ml/2 tbs. oil	2 tbs. oil
2 onions, sliced into rings	2 onions, sliced into rings
1 garlic clove, finely chopped	1 garlic clove, finely chopped
4 celery stalks, chopped	4 celery stalks, chopped
1 small turnip, chopped	1 small turnip, chopped
175ml/6floz beef stock	¾ cup beef stock

Cut the meat across the grain into three equal slices. Pound each until thin, then lay flat, overlapping the edges. Roll up and secure with string. Place the meat roll in a shallow dish and pour over the vinegar. Add the bay leaves, peppercorns, sage leaves and 5ml/1 teaspoon salt. Marinate for 2 hours.

Drain the meat roll. Strain the marinade and reserve.

Melt the butter with the oil in a flameproof casserole. Add the meat roll and brown on all sides. Remove it from the pot. Add the onions, garlic, celery and turnip to the casserole and fry until the onions are softened. Return the meat roll to the casserole and pour over the stock and reserved marinade.

Bring to the boil, then cover and simmer for 1½ hours or until the meat roll is tender. Serve cut into thick slices. **SERVES 8**

Beef pot roast with peppers

Metric/Imperial	American
1 x 2kg/4lb top rump of beef	1 x 4lb bottom round of beef
60ml/4 tbs. oil	¼ cup oil
2 large green peppers, cored, seeded and sliced	2 large green peppers, cored, seeded and sliced
2 large red peppers, cored, seeded and sliced	2 large red peppers, cored, seeded and sliced
1 onion, sliced into rings	1 onion, sliced into rings
900ml/1½ pints beef stock	2 pints beef stock
2 garlic cloves, crushed	2 garlic cloves, crushed
2.5ml/½ tsp. dried oregano	½ tsp. dried oregano

Rub the meat all over with salt and pepper. Heat the oil in a flame-proof casserole. Add the meat and brown on all sides. Put half the peppers and all the onion in the casserole and fry until the onion is softened. Stir in the stock, garlic, oregano and seasoning to taste. Bring to the boil, then cover and cook for 2½ to 3 hours or until the meat is tender.

Transfer the meat to a warmed serving platter and keep hot. Strain the cooking liquid and return it to the casserole. Add the remaining peppers and bring the liquid to the boil. Boil for 15 to 20 minutes to reduce well and until the peppers are tender.

Remove the string from the meat and carve it into thick slices. Spoon over the peppers with a little of the liquid and serve the remaining liquid separately as a gravy. **SERVES 6**

Tournedos with herb butter

Metric/Imperial	American
6 tournedos, about 2.5cm/1in thick	6 filet mignon, about 1in thick
watercress to garnish	watercress to garnish
Herb butter	**Herb butter**
75g/3oz butter	6 tbs. butter
15ml/1 tbs. chopped parsley	1 tbs. chopped parsley
7.5ml/1½ tsp. lemon juice	1½ tsp. lemon juice

First make the butter. Cream the butter until softened, then beat in the parsley, lemon juice and seasoning to taste. Form the butter into a roll, wrap in greaseproof or waxed paper and chill until firm. Preheat the grill (broiler) to moderately high.

Rub the steaks with salt and pepper and place on the grill (broiler) rack. Cook for about 4 minutes on each side (for rare steaks). Transfer the steaks to a warmed serving platter and top each with a pat of the butter. Garnish with watercress and serve with straw potatoes.

SERVES 6

Boned lamb chops milanaise

Metric/Imperial	American
30ml/2 tbs. oil	2 tbs. oil
1 onion, finely chopped	1 onion, finely chopped
1 garlic clove, crushed	1 garlic clove, crushed
400g/14oz canned tomatoes	14oz canned tomatoes
30ml/2 tbs. tomato purée	2 tbs. tomato paste
1 bay leaf	1 bay leaf
5ml/1 tsp. dried oregano	1 tsp. dried oregano
100g/4oz butter	½ cup butter
50g/2oz mushrooms, sliced	½ cup sliced mushrooms
50g/2oz lean cooked ham, cut	2 slices lean cooked ham,
into short strips	cut into short strips
250g/8oz spaghetti	½lb spaghetti
8 boned lamb chops (noisettes)	8 boneless lamb chops (noisettes)

Heat the oil in a saucepan. Add the onion and garlic and fry until they are softened. Stir in the undrained tomatoes, tomato purée (paste), bay leaf, seasoning to taste and oregano and bring to the boil. Simmer for 20 minutes. Meanwhile, melt 25g/1oz (2 tablespoons) of the butter in a frying pan. Add the mushrooms and fry for 3 minutes. Stir in the ham and cook for a further 3 minutes. Using a slotted spoon, transfer the mushrooms and ham to the tomato sauce.

Cook the spaghetti in boiling salted water until al dente. Drain and return to the saucepan. Stir in 25g/1oz (2 tablespoons) of the butter. Keep warm.

Add the remaining butter to the frying pan and melt it. Add the chops and fry for 4 to 6 minutes on each side or until tender but still slightly pink inside. Transfer to a warmed serving platter, arranging them in a large circle. Pile the spaghetti in the centre and spoon over the tomato sauce. **SERVES 4**

Moussaka

Metric/Imperial	American
½kg/1lb aubergines, sliced	1lb eggplants, sliced
25g/1oz butter	2 tbs. butter
1 onion, finely chopped	1 onion, finely chopped
1 garlic clove, crushed	1 garlic clove, crushed
½kg/1lb lean minced lamb	1lb lean ground lamb
4 medium tomatoes, chopped	4 medium tomatoes, chopped
30ml/2 tbs. tomato purée	2 tbs. tomato paste
5ml/1 tsp. dried thyme	1 tsp. dried thyme
45ml/3 tbs. flour	3 tbs. flour
120ml/4floz oil	½ cup oil
300ml/½ pint béchamel or white sauce	1¼ cups béchamel or white sauce
2 egg yolks	2 egg yolks
25g/1oz Parmesan cheese, grated	¼ cup grated Parmesan cheese

Sprinkle the aubergine (eggplant) slices with salt and set aside for 30 minutes.

Preheat the oven to 190°C/375°F, Gas Mark 5.

Melt the butter in a frying pan. Add the onion and garlic and fry until softened. Add the lamb and fry until it loses its pinkness. Stir in the tomatoes, tomato purée (paste), thyme and seasoning to taste and cook for a further 4 minutes. Remove from the heat.

Rinse the aubergine (eggplant) slices and pat dry. Coat them with the flour. Heat a little of the oil in another frying pan and fry the aubergine (eggplant) slices in batches until they are brown on both sides. Add more oil to the pan as necessary.

Cover the bottom of a baking dish with half the aubergine (eggplant) slices. Spoon over the lamb mixture and cover with the remaining aubergine (eggplant) slices. Beat together the béchamel sauce and egg yolks and pour over the top. Sprinkle with the cheese. Bake for 35 to 40 minutes or until the top is lightly browned. **SERVES 4**

Broiled pork chops

Metric/Imperial	American
1 large onion, thinly sliced into rings	*1 large onion, thinly sliced into rings*
6 thick pork chops	*6 thick pork chops*
50ml/2fl oz red wine vinegar	*¼ cup red wine vinegar*
125ml/4fl oz tomato ketchup	*½ cup ketchup*
10ml/2 tsp. sugar	*2 tsp. sugar*
2.5ml/½ tsp. ground cloves	*½ tsp. ground cloves*
5ml/1 tsp. celery seed	*1 tsp. celery seed*
2.5ml/½ tsp. mustard powder	*½ tsp. dry mustard*
1 bay leaf	*1 bay leaf*

Preheat the oven to 180°C/350°F, Gas Mark 4.

Spread the onion rings over the bottom of a greased shallow ovenproof dish that is large enough to hold the chops in one layer. Rub the chops with salt and pepper and place them in the dish.

Mix together all the ingredients for the sauce and pour over the chops. Bake for 1 hour or until the chops are cooked through and tender. Discard the bay leaf before serving.

SERVES 6

Pork & pineapple casserole

Metric/Imperial	American
4 small pork fillets	4 small pork tenderloins
1 garlic clove, halved	1 garlic clove, halved
15ml/1 tbs. grated orange rind	1 tbs. grated orange rind
2.5ml/½ tsp. dried marjoram	½ tsp. dried marjoram
2.5ml/½ tsp. dried sage	½ tsp. dried sage
25g/1oz butter	2 tbs. butter
2 medium green peppers, cored, seeded and shredded	2 medium green peppers, cored, seeded and shredded
300ml/½ pint dry white wine or stock	1¼ cups dry white wine or stock
½kg/1lb canned pineapple rings, drained and chopped	1lb canned pineapple rings, drained and chopped
15ml/1 tbs. cornflour	1 tbs. cornstarch
30ml/2 tbs. orange juice	2 tbs. orange juice

Beat the pork fillets (tenderloins) until flat, then rub all over with the garlic and salt and pepper. Discard the garlic. Sprinkle with the orange rind and herbs and roll up. Tie into shape with string.

Melt the butter in a flameproof casserole. Add the green peppers and fry until softened. Remove them from the casserole. Add the pork rolls to the casserole and brown on all sides. Pour in the wine or stock and add the pineapple and peppers. Stir well and season to taste. Bring to the boil, cover and simmer for 1 hour or until the pork is cooked. Transfer the pork rolls to a warmed serving dish and discard the string. Arrange the green peppers and pineapple around the pork. Keep hot.

Dissolve the cornflour (cornstarch) in the orange juice and stir into the cooking liquid. Simmer, stirring, until thickened. Pour this sauce over the pork and serve. **SERVES 4**

Vitello tonnato

Metric/Imperial	American
1 x 1½kg/3lb boned leg or loin of veal	*1 x 3lb boned leg of loin of veal*
3 anchovy fillets, halved	*3 anchovy fillets, halved*
3 garlic cloves, halved	*3 garlic cloves, halved*
200g/7oz canned tuna fish	*7oz canned tuna fish*
1 onion, thinly sliced	*1 onion, thinly sliced*
2 carrots, sliced	*2 carrots, sliced*
300ml/½ pint veal stock	*1¼ cups veal stock*
175ml/6floz dry white wine	*¾ cup dry white wine*
45ml/3 tbs. wine vinegar	*3 tbs. wine vinegar*
2 bay leaves	*2 bay leaves*
5ml/1 tsp. dried basil	*1 tsp. dried basil*
120ml/4floz mayonnaise	*½ cup mayonnaise*
2 hard-boiled egg yolks, sieved	*2 hard-cooked egg yolks, strained*
45ml/3 tbs. whipped cream	*3 tbs. whipped cream*

Preheat the oven to 180°C/350°F, Gas Mark 4.

Make six incisions in the veal and insert half an anchovy fillet and half a garlic clove in each. Place the veal in a flameproof casserole and add the tuna fish with its oil, the onion, carrots, stock, wine, vinegar, bay leaves, basil and seasoning to taste. Bring to the boil.

Cover the casserole and place it in the oven. Cook for 1½ to 1¾ hours or until the veal is tender. Remove from the oven and cool in the casserole.

Remove the veal from the casserole and carve it into thin slices. Arrange these, overlapping, in a serving platter. Strain the cooking liquid, rubbing as much of the vegetable through as possible, and reserve 250ml/8floz (1 cup). Into this beat the mayonnaise, egg yolks and cream. Pour this sauce over the veal and chill overnight before serving. **SERVES 6-8**

Kidneys with sausages & wine

Metric/Imperial	American
50g/2oz butter	¼ cup butter
12 lambs' kidneys, halved	12 lamb kidneys, halved
4 pork chipolata sausages, twisted and halved	4 pork link sausages, twisted and halved
15ml/1 tbs. flour	1 tbs. flour
120ml/4floz red wine	½ cup red wine
250ml/8floz beef stock	1 cup beef stock
15ml/1 tbs. tomato purée	1 tbs. tomato paste
30ml/2 tbs. brandy	2 tbs. brandy
12 button onions, blanched	12 pearl onions, blanched
chopped parsley	chopped parsley

Melt the butter in a frying pan. Add the kidneys and sausages and fry until the kidneys are tender and the sausages brown on all sides. Remove from the pan and keep warm.

Stir the flour into the fat in the pan, then gradually stir in the wine and stock. Bring to the boil. Add the tomato purée (paste), brandy and seasoning to taste and stir well.

Return the kidneys and sausages to the pan with the onions. Mix well, then cover and cook gently for 25 minutes.

Serve hot, sprinkled with parsley.　**SERVES 4**

POULTRY & GAME

Chicken fricassée

Metric/Imperial	American
4 chicken quarters	*4 chicken quarters*
40g/1½oz butter	*3 tbs. butter*
30ml/2 tbs. oil	*2 tbs. oil*
2 large onions, chopped	*2 large onions, chopped*
1 garlic clove, crushed	*1 garlic clove, crushed*
1 large green pepper, cored,	*1 large green pepper, cored,*
seeded and thinly sliced	*seeded and thinly sliced*
15ml/1 tbs. flour	*1 tbs. flour*
450ml/¾ pint chicken stock	*1 pint chicken stock*
60ml/4 tbs. tomato purée	*¼ cup tomato paste*

Rub the chicken quarters with seasoning to taste. Melt the butter with the oil in a saucepan. Add the chicken quarters, two at a time, and brown on all sides. Remove the chicken quarters from the pan as they brown.

Add the onions and garlic to the pan and fry until softened. Add the green pepper and fry for a further 2 to 3 minutes. Sprinkle over the flour and cook, stirring, until it is golden brown. Gradually stir in the stock and then the tomato purée (paste) and bring to the boil.

Return the chicken quarters to the pan and spoon the liquid over them. Cover and simmer for 1 hour or until the chicken is tender.

SERVES 4

Chicken in white wine

Metric/Imperial	American
8 chicken pieces	8 chicken pieces
25g/1oz butter	2 tbs. butter
2 onions, thinly sliced	2 onions, thinly sliced
250ml/8floz chicken stock	1 cup chicken stock
150ml/¼ pint sparkling white wine	⅔ cup sparkling white wine
2.5ml/½ tsp. dried thyme	½ tsp. dried thyme
1.25ml/¼ tsp. ground mace	¼ tsp. ground mace
45ml/3 tbs. flour	3 tbs. flour
175ml/6floz double cream	¾ cup heavy cream
250g/8oz mushrooms, sliced	½lb mushrooms, sliced
5ml/1 tsp. cornflour	1 tsp. cornstarch
5ml/1 tsp. water	1 tsp. water

Preheat the oven to 220°C/425°F, Gas Mark 7.
Rub the chicken pieces with salt and pepper. Melt the butter in a flameproof casserole. Add the onions and fry until softened. Add the chicken pieces and turn to coat in the butter. Transfer the casserole to the oven and cook for 35 minutes. Remove the casserole from the oven and add the stock, wine, thyme and mace. Sprinkle over the flour and stir vigorously to mix the ingredients together. Warm the cream with the mushrooms without boiling, then add to the casserole. Mix well and bring to the boil on top of the stove. Cover and return to the oven. Cook for a further 40 minutes.
Transfer the chicken pieces to a warmed serving dish and keep hot. Boil the cooking liquid until reduced by one-third. Adjust the seasoning. Dissolve the cornflour (cornstarch) in the water and stir in. Cook, stirring, until thickened, then pour this sauce over the chicken pieces. **SERVES 4**

Marbled chicken

Metric/Imperial	American
1 x 1½kg/3lb chicken, boned and slit open	*1 x 3lb chicken, boned and slit open*
60ml/4 tbs. dry sherry	*¼ cup dry sherry*
250g/8oz sausagemeat	*½lb sausagemeat*
100g/4oz salami, sliced	*¼lb salami, sliced*
100g/4oz pistachio nuts	*1 cup pistachio nuts*
2 hard-boiled eggs, sliced	*2 hard-cooked eggs, sliced*
100g/4oz chicken livers, sliced	*¼lb chicken livers, sliced*
100/4oz mushrooms, sliced	*¼lb mushrooms, sliced*
1 large red pepper, cored, seeded and sliced	*1 large red pepper, cored, seeded and sliced*
50g/2oz butter	*¼ cup butter*

Preheat the oven to 170°C/325°F, Gas Mark 3.
Lay the chicken flat, skin side down, on a sheet of foil. Sprinkle with salt and pepper, then brush with 7.5ml/1½ teaspoons of the sherry. Cover with half the sausagemeat, leaving a 1cm/½in border. Add layers of the salami, pistachio nuts, eggs, chicken livers, mushrooms and red pepper. Top with the remaining sausagemeat. Push the legs inside out so the shape of the chicken is square. Tuck in the wings. Pour over the remaining sherry, then fold over the ends and sides of the chicken to make a neat parcel. Sew the joins with a trussing needle and string.
Dot the chicken with the butter, then wrap in the foil. Put into a roasting pan and cook for 2½ to 3 hours or until the juices that run out of the chicken when it is pierced with a skewer are clear. Cool in the foil and serve cold, in slices. **SERVES 4-6**

Spanish chicken

Metric/Imperial	American
60ml/4 tbs. olive oil	*¼ cup olive oil*
8 chicken pieces	*8 chicken pieces*
2 onions, thinly sliced	*2 onions, thinly sliced*
2 garlic cloves, crushed	*2 garlic cloves, crushed*
1 large red pepper, cored,	*1 large red pepper, cored,*
seeded and chopped	*seeded and chopped*
400g/14oz canned artichoke	*14oz canned artichoke*
hearts, drained	*hearts, drained*
500ml/16floz chicken stock	*1 pint chicken stock*
1.25ml/¼ tsp. cayenne	*¼ tsp. cayenne*
1.25ml/¼ tsp. saffron powder	*¼ tsp. saffron powder*
16 stuffed olives, halved	*16 stuffed olives, halved*

Preheat the oven to 180°C/350°F, Gas Mark 4.

Heat the oil in a frying pan. Add the chicken pieces and brown on all sides. Remove from the pan and place the chicken in a flameproof casserole.

Add the onions, garlic and red pepper to the frying pan and fry until softened. Stir in the artichoke hearts followed by the stock, cayenne, saffron and seasoning to taste. Bring to the boil and pour over the chicken in the casserole. Place the casserole in the oven and cook for 45 to 55 minutes or until the chicken is tender.

Transfer the chicken pieces to a warmed serving dish and keep hot. Boil the cooking liquid to reduce well. Stir in the olives and heat through, then pour this sauce over the chicken. **SERVES 4**

Roast chicken with apricots

Metric/Imperial	American
1kg/2lb canned apricots	*2lb canned apricots*
40g/1½oz butter	*3 tbs. butter*
2 shallots, finely chopped	*2 shallots, finely chopped*
300g/10oz pork sausagemeat	*1¼ cups pork sausagemeat*
15g/½oz fresh breadcrumbs	*¼ cup fresh breadcrumbs*
30ml/2 tbs. double cream	*2 tbs. heavy cream*
5ml/1 tsp. mixed herbs	*1 tsp. mixed herbs*
15ml/1 tbs. chopped toasted	*1 tbs. chopped toasted*
hazelnuts	*hazelnuts*
1 x 2.5kg/5lb chicken	*1 x 5lb chicken*
15ml/1 tbs. brown sugar	*1 tbs. brown sugar*
250ml/8floz dry white wine	*1 cup dry white wine*

Drain the apricots, reserving 150ml/¼ pint (⅔ cup) of the can syrup. Chop the apricots finely. Preheat the oven to 220°C/425°F, Gas Mark 7.

Melt 25g/1oz (2 tablespoons) of the butter in a saucepan. Add the shallots and fry until softened. Stir in the sausagemeat and fry until it loses its pinkness. Add the breadcrumbs, cream, herbs, hazelnuts and 30ml/2 tablespoons of the chopped apricots and mix well. Cook gently for a further 5 minutes. Season to taste, then use to stuff the chicken. Truss and rub the chicken all over with salt and pepper. Place it in a roasting pan and roast for 15 minutes.

Meanwhile put the reserved apricot can syrup, sugar, wine and remaining butter in a saucepan and bring to the boil. Add the rest of the apricots and simmer for 5 minutes or until they are beginning to pulp. Rub the mixture through a strainer to make a smooth purée. Pour this over the chicken. Reduce the temperature to 180°C/350°F, Gas Mark 4 and continue roasting for 1¼ to 1½ hours or until the chicken is cooked. Skim any fat from the cooking liquid and serve as a sauce. **SERVES 6**

Venison chops

Metric/Imperial
4 venison chops
1 garlic clove, halved
60ml/4 tbs. oil
175ml/6floz soured cream
5ml/1 tsp. grated horseradish
Marinade
120ml/4floz dry white wine
60ml/4 tbs. olive oil
1 onion, thinly sliced
12 black peppercorns
5ml/1 tsp. dried thyme

American
4 venison chops
1 garlic clove, halved
¼ cup oil
¾ cup sour cream
1 tsp. grated horseradish
Marinade
½ cup dry white wine
¼ cup olive oil
1 onion, thinly sliced
12 black peppercorns
1 tsp. dried thyme

Mix together the marinade ingredients in a shallow dish. Add the venison chops and marinate for 24 hours, turning occasionally. Remove the chops from the marinade and pat dry. Rub them with the garlic clove and salt and pepper. Discard the garlic. Reserve the marinade.

Heat the oil in a frying pan. Add the chops and brown on both sides. Pour in the marinade and bring to the boil. Cover and simmer for 20 minutes or until the chops are tender. Remove from the heat and cool. Leave the chops to marinate for a further 24 hours.

Return the pan to the heat and bring to the boil. Simmer for 15 minutes.

Transfer the chops to a warmed serving platter. Keep hot. Strain the cooking liquid into a saucepan. Stir in the sour cream and horseradish and heat through gently. Pour this sauce over the chops and serve.   **SERVES 4**

Jugged hare

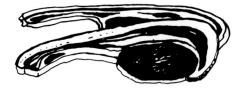

Metric/Imperial	American
50g/2oz flour	*½ cup flour*
1 x 2-2½kg/4-5lb hare, cut into 6 pieces and skinned, blood reserved	*1 x 4-5lb hare, cut into 6 pieces and skinned, blood reserved*
8 streaky bacon rashers, chopped	*8 bacon slices, chopped*
50g/2oz butter	*¼ cup butter*
300ml/½ pint beef stock	*1¼ cups beef stock*
300ml/½ pint dry red wine	*1¼ cups dry red wine*
1 bouquet garni	*1 bouquet garni*
250g/8oz button onions	*½lb pearl onions*
250g/8oz small button mushrooms	*½lb small button mushrooms*
120ml/4floz port wine	*½ cup port wine*

Mix the flour with salt and pepper and use to coat the hare pieces. Preheat the oven to 150°C/300°F, Gas Mark 2.

Fry the bacon in a flameproof casserole until it has rendered most of its fat. Remove the bacon from the pan with a slotted spoon. Add 25g/1oz (2 tablespoons) of the butter to the casserole. When it has melted, add the hare pieces and fry until they are browned on all sides. Stir in the stock and wine and bring to the boil. Add the bouquet garni and seasoning to taste. Cover the casserole and transfer it to the oven. Cook for 2½ hours.

Melt the remaining butter in a saucepan. Add the onions and mushrooms and fry until lightly browned. Add to the casserole with the port. Stir well and cook in the oven for a further 30 to 40 minutes or until the hare is tender.

Place the hare pieces and vegetables in a warmed serving dish. Discard the bouquet garni from the casserole and boil the cooking liquid to reduce. Stir in the reserved blood and cook gently until the sauce is thickened and smooth. Pour over the hare pieces and serve.

SERVES 4-6

Roast pheasant

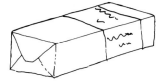

Metric/Imperial
2 young pheasants
50g/2oz butter, melted

American
2 young pheasants
¼ cup butter, melted

Preheat the oven to 180°C/350°F, Gas Mark 4.
Place the trussed pheasants in a roasting pan. Brush with a little of the melted butter and sprinkle with salt and pepper. Roast for 1 hour, basting frequently with more of the melted butter. The pheasants are cooked when the juices run clear when the thigh is pierced with a skewer.
Serve with game chips and bread sauce, garnished with watercress.

SERVES 4

Chestnut Charlotte

Metric/Imperial	American
200ml/⅓ pint milk	⅞ cup milk
150ml/¼ pint water	⅔ cup water
30 sponge fingers	30 ladyfingers
75g/3oz sugar	6 tbs. sugar
15g/½oz gelatine	2 envelopes unflavoured gelatin
160g/5½oz canned unsweetened chestnut purée	5½oz canned unsweetened chestnut purée
30ml/2 tbs. orange liqueur	2 tbs. orange liqueur
100/4oz canned preserved chestnuts	¼lb canned preserved chestnuts
300ml/½ pint double cream	1¼ cups heavy cream

Mix together 75ml/3floz (6 tablespoons) of the milk and water. Dip the sponge fingers (ladyfingers) in to moisten them, then use them to line the sides of a 1.2 litre/2 pint (2½ pint) capacity mould. Trim the ends of the fingers if necessary. Place a circle of greaseproof or waxed paper on the bottom of the mould.

Put the sugar and remaining milk in a saucepan and stir to dissolve the sugar. Heat the remaining water, then add stirring until it is dissolved. Add to the pan with the chestnut purée and liqueur. Mix well. Remove from the heat. Cool, then chill until the mixture is beginning to set.

Drain the preserved chestnuts, reserving the syrup. Chop the chestnuts.

Whip the cream until it is thick and fold it into the chestnut purée mixture with the chopped chestnuts. Spoon into the lined mould. Chill for at least 6 hours or overnight. Turn out to serve, with the reserved chestnut syrup poured over. **SERVES 10**

Orange caramel trifle

Metric/Imperial	American
6 trifle sponge squares, each cut into two layers	12 thin square slices sponge cake
45ml/3 tbs. orange liqueur or sweet sherry	3 tbs. orange liqueur or sweet sherry
45ml/3 tbs. orange juice	3 tbs. orange juice
300g/10oz sugar	1¼ cups sugar
300ml/½ pint thick custard sauce	1¼ cups thick custard sauce
4 large oranges, thinly sliced	4 large oranges, thinly sliced
150ml/¼ pint double cream	⅔ cup heavy cream

Lay the sponge cake squares flat on a tray and sprinkle over the liqueur or sherry and orange juice. Leave for 30 minutes to absorb the liquid.

Melt the sugar in a saucepan, then boil the syrup until it turns golden brown. Remove from the heat and keep warm.

Arrange one-third of the sponge squares in a glass serving dish. Cover with one-third of the custard, then make a layer of one-third of the orange slices. Trickle over one-third of the caramel. Continue making layers in this way, ending with caramel-coated orange slices. Chill for 2 hours.

Whip the cream and pipe stars over the top of the trifle. **SERVES 4-6**

Pears with cardamom

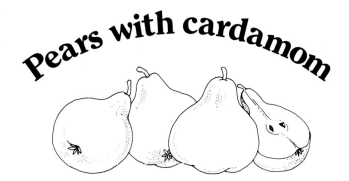

Metric/Imperial	American
3 large pears, peeled, cored and sliced	*3 large pears, peeled, cored and sliced*
30ml/2 tbs. brown sugar	*2 tbs. brown sugar*
120ml/4floz orange liqueur	*½ cup orange liqueur*
10ml/2 tsp. ground cardamom	*2 tsp. ground cardamom*
250ml/8floz double cream	*1 cup heavy cream*

Preheat the oven to 180°C/350°F, Gas Mark 4.

Put the pears in a shallow baking dish. Sprinkle with the sugar, then with the liqueur and cardamom. Bake for 35 to 40 minutes or until the pears are tender. Allow to cool.

Divide the pears and liquid between four serving dishes. Whip the cream and spoon on top. **SERVES 4**

Peaches with marzipan

Metric/Imperial	American
250g/8oz marzipan	½lb marzipan
250g/8oz sugar	1 cup sugar
350ml/12floz water	1½ cups water
5ml/1 tsp. grated lemon rind	1 tsp. grated lemon rind
4 peaches, peeled, halved and stoned	4 peaches, peeled, halved and pitted
100g/4oz apricot jam	½ cup apricot jam
150ml/¼ pint double cream	⅔ cup heavy cream
30ml/2 tbs. chopped pistachio nuts	2 tbs. chopped pistachio nuts

Preheat the oven to 180°C/350°F, Gas Mark 4.
Roll out the marzipan on a surface sprinkled with cornflour (cornstarch) to about 5mm/¼in thick. Cut out eight 7.5cm/3in circles. Use these to line eight patty tins (shallow muffin pans). Bake for 15 minutes.
Meanwhile, dissolve the sugar in the water in a saucepan. Add the lemon rind and bring to the boil. Add the peach halves and poach gently for 3 to 5 minutes or until just tender. Drain the peach halves. Remove the marzipan cases from the oven and cool.
Heat the jam until it is liquid, then strain it.
Remove the marzipan cases from the tins (pans). Divide the apricot jam between the cases, then place a peach half, cut side up, in each. Whip the cream and pipe in a swirl on each peach half. Decorate with pistachio nuts. **SERVES 4**

Rhubarb tart

Metric/Imperial
100g/4oz sugar
250ml/8floz water
½kg/1lb rhubarb, chopped
2.5ml/½ tsp. ground cinnamon
shortcrust pastry made with
  250g/8oz flour and 100g/4oz fat
beaten egg

American
½ cup sugar
1 cup water
1lb rhubarb, chopped
½ tsp. ground cinnamon
pie pastry made with 2 cups flour
  and ½ cup fat
beaten egg

Dissolve the sugar in the water in a saucepan. Bring to the boil. Add the rhubarb and cinnamon and return to the boil, then cook gently for 30 minutes or until the rhubarb is very tender. Cool.
Preheat the oven to 180°C/350°F, Gas Mark 4.
Roll out two-thirds of the dough and use to line a 23cm/9in flan tin (tart pan). Spoon the rhubarb mixture into the pastry case.
Roll out the remaining dough to about 5mm/¼in thick and cut into eight strips 1cm/½in wide. Lay these over the rhubarb filling to make a lattice. Brush the dough with beaten egg. Bake for 40 minutes or until the pastry is golden brown. Serve hot or cold. **SERVES 4-6**

Soufflé Grand Marnier

Metric/Imperial	American
100g/4oz caster sugar	*½ cup superfine sugar*
5 egg yolks	*5 egg yolks*
60ml/4 tbs. Grand Marnier	*¼ cup Grand Marnier*
15ml/1 tbs. grated orange rind	*1 tbs. grated orange rind*
7 egg whites	*7 egg whites*
icing sugar	*confectioners' sugar*

Preheat the oven to 200°C/400°F, Gas Mark 6.

Sprinkle 30ml/2 tablespoons of the sugar over the bottom and sides of a greased 1.5 litre/2½ pint (1½ quart) capacity soufflé dish. Put the remaining sugar in a heatproof bowl with the egg yolks. Place the bowl over a pan of hot water and beat until the mixture is thick and pale. Stir in the liqueur and orange rind and remove from the heat. Place the bowl in another bowl filled with ice cubes and stir until cool. Beat the egg whites until stiff. Fold into the egg yolk mixture. Spoon into the soufflé dish.

Place in the oven and reduce the temperature to 190°C/375°F, Gas Mark 5. Bake for 25 to 30 minutes or until risen and golden brown. Sprinkle over a little icing (confectioners') sugar and serve immediately. **SERVES 4-6**

Ice cream peach meringue

Metric/Imperial	American
4 egg whites	*4 egg whites*
250g/8oz icing sugar	*2 cups confectioners' sugar*
apricot jam	*apricot jam*
1 x 23cm/9in sponge cake	*1 x 9in sponge cake*
60ml/4 tbs. orange juice	*¼ cup orange juice*
3 large peaches, peeled, halved	*3 large peaches, peeled, halved*
and stoned	*and pitted*
350ml/12floz sweet white wine	*1½ cups sweet white wine*
6 scoops vanilla ice cream	*6 scoops vanilla ice cream*
60ml/4 tbs. orange liqueur	*¼ cup orange liqueur*

Preheat the oven to 130°C/250°F, Gas Mark ½.

Put the egg whites and sugar in a heatproof bowl placed over a pan of simmering water. Beat until the mixture forms stiff glossy peaks. Remove from the heat and continue beating for 2 minutes.

Draw a 25cm/10in circle on three sheets of non-stick (parchment) paper and place them on baking sheets. Pipe the meringue mixture into one circle to fill it, then pipe rings on the other circles. Bake for 1½ hours or until firm. Cool, then peel off the paper.

Place the meringue base on a flat serving plate. Arrange the rings on top to form the sides of the basket. Secure them with a little apricot jam. Put the cake inside the meringue basket, trimming it if necessary Sprinkle over the orange juice and leave for 30 minutes.

Meanwhile, poach the peach halves in the wine for 15 minutes. Drain and cool.

Soften the ice cream a little and spread it over the cake. Place the peach halves on top, cut sides down. Warm the liqueur and pour it over the peaches. Ignite it and serve while still flaming. **SERVES 6**

Punch

Metric/Imperial	American
725ml/1 pint 4floz lemon juice	*1½ pints lemon juice*
350g/12oz brown sugar	*2 cups brown sugar*
2 bottles Jamaican rum	*2 bottles Jamaican rum*
1 bottle brandy	*1 bottle brandy*
1.8 litres/3 pints water	*3¾ pints water*
175ml/6floz peach bitters	*¾ cup peach bitters*
250g/8oz peaches, peeled, stoned and chopped	*½lb peaches, peeled, pitted and chopped*

Put the lemon juice and sugar in a punch bowl and stir to dissolve the sugar. Add the remaining ingredients and mix well. Leave for at least 3 hours, stirring occasionally, before serving. **SERVES 36**

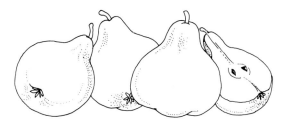

COLD DESSERTS

Pear condé

Metric/Imperial	American
100g/4oz round-grain rice	⅔ cup round-grain rice
900ml/1½ pints milk	2 pints milk
300g/10oz sugar	1¼ cups sugar
25g/1oz butter	2 tbs. butter
5ml/1 tsp. vanilla essence	1 tsp. vanilla extract
6 egg yolks	6 egg yolks
1kg/2lb firm pears, peeled, cored and halved	2lb firm pears, peeled, cored and halved
250ml/8fl oz water	1 cup water
45ml/3 tbs. brandy	3 tbs. brandy

Preheat the oven to 150°C/300°F, Gas Mark 2.

Mix together the rice, milk, 50g/2oz (¼ cup) of the sugar, the butter, vanilla and a pinch of salt in a flameproof casserole. Bring to the boil on top of the stove, then cover and transfer to the oven. Cook for 1 hour or until the rice is tender and has absorbed all the liquid. Remove from the oven and stir in the egg yolks. Place over gentle heat on top of the stove and cook, stirring, for 3 minutes. Remove from the heat and allow to cool.

Cut about one-quarter of the pear halves into thin slices. Spoon one-third of the rice mixture into a greased 1.2 litre/2 pint (2½ pint) capacity soufflé dish. Cover with half the pear slices. Continue making layers in this way, ending with the rest of the rice mixture. Chill for 2 hours or until firm.

Meanwhile, make the sauce. Dissolve the remaining sugar in the water in a saucepan. Add the remaining pear halves and poach gently until tender. Remove half the pear halves from the pan and purée the remainder with the poaching syrup. Boil this sauce for 3 minutes. Stir in the brandy and cool.

Turn out the condé. Decorate with the reserved pear halves, sliced, and glacé (candied) cherries. Serve with the sauce. **SERVES 6**

Baked Alaska

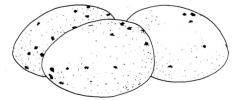

Metric/Imperial	American
2 x 20cm/8in sponge cake layers	*2 x 8in sponge cake layers*
250g/8oz apricot jam	*¾ cup apricot jam*
1 litre/1 quart vanilla ice cream	*1¼ quarts vanilla ice cream*
MERINGUE	**MERINGUE**
6 egg whites	*6 egg whites*
175g/6oz caster sugar	*¾ cup superfine sugar*

Sandwich the cake layers together with the jam. Place on an oven-proof serving plate.

Allow the ice cream to soften. Unwrap it and place it on a sheet of foil. Shape it into a 20cm/8in diameter circle. Wrap in the foil and freeze until firm.

Preheat the oven to 230°C/450°F, Gas Mark 8.

Beat the egg whites until stiff. Add 30ml/2 tablespoons of the sugar and continue beating for 1 minute. Fold in the rest of the sugar.

Place the ice cream circle on top of the cake, then quickly mask the whole in meringue, bringing it down to the plate to seal in the ice cream and cake. Bake for 3 to 4 minutes or until the meringue turns a pale golden brown. Serve immediately. **SERVES 6**

Ice cream bombe

Metric/Imperial	American
450ml/¾ pint raspberry ice cream	1 pint raspberry ice cream
40g/1½oz caster sugar	3 tbs. sugar
150ml/¼ pint water	⅔ cup water
2 large egg yolks	2 egg yolks
10ml/2 tsp. orange juice	2 tsp. orange juice
5ml/1 tsp. lemon juice	1 tsp. lemon juice
5ml/1 tsp. grated orange rind	1 tsp. grated orange rind
1 egg white	1 egg white

Beat the ice cream until it is slightly softened, then use it to line a chilled 600ml/1 pint (2½ cup) capacity mould. Cover and freeze for 1½ hours (for a china mould) or 45 minutes (for a metal mould).

Meanwhile, dissolve the sugar in the water in a saucepan. Bring to the boil and boil until the syrup reaches 102°C/127°F on a sugar thermometer. Remove from the heat and cool quickly. Beat the egg yolks in the top of a double boiler until they are thick and light. Gradually beat in the cooling syrup. When all the syrup has been incorporated, continue cooking gently, beating, for 15 minutes or until the mixture has doubled in bulk. Remove from the heat and continue beating until cold.

Stir the fruit juices and orange rind into the egg yolk mixture. Beat the egg white until stiff and fold in. Spoon into the ice cream-lined mould. Cover and freeze for 1½ to 2 hours.   **SERVES 6**

Cassata Napoletaine

Metric/Imperial	American
200ml/⅓ pint strawberry ice cream	½ pint strawberry ice cream
200ml/⅓ pint lemon or lime sorbet	½ pint lemon or lime sherbet
75ml/3fl oz double cream	⅓ cup heavy cream
2.5ml/½ tsp. icing sugar	½ tsp. confectioners' sugar
25g/1oz candied angelica, finely chopped	3 tbs. finely chopped candied angelica
25g/1oz glacé cherries, finely chopped	3 tbs. finely chopped candied cherries
40g/1½oz pistachio nuts or toasted almonds, finely chopped	⅓ cup finely chopped pistachio nuts or toasted almonds

Beat the ice cream until it is slightly softened, then use it to line a chilled 600ml/1 pint (2½ cup) capacity mould. Cover and freeze for 1½ hours (for a china mould) or 45 minutes (for a metal mould).
Beat the sorbet (sherbet) to soften it, then make a second layer in the mould on top of the ice cream. Cover and freeze for 45 minutes.
Whip the cream until thick and fold in the sugar, fruit and nuts. Spoon into the hollow left in the centre of the mould. Cover and freeze for 1 to 2 hours (or 3 hours for a china mould). **SERVES 6**

Coupe Jacques

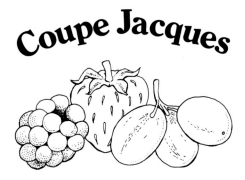

Metric/Imperial	American
½-¾kg/1-1½lb assorted fresh fruit, cut into small pieces	1-1½lb assorted fresh fruit, cut into small pieces
30ml/2 tbs. caster sugar	2 tbs. superfine sugar
10ml/2 tsp. lemon juice	2 tsp. lemon juice
60ml/4 tbs. water	¼ cup water
45ml/3 tbs. kirsch	3 tbs. kirsch
600ml/1 pint lemon sorbet	1¼ pints lemon sherbet
600ml/1 pint raspberry sorbet	1¼ pints raspberry sherbet

Mix together the fruit, sugar, lemon juice, water and kirsch. Chill for 1 hour.

Divide the lemon and raspberry sorbets (sherbets) between six glass serving dishes. Spoon over the fruit mixture and serve immediately.   **SERVES 6**

Chocolate cream

Metric/Imperial	American
600ml/1 pint milk	*2½ cups milk*
4 eggs, separated	*4 eggs, separated*
75ml/5 tbs. caster sugar	*5 tbs. superfine sugar*
45ml/3 tbs. flour	*3 tbs. flour*
5ml/1 tsp. vanilla essence	*1 tsp. vanilla extract*
15g/½oz butter	*1 tbs. butter*
100g/4oz dark cooking chocolate,	*4 squares semi-sweet chocolate,*
melted in 30ml/2 tbs. water	*melted in 2 tbs. water*
whipped cream	*whipped cream*
walnut halves	*walnut halves*

Scald the milk. Beat together the egg yolks and 60ml/4 tablespoons of the sugar until pale. Beat in the flour, then gradually beat in the milk. Return to the saucepan in which you scalded the milk and cook gently, stirring, for 2 minutes. Remove from the heat and stir in the vanilla and butter.
Beat the egg whites with a pinch of salt until stiff. Add the remaining sugar and continue beating for 1 minute. Fold the melted chocolate into the egg yolk mixture, followed by the egg whites. Spoon into a serving bowl or six individual glass serving dishes and chill until set. Serve decorated with whipped cream and walnut halves. **SERVES 6**

Old English flummery

Metric/Imperial	American
100g/4oz round-grain rice	*⅔ cup round-grain rice*
300ml/½ pint milk	*1¼ cups milk*
300ml/½ pint double cream	*1¼ cups heavy cream*
50g/2oz sugar	*¼ cup sugar*
15ml/1 tbs. grated lemon rind	*1 tbs. grated lemon rind*
5ml/1 tsp. ground cinnamon	*1 tsp. ground cinnamon*

Put all the ingredients in a heatproof bowl placed over a saucepan of hot water or in the top of a double boiler. Cover and cook for 50 to 55 minutes, stirring occasionally, until the rice is soft and has absorbed most of the liquid.

Remove from the heat and pour into a serving dish or four individual glass serving dishes. Allow to cool, then chill until set. **SERVES 4**

Knickerbocker glory

Metric/Imperial	American
250g/8oz strawberries, halved	½lb strawberries, halved
4 scoops vanilla ice cream	4 scoops vanilla ice cream
2 large peaches, peeled, stoned and sliced	2 large peaches, peeled, pitted and sliced
4 scoops chocolate ice cream	4 scoops chocolate ice cream
60ml/4 tbs. chocolate sauce or melted chocolate	¼ cup chocolate sauce or melted chocolate
whipped cream	whipped cream
4 maraschino cherries	4 maraschino cherries

Divide the strawberries between four tall sundae glasses. Top each with a scoop of vanilla ice cream, then peaches followed by a scoop of chocolate ice cream. Spoon chocolate sauce or melted chocolate over each, then a swirl of whipped cream and finally a cherry.

SERVES 4

Sherry jelly (gelatin)

Metric/Imperial	American
40g/1½oz gelatine	3 envelopes unflavored gelatin
120ml/4fl oz warm water	½ cup warm water
250ml/8fl oz boiling water	1 cup boiling water
100g/4oz sugar	½ cup sugar
120ml/4fl oz orange juice	½ cup orange juice
30ml/2 tbs. lemon juice	2 tbs. lemon juice
350ml/12fl oz medium sherry	1½ cups medium sherry

Soften the gelatine in the water, then stir in the boiling water to dissolve it. Stir in the sugar and 1.25ml/¼ teaspoon salt until dissolved. Allow to cool for 10 minutes.

Mix together the orange and lemon juices and sherry. Stir in the gelatine mixture. Pour into a dampened 900ml/1½ pint (1 quart) capacity mould. Chill for at least 4 hours or until set.

Turn out to serve, decorated with whipped cream, if you like.

SERVES 4-6

Apricot sorbet

Metric/Imperial	American
½kg/1lb canned apricot halves	1lb canned apricot halves
50g/2oz caster sugar	¼ cup superfine sugar
30ml/2 tbs. orange juice	2 tbs. orange juice
30ml/2 tbs. lemon juice	2 tbs. lemon juice
2 egg whites	2 egg whites
2 drops of vanilla essence	2 drops of vanilla extract

Drain the apricots, reserving the can syrup. Purée the apricots, then add enough of the reserved syrup to make up to 500ml/16fl oz (1 pint). Stir the sugar and fruit juices into the purée.

Beat the egg whites until stiff. Beat them into the apricot mixture with the vanilla until smooth. Pour into a freezer tray and freeze until mushy.

Beat the apricot mixture until it is smooth again and return to the freezer tray. Freeze for a further 4 hours or until the sorbet is firm.

SERVES 4

Strawberry & chestnut pudding

Metric/Imperial	American
200g/7oz unsalted butter	¾ cup plus 2 tbs. unsalted butter
200g/7oz sugar	¾ cup plus 2 tbs. sugar
300g/10oz dark cooking chocolate	10 squares semi-sweet chocolate
1kg/2lb unsweetened canned chestnut purée	2lb unsweetened canned chestnut purée
75ml/3fl oz brandy	6 tbs. brandy
300ml/½ pint double cream	1¼ cups heavy cream
10-12 strawberries	10-12 strawberries

Cream the butter and sugar together until pale and fluffy. Melt the chocolate. Allow to cool slightly, then stir into the creamed mixture. Beat in the chestnut purée, followed by the brandy. Spoon into a greased 1kg/2lb loaf pan and chill overnight.

Just before serving, turn out of the pan. Whip the cream and use to decorate the pudding with the strawberries. **SERVES 8-10**

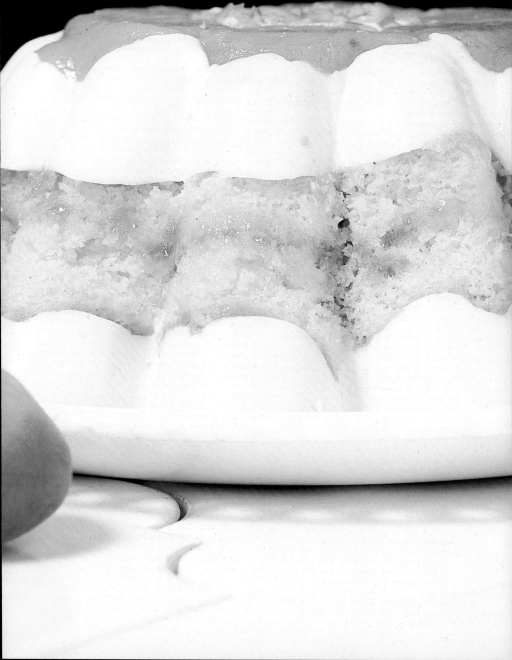

Apricot & jelly (gelatin) trifle

Metric/Imperial	American
¾kg/1½lb apricots, halved and stoned	1½lb apricots, halved and pitted
120ml/4fl oz water	½ cup water
75ml/5 tbs. sugar	5 tbs. sugar
20g/¾oz gelatine	1½ envelopes unflavored gelatin
30ml/2 tbs. apricot brandy	2 tbs. apricot brandy
1 x 18cm/7in sponge cake	1 x 7in sponge cake
60ml/4 tbs. apricot jam	¼ cup apricot jam
60ml/4 tbs. sherry	¼ cup sherry
75g/3oz pistachio nuts, chopped	¾ cup chopped pistachio nuts
450ml/¾ pint double cream	1 pint heavy cream
175ml/6fl oz milk	¾ cup milk

Put the apricots, water and 60ml/4 tablespoons of the sugar in a saucepan and poach gently until the apricots are tender but still firm. Remove the apricots from the pan with a slotted spoon. Add the gelatine to the cooking liquid and stir to dissolve. Stir in the remaining sugar and the brandy. Remove from the heat.

Cut the cake into two layers, then sandwich back together again with the jam. Cut the cake into 2.5cm/1in squares and sprinkle with the sherry.

Arrange the apricot halves and pistachio nuts decoratively in a greased 1.8 litre/3 pint (2 quart) capacity mould. Beat the cream until thick, then fold in the milk and apricot jelly (gelatin) mixture. Spoon half into the mould and chill until set.

Make a layer of the cake cubes in the mould and cover with the remaining cream mixture. Chill until set and turn out to serve.

SERVES 6

Sugar & cream cheese dessert

Metric/Imperial	American
250g/8oz brandy snaps, crushed	½lb brandy snaps, crushed
100g/4oz butter, melted	½ cup butter, melted
2.5ml/½ tsp. ground ginger	½ tsp. ground ginger
½kg/1lb cream cheese	1lb cream cheese
50g/2oz caster sugar	¼ cup superfine sugar
120ml/4fl oz single cream	½ cup light cream
30ml/2 tbs. lemon juice	2 tbs. lemon juice
2.5ml/½ tsp. ground cinnamon	½ tsp. ground cinnamon
15g/½oz gelatine	1 envelope unflavored gelatin
30ml/2 tbs. warm water	2 tbs. warm water
425g/15oz canned apricot halves, drained	15oz canned apricot halves, drained
60ml/4 tbs. preserved ginger, chopped	¼ cup chopped preserved ginger
450ml/¾ pint double cream	1 pint heavy cream
50g/2oz dark brown sugar	⅓ cup dark brown sugar

Mix together the crushed brandy snaps, butter and ground ginger and use to line the bottom of a greased 23cm/9in loose-bottomed cake pan. Beat together the cream cheese, sugar, single (light) cream, lemon juice and cinnamon. Dissolve the gelatine in the water and stir into the cheese mixture. Spoon into the pan on top of the crumb crust. Chill until set.

Preheat the grill (broiler) to moderate.

Arrange the apricot halves over the cheese mixture and scatter with the chopped ginger. Whip the double (heavy) cream and spread over the apricots. Sprinkle with the brown sugar. Grill (broil) until the sugar caramelizes. Remove from the pan and serve. **SERVES 6**

Zuccotto

Metric/Imperial

600ml/1 pint double cream
40g/1½oz icing sugar
50g/2oz hazelnuts, toasted
250g/8oz cherries, halved and stoned
100g/4oz plain dessert chocolate,
  grated
60ml/4 tbs. brandy
60ml/4 tbs. orange juice
2 x 20cm/8in chocolate sponge cakes
30ml/2 tbs. cocoa powder

American

2½ cups heavy cream
¼ cup plus 2 tbs. confectioners' sugar
½ cup toasted hazelnuts
½lb cherries, halved and pitted
4oz plain dessert chocolate,
  grated
¼ cup brandy
¼ cup orange juice
2 x 8in chocolate sponge cakes
2 tbs. unsweetened cocoa

Whip the cream with 25g/1oz (¼ cup) of the icing (confectioners') sugar. Fold in the hazelnuts, cherries and chocolate. Chill well.
Mix together the brandy and orange juice.
Cut the sponge cakes into two layers each and use three of these layers to line a 1.2 litre/2 pint (2½ pint) capacity mould. Cut the cake into pieces so that it fits the shape of the mould. Sprinkle the brandy mixture over the cake lining. Spoon in the cream mixture and cover with the remaining cake layer. Chill for 2 hours.
Turn the dessert out of the mould. Sprinkle two opposite quarters with the cocoa and the remaining quarters with the rest of the icing (confectioners') sugar. **SERVES 8-10**

HOT DESSERTS

Cherry clafoutis

Metric/Imperial

175ml/6fl oz milk
2 eggs
10ml/2 tsp. vanilla essence
75ml/5 tbs. icing sugar
105ml/7 tbs. flour
600g/1¼lb fresh or canned black
  cherries, stoned

American

¾ cup milk
2 eggs
2 tsp. vanilla extract
5 tbs. confectioners' sugar
7 tbs. flour
1¼lb fresh or canned black
  cherries, pitted

Preheat the oven to 180°C/350°F, Gas Mark 4.
Beat together the milk, eggs and vanilla. Beat in 60ml/4 tablespoons of
the sugar, 15ml/1 tablespoon at a time, then beat in the flour in the
same way, adding a pinch of salt with the last spoonful. When all the
sugar and flour have been incorporated, the batter should be smooth
and light.
Pour the batter into a greased baking dish. Add the cherries and
spread them out in the batter. Bake for 50 minutes to 1 hour or until
a knife inserted into the centre of the clafoutis comes out clean.
Sprinkle over the remaining sugar and serve.   **SERVES 6**

Gooseberry crumble

Metric/Imperial

¾kg/1½lb gooseberries
100g/4oz sugar
30ml/2 tbs. water
CRUMBLE TOPPING
100g/4oz flour
75g/3oz butter
50g/2oz sugar

American

1½lb gooseberries
½ cup sugar
2 tbs. water
CRUMBLE TOPPING
1 cup flour
6 tbs. butter
¼ cup sugar

Preheat the oven to 180°C/350°F, Gas Mark 4.
Put the gooseberries in a greased baking dish and sprinkle with the sugar and water.
For the topping, sift the flour into a mixing bowl. Rub in the butter until the mixture resembles breadcrumbs, then stir in the sugar. Cover the gooseberries with the crumble topping. Bake for 45 minutes or until golden brown.   **SERVES 4**

Fruit cobbler

Metric/Imperial	American
½kg/1lb blackberries	1lb blackberries
2 cooking apples, peeled, cored and chopped	2 cooking apples, peeled, cored and chopped
45ml/3 tbs. water	3 tbs. water
50g/2oz dark brown sugar	⅓ cup dark brown sugar
grated rind of 1 orange	grated rind of 1 orange
1.25ml/¼ tsp. ground cinnamon	¼ tsp. ground cinnamon
10ml/2 tsp. arrowroot	2 tsp. arrowroot
15ml/1 tbs. orange juice	1 tbs. orange juice
shortcrust pastry made with 175g/6oz flour, 75g/3oz butter, 30ml/2 tbs. sugar and 1 egg	pie pastry made with 1½ cups flour, 6 tbs. butter, 2 tbs. sugar and 1 egg
1 egg yolk	1 egg yolk

Preheat the oven to 200°C/400°F, Gas Mark 6.

Put the blackberries, apples, water, sugar, orange rind and cinnamon in a saucepan and bring to the boil, stirring. Cover and cook for 6 to 8 minutes or until the fruit is tender.

Dissolve the arrowroot in the orange juice and stir into the fruit mixture. Cook, stirring, until thickened. Spoon into a pie dish and allow to cool.

Roll out the dough to about 5mm/¼in thick. Cut out 5cm/2in circles as well as a 1cm/½in wide strip long enough to cover the rim of the pie dish. Dampen the rim of the dish and press on the dough strip. Dampen the dough strip and press on the dough circles, arranging them in an overlapping pattern. Leave a gap in the middle to expose the filling. Brush the dough with the egg yolk. Bake for 20 to 30 minutes or until the pastry is golden. **SERVES 4**

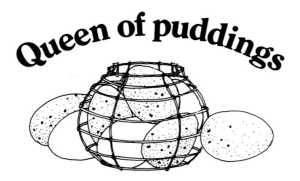

Queen of puddings

Metric/Imperial	American
50g/2oz butter	*¼ cup butter*
175g/6oz caster sugar	*¾ cup superfine sugar*
finely grated rind of 2 lemons	*finely grated rind of 2 lemons*
100g/4oz fresh breadcrumbs	*2 cups fresh breadcrumbs*
600ml/1 pint milk	*2½ cups milk*
2 eggs, separated	*2 eggs, separated*
45ml/3 tbs. jam	*3 tbs. jam*

Preheat the oven to 180°C/350°F, Gas Mark 4.
Cream the butter, 50g/2oz (¼ cup) of the sugar and the lemon rind together until pale and fluffy. Beat in the breadcrumbs. Scald the milk, then stir into the breadcrumb mixture. Leave to cool for 10 minutes, then beat in the egg yolks.
Spoon into a greased baking dish and bake for 35 to 40 minutes or until firm. Remove from the oven and cool slightly, then spread over the jam.
Reduce the oven temperature to 140°C/275°F, Gas Mark 1.
Beat the egg whites until stiff. Add 15ml/1 tablespoon of the remaining sugar and continue beating for 1 minute. Fold in the rest of the sugar. Spread the meringue over the jam and return to the oven. Bake for 20 to 25 minutes or until the meringue is set and golden brown on top.   **SERVES 4**

Railway pudding

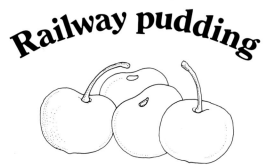

Metric/Imperial	American
100g/4oz butter	*½ cup butter*
100g/4oz sugar	*½ cup sugar*
2 eggs	*2 eggs*
30ml/2 tbs. cream	*2 tbs. cream*
grated rind of 1 lemon	*grated rind of 1 lemon*
2.5ml/½ tsp. vanilla essence	*½ tsp. vanilla extract*
175g/6oz flour	*1½ cups flour*
5ml/1 tsp. baking powder	*1 tsp. baking powder*
250g/8oz sweet red cherries,	*½lb sweet red cherries, halved*
halved and stoned	*and pitted*

Cream the butter with the sugar until pale and fluffy. Beat in the eggs one at a time, followed by the cream, lemon rind and vanilla. Sift over the flour and baking powder and fold in. Stir in the cherries.

Spoon into a greased 1.2 litre/2 pint (2½ pint) capacity pudding basin (steaming mold). Cover with greased greaseproof or waxed paper and foil, making a pleat in the centre to allow for expansion, then steam the pudding for 2 hours. **SERVES 6**

Rhubarb brown Betty

Metric/Imperial	American
100g/4oz fresh brown breadcrumbs	2 cups fresh brown breadcrumbs
175g/6oz digestive biscuits, crushed	1½ cups crushed graham crackers
100g/4oz dark brown sugar	⅔ cup dark brown sugar
5ml/1 tsp. ground cinnamon	1 tsp. ground cinnamon
1.25ml/¼ tsp. grated nutmeg	¼ tsp. grated nutmeg
grated rind of 1 lemon	grated rind of 1 lemon
grated rind of 1 orange	grated rind of 1 orange
175g/6oz butter, melted	¾ cup butter, melted
¾kg/1½lb rhubarb, chopped	1½lb rhubarb, chopped
100g/4oz sultanas	⅔ cup seedless white raisins

Preheat the oven to 190°C/375°F, Gas Mark 5.
Mix together the breadcrumbs, crushed biscuits (crackers), sugar, spices, lemon and orange rinds and melted butter. Use about one-third of the mixture to cover the bottom of a greased baking dish. Cover with half the rhubarb and sultanas (raisins). Continue making layers in this way, ending with the breadcrumb mixture.
Bake for 30 minutes or until golden brown. **SERVES 4-6**

Sago pudding

Metric/Imperial	American
500ml/16fl oz milk	*1 pint milk*
50g/2oz sago	*⅓ cup sago*
50g/2oz sugar	*¼ cup sugar*
2.5ml/½ tsp. ground cinnamon	*½ tsp. ground cinnamon*
10ml/2 tsp. grated lemon rind	*2 tsp. grated lemon rind*
2 egg yolks	*2 egg yolks*

Scald the milk in a saucepan, then sprinkle over the sago. Cook, stirring, for 10 minutes or until the mixture thickens and the sago becomes clear. Stir in the sugar, cinnamon and lemon rind. When the sugar has dissolved, remove from the heat and stir in the egg yolks.

Preheat the oven to 180°C/350°F, Gas Mark 4.

Pour into a greased 1.8 litre/3 pint (2 quart) capacity baking dish. Bake for 30 to 35 minutes or until the pudding is thick and creamy and lightly browned on top. Serve hot or cold. **SERVES 2-3**

Soufflé omelette

Metric/Imperial	American
15ml/1 tbs. icing sugar	*1 tbs. confectioners' sugar*
100g/4oz sugar	*½ cup sugar*
6 egg yolks	*6 egg yolks*
5ml/1 tsp. vanilla essence	*1 tsp. vanilla extract*
8 egg whites	*8 egg whites*
300ml/½ pint double cream, whipped	*1¼ cups heavy cream, whipped*

Preheat the oven to 220°C/425°F, Gas Mark 7.

Sprinkle the icing (confectioners') sugar over the bottom and sides of a greased shallow round baking dish.

Beat the sugar, egg yolks and vanilla together. In another bowl, beat the egg whites until stiff. Fold the egg whites into the egg yolk mixture and pour into the baking dish. Bake for 8 to 10 minutes or until the omelette is lightly browned.

Spoon the whipped cream onto half the omelette and fold over the other half. Slide onto a plate and serve. **SERVES 4-6**

Spotted Dick

Metric/Imperial	American
250g/8oz flour	2 cups flour
30ml/2 tbs. sugar	2 tbs. sugar
10ml/2 tsp. baking powder	2 tsp. baking powder
pinch of ground cloves	pinch of ground cloves
75g/3oz shredded suet	6 tbs. shredded suet
100g/4oz currants	⅔ cup currants
50g/2oz sultanas	⅓ cup seedless white raisins
90-120ml/6-8 tbs. water	6-8 tbs. water
90ml/6 tbs. strawberry jam	6 tbs. strawberry jam
45ml/3 tbs. milk	3 tbs. milk

Sift the flour, sugar, baking powder, cloves and 5ml/1 teaspoon salt into a mixing bowl. Stir in the suet, currants and sultanas (raisins), then add enough of the water to bind the mixture to a light and pliable dough.

Roll out the dough to a rectangle about 5mm/¼in thick. Spread over the jam to within 5mm/¼in of the edges. Brush the edges with the milk, then roll up like a Swiss (jelly) roll, pressing the edges together to seal. Wrap the roll loosely in foil, making a pleat to allow for expansion.

Steam for 2½ hours.   **SERVES 6-8**

Zabaglione Creole

Metric/Imperial

60ml/4 tbs. brown sugar
30ml/2 tbs. water
4 eggs, separated
60ml/4 tbs. rum
2.5ml/½ tsp. grated nutmeg
120ml/4 fl oz double cream, whipped

American

¼ cup brown sugar
2 tbs. water
4 eggs, separated
¼ cup rum
½ tsp. grated nutmeg
½ cup heavy cream, whipped

Dissolve the sugar in the water in a saucepan, then bring to the boil. Boil until the syrup is golden brown, then remove from the heat and cool.
Beat the egg whites until stiff. Fold in the syrup.
Beat the egg yolks, rum and nutmeg together in a heatproof bowl over a pan of simmering water until thick and pale. Remove from the heat and fold in the egg white mixture and the whipped cream. Pour into a serving bowl and chill for 20 minutes before serving.   **SERVES 4-6**

FRUIT DESSERTS

Bananas baked in orange juice

Metric/Imperial	American
6 bananas, halved lengthways and then crossways	6 bananas, halved lengthwise and then crosswise
10ml/2 tsp. cornflour	2 tsp. cornstarch
150ml/¼ pint orange juice	⅔ cup orange juice
grated rind of 1 orange	grated rind of 1 orange
50g/2oz desiccated coconut	½ cup shredded coconut
30ml/2 tbs. dark brown sugar	2 tbs. dark brown sugar
15g/½oz butter	1 tbs. butter

Preheat the oven to 190°C/375°F, Gas Mark 5.
Arrange the banana pieces in a greased baking dish. Dissolve the cornflour (cornstarch) in the orange juice and pour over the bananas. Mix together the orange rind, coconut and sugar and sprinkle over the top. Dot with the butter cut into small pieces.
Bake for 30 minutes or until the bananas are tender and the sauce is thick. **SERVES 4**

Cherries jubilee

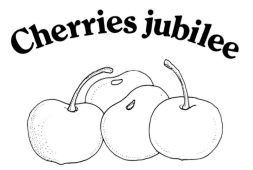

Metric/Imperial	American
400g/14oz canned unsweetened stoned black cherries	*14oz canned unsweetened pitted black cherries*
pinch of ground cinnamon	*pinch of ground cinnamon*
15ml/1 tbs. caster sugar	*1 tbs. superfine sugar*
10ml/2 tsp. arrowroot	*2 tsp. arrowroot*
60ml/4 tbs. brandy	*¼ cup brandy*

Drain the cherries, reserving 250ml/8fl oz (1 cup) of the can syrup (or make it up to this amount with water). Put the syrup, cinnamon, sugar and arrowroot in a saucepan and heat gently, stirring, until warm and slightly thickened. Add the cherries and cook gently for a further 1 to 2 minutes to heat through.

Pour the cherry mixture into a warmed flameproof serving dish or chafing dish and keep hot.

Warm the brandy. Pour it over the cherry mixture and ignite it. Serve as soon as the flames have died away, with vanilla ice cream.

SERVES 6

Strawberries Romanoff

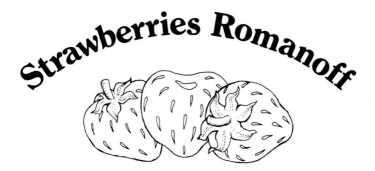

Metric/Imperial

1kg/2lb strawberries
150ml/¼ pint orange juice
30ml/2 tbs. orange liqueur (optional)
300ml/½ pint double cream
2.5ml/½ tsp. vanilla essence
15ml/1 tbs. caster sugar

American

2lb strawberries
⅔ cup orange juice
2 tbs. orange liqueur (optional)
1¼ cups heavy cream
½ tsp. vanilla extract
1 tbs. superfine sugar

Mix together the strawberries, orange juice and liqueur, if using. Chill for 2 hours.

Whip the cream with the vanilla and sugar. Spoon the strawberry mixture into a serving dish and decorate with swirls of cream.

SERVES 4-6

Lemon meringue pie

Metric/Imperial	American
shortcrust pastry made with 175g/6oz flour and 75g/3oz fat	*pie pastry made with 1½ cups flour and 6 tbs. fat*
grated rind and juice of 2 lemons	*grated rind and juice of 2 lemons*
300ml/½ pint water	*1¼ cups water*
250g/8oz caster sugar	*1 cup superfine sugar*
45ml/3 tbs. arrowroot dissolved in 30ml/2 tbs. water	*3 tbs. arrowroot dissolved in 2 tbs. water*
4 eggs, separated	*4 eggs, separated*

Preheat the oven to 200°C/400°F, Gas Mark 6.
Roll out the dough and use to line a 23cm/9in flan dish (pie pan). Bake blind (unfilled) for about 10 minutes or until the pastry is just set. Allow to cool and reduce the oven temperature to 180°C/350°F, Gas Mark 4.
Mix together the lemon rind and juice, water and 50g/2oz (¼ cup) of the sugar in a saucepan. Heat, stirring, until the sugar has dissolved, then stir in the arrowroot and continue cooking, stirring, until thickened. Remove from the heat. Cool slightly, then beat in the egg yolks.
Pour the lemon mixture into the pastry case. Bake for 5 minutes or until the filling has set.
Meanwhile, beat the egg whites until frothy. Gradually beat in the remaining sugar and continue beating until the meringue is stiff. Spread the meringue over the lemon filling to cover it completely. Return to the oven and continue baking for 20 to 25 minutes or until the meringue is golden brown. **SERVES 8**

Raspberry mousse

Metric/Imperial	American
50g/2oz caster sugar	¼ cup superfine sugar
60ml/4 tbs. orange juice	½ cup orange juice
½kg/1lb raspberries	1lb raspberries
350ml/12fl oz double cream	1½ cups heavy cream
4 eggs, separated	4 eggs, separated
15g/½oz gelatine	1 envelope unflavoured gelatin
60ml/4 tbs. warm water	¼ cup warm water

Dissolve the sugar in the orange juice in a saucepan, then bring to the boil and boil for 1 minute. Stir in the raspberries, cover and cook gently for 10 minutes or until pulped. Rub the raspberry mixture through a strainer to make a smooth purée. (Alternatively, purée the mixture in a blender and strain to remove the pips.)

Mix the cream and egg yolks together in a heatproof bowl placed over a saucepan of simmering water. Cook, stirring, until the custard is thick and smooth. Remove from the heat and beat the custard into the raspberry purée. Dissolve the gelatine in the water and stir into the raspberry mixture.

Beat the egg whites until stiff and fold into the raspberry mixture. Spoon into a lightly greased decorative mould or serving dish and chill for 4 hours or until set.

Turn out to serve, decorated with whipped cream and raspberries, if liked. **SERVES 6**

Strawberry shortcake

Metric/Imperial	American
250g/8oz flour	2 cups flour
50g/2oz icing sugar	½ cup confectioners' sugar
175g/6oz butter	¾ cup butter
1 egg yolk	1 egg yolk
300ml/½ pint double cream	1¼ cups heavy cream
½kg/1lb strawberries, sliced	1lb strawberries, sliced
30ml/2 tbs. sugar	2 tbs. sugar

Sift the flour and icing (confectioners') sugar into a mixing bowl. Rub in the butter, then bind to a smooth dough with the egg yolk and 30ml/2 tablespoons of the cream. Chill for 30 minutes.

Preheat the oven to 190°C/375°F, Gas Mark 5.

Divide the dough in half and roll out each portion to a 23cm/9in circle. Place the circles on greased baking sheets. Bake for 12 to 15 minutes or until the edges of the shortcakes are golden brown. Allow to cool.

Whip the remaining cream until thick. Fold in the strawberries and sugar.

Place one shortcake layer on a serving plate and cover with the strawberry mixture, piling it up in the centre. Cut the other shortcake layer into eight triangles and arrange on the strawberry mixture as shown.   **SERVES 8**

Summer pudding

Metric/Imperial	American
1kg/2lb raspberries	*2lb raspberries*
100g/4oz caster sugar	*½ cup superfine sugar*
120ml/4fl oz milk	*½ cup milk*
8 slices stale white bread,	*8 slices stale white bread,*
crusts removed	*crusts removed*

Mix together the raspberries and sugar. Sprinkle the milk over the bread slices to moisten them. Line a greased pudding basin or mould with two-thirds of the bread slices, overlapping them. Pour the raspberries into the basin and arrange the remaining bread slices on top to cover completely.

Cover with a piece of foil and put a weight on top. Chill for at least 8 hours. Turn out to serve. **SERVES 4-6**

Toffee apples

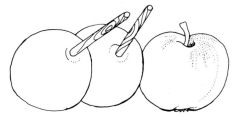

Metric/Imperial

½kg/1lb soft brown sugar
50g/2oz butter
10ml/2 tsp. malt vinegar
150ml/¼ pint water
30ml/2 tbs. golden syrup
10 green eating apples

American

1lb (2⅔ cups) brown sugar
¼ cup butter
2 tsp. malt vinegar
⅔ cup water
2 tbs. light corn syrup
10 green eating apples

Put the sugar, butter, vinegar, water and syrup in a saucepan and stir over gentle heat until the sugar has dissolved. Bring to the boil and boil until the syrup measures 160°C/325°F on a sugar thermometer, or until a little dropped into cold water forms a hard crack.

Spear the apples on wooden sticks and dip them into the toffee. Place them, stick up, on greaseproof or waxed paper. Leave to cool and set.

MAKES 10

Oriental fruit salad

Metric/Imperial	American
1 medium round watermelon	*1 medium watermelon*
20 canned lychees, drained	*20 canned lychees, drained*
4 peaches, peeled, stoned and sliced	*4 peaches, peeled, pitted and sliced*
½ kg/1 lb seedless grapes, peeled	*1 lb seedless grapes, peeled*

Halve the watermelon and scoop out all the flesh. Discard the seeds and cut the flesh into cubes (or into balls). Mix the watermelon flesh with the lychees, peaches and grapes and pile back into the water-melon halves. Chill for 30 minutes. **SERVES 4**

Dried fruit crumble

Metric/Imperial	American
300ml/½ pint water	*1¼ cups water*
250ml/8fl oz white wine	*1 cup white wine*
150g/5oz sugar	*⅔ cup sugar*
100g/4oz each dried apricots, figs, peaches, prunes, pears and apples, soaked overnight and drained	*⅔ cup each dried apricots, figs, peaches, prunes, pears and apples, soaked overnight and drained*
50g/2oz pistachio nuts	*½ cup pistachio nuts*
50g/2oz Brazil nuts	*½ cup Brazil nuts*
75g/3oz desiccated coconut	*¾ cup shredded coconut*
75g/3oz flour	*¾ cup flour*
75g/3oz butter	*6 tbs. butter*

Put the water, wine and 50g/2oz (¼ cup) of the sugar in a saucepan. Bring to the boil, stirring to dissolve the sugar. Add the dried fruits and nuts and simmer for 20 minutes.

Preheat the oven to 180°C/350°F, Gas Mark 4.

Drain the dried fruits and nuts, if necessary, and place them in a baking dish. Mix together the coconut, flour, butter and remaining sugar, rubbing the ingredients together until the mixture resembles breadcrumbs. Sprinkle over the fruit.

Bake for 20 to 30 minutes or until the crumble topping is golden brown.   **SERVES 6**

PIES & TARTS

Double crust apple pie

Metric/Imperial	American
rich shortcrust pastry made with 300g/10oz flour and 150g/5oz mixed fats	*pie pastry made with 2½ cups flour and ¾ cup mixed fats*
1kg/2lb cooking apples, peeled, cored and sliced	*2lb cooking apples, peeled, cored and sliced*
15ml/1 tbs. lemon juice	*1 tbs. lemon juice*
175g/6oz sugar	*¾ cup sugar*
7.5ml/1½ tsp. mixed spice	*1½ tsp. apple pie spice*
15ml/1 tbs. cornflour	*1 tbs. cornstarch*
25g/1oz butter	*2 tbs. butter*
15ml/1 tbs. cream	*1 tbs. cream*

Preheat the oven to 190°C/375°F, Gas Mark 5.

Divide the dough in half. Roll out one half and use to line a 23cm/9in deep pie dish. Mix together the apples, lemon juice, sugar, spice and cornflour (cornstarch) and spoon into the pastry case, piling it higher in the centre. Dot with the butter cut into small pieces.

Roll out the remaining dough and place it over the apple filling. Trim the edges and press together to seal. Make a crimped design on the rim and cut two gashes in the centre. Brush with the cream.

Bake for 40 minutes or until the pastry is golden brown. Sprinkle with sugar before serving. **SERVES 6**

Fruit & almond tart

Metric/Imperial	American
1 x 23cm/9in baked flan case, made from shortcrust pastry, with trimmings reserved	*1 x 9in baked pastry shell, made from pie pastry, with trimmings reserved*
250g/8oz marzipan	*8oz marzipan*
50g/2oz slivered almonds	*⅓ cup slivered almonds*
30ml/2 tbs. sultanas	*2 tbs. seedless raisins*
30ml/2 tbs. currants	*2 tbs. currants*
30ml/2 tbs. chopped candied lemon peel	*2 tbs. chopped candied lemon peel*
grated rind of 1 lemon	*grated rind of 1 lemon*
350ml/12floz custard	*1½ cups custard*
15ml/1 tbs. water	*1 tbs. water*
50g/2oz icing sugar	*½ cup confectioners' sugar*
1-2 drops of lemon essence	*1-2 drops of lemon extract*

Roll the marzipan into a 20cm/8in circle and carefully lift into the flan case (pastry shell). Sprinkle with half of the almonds, the dried fruits, lemon peel and rind. Pour over the custard and smooth it over. Roll out the dough trimmings. Cut out 6 crescent-shaped pieces, 5cm/2in x 2cm/¾in, and one 5cm/2in circle. Arrange the crescents, convex edges outwards, in a circle on top of the custard and place the circle in the centre. Chill the tart for 15 minutes.

Preheat the oven to 180°C/350°F, Gas Mark 4.

Place the tart in the oven and bake for 20 to 25 minutes or until the pastry trimmings are golden brown and crisp. Remove from the oven and cool completely.

To make the icing, gradually stir the water into the icing (confectioners') sugar, beating until the icing is thin and of a dropping consistency. Beat in the lemon essence (extract).

When the tart is cold, drop equal amounts of the icing over the pastry crescents and circle. Sprinkle with the remaining almonds. Set aside for 30 minutes to allow the icing to harden slightly before serving.

SERVES 6

Unbaked lemon cheesecake

Metric/Imperial	American
100g/4oz digestive biscuits, crushed	1 cup crushed graham crackers
40g/1½oz butter, melted	3 tbs. butter, melted
15g/½oz gelatine	1 envelope unflavored gelatin
60ml/4 tbs. warm water	¼ cup warm water
3 eggs	3 eggs
115g/4½oz sugar	½ cup plus 2 tbs. sugar
60ml/4 tbs. milk	¼ cup milk
grated rind and juice of 1 lemon	grated rind and juice of 1 lemon
350g/12oz cottage cheese	1½ cups cottage cheese
150ml/¼ pint double cream, whipped	⅔ cup heavy cream, whipped

Mix together the crushed biscuits (crackers) and butter and use to line the bottom of a 20cm/8in loose-bottomed pan. Chill until set.

Dissolve the gelatine in the water. Put 1 whole egg and the remaining 2 yolks, 100g/4oz (½ cup) of the sugar, a pinch of salt and the milk in a saucepan and beat well together. Heat gently, stirring, until the custard thickens. Do not allow to boil. Remove from the heat and stir in the gelatine. Allow to cool.

Stir the lemon rind and juice, cottage cheese and remaining sugar into the custard, then fold in the cream. Beat the egg whites until stiff and fold in. Spoon into the pan on top of the crumb base and chill until set.

Remove from the pan for serving, and decorate with whipped cream and crystallized lemon slices, if you like.   **SERVES 6-8**

Austrian sponge cake

Metric/Imperial	American
350g/12oz almonds, chopped	3 cups chopped almonds
175g/6oz sugar	¾ cup sugar
100g/4oz butter	½ cup butter
3 egg yolks	3 egg yolks
120ml/4fl oz brandy	½ cup brandy
60ml/4 tbs. milk	¼ cup milk
30 sponge finger biscuits	30 ladyfingers
300ml/½ pint double cream	1¼ cups heavy cream

Put 225g/8oz (2 cups) of the almonds and half the sugar in a saucepan. Cook gently, stirring, for about 10 minutes or until the sugar caramelizes and the almonds are pale golden. Remove from the heat and cool, then crush the caramelized almonds into pieces.

Cream the butter and remaining sugar together until pale and fluffy. Beat in the egg yolks and half the brandy, then fold in the caramelized almonds.

Mix together the remaining brandy and milk. Dip the sponge fingers (ladyfingers) into the liquid to moisten them. Use about one-third of the fingers to cover the bottom of a 15cm/6in round deep cake pan lined with greaseproof or waxed paper. Spoon over half the caramelized almond mixture, then another layer of fingers, the remaining almond mixture and the rest of the fingers. Cover the top with a sheet of foil and place a weight on top. Chill for at least 6 hours or overnight.

Turn out the cake onto a serving plate. Whip the cream and spread all over the top and sides of the cake. Decorate with the remaining chopped almonds and serve. **SERVES 6**

Meringue jam tart

Metric/Imperial	American
shortcrust pastry made with 175g/	*pie pastry made with 1½ cups*
6oz flour and 75g/3oz fat	*flour and 6 tbs. fat*
60ml/4 tbs. apricot jam	*¼ cup apricot jam*
300ml/½ pint milk	*1¼ cups milk*
thinly pared rind of 1 lemon	*thinly pared rind of 1 lemon*
50g/2oz fresh breadcrumbs	*1 cup fresh breadcrumbs*
50g/2oz butter	*¼ cup butter*
50g/2oz caster sugar	*¼ cup superfine sugar*
2 eggs, separated	*2 eggs, separated*
1.25ml/¼ tsp. grated nutmeg	*¼ tsp. grated nutmeg*

Preheat the oven to 200°C/400°F, Gas Mark 6.
Roll out the dough and use to line a 23cm/9in flan dish (pie pan).
Bake blind (unfilled) for about 10 minutes or until the pastry is just set. Remove from the oven and allow to cool. Reduce the oven temperature to 150°C/300°F, Gas Mark 2.
Spread the jam over the bottom of the pastry case.
Put the milk and lemon rind in a saucepan. Scald the milk, then remove from the heat, cover and leave to infuse for 20 minutes.
Remove the lemon rind and stir the breadcrumbs into the milk. Soak for 5 minutes. Cream the butter and half the sugar together until pale and fluffy. Beat in the egg yolks and nutmeg, then mix in the milk and breadcrumbs.
Pour over the jam in the pastry case. Bake for 45 minutes.
Remove the tart from the oven. Increase the temperature to 190°C/375°F, Gas Mark 5.
Beat the egg whites until frothy. Gradually beat in the remaining sugar and continue beating until stiff. Spoon the meringue over the tart filling and return to the oven. Bake for 10 to 15 minutes or until the meringue is lightly browned. **SERVES 8**

Mulberry & apple pie

Metric/Imperial	American
300g/10oz shortbread, crushed	2½ cups crushed shortbread
50g/2oz unsalted butter, melted	¼ cup unsalted butter, melted
50g/2oz ground almonds	½ cup ground almonds
50g/2oz caster sugar	¼ cup superfine sugar
1 egg	1 egg
30ml/2 tbs. double cream	2 tbs. heavy cream
¾kg/1½lb canned mulberries	1½lb canned mulberries
15ml/1 tbs. arrowroot	1 tbs. arrowroot
pinch of ground allspice	pinch of ground allspice
1.25ml/¼ tsp. ground cloves	¼ tsp. ground cloves
2 large cooking apples, peeled, cored and sliced	2 large cooking apples, peeled, cored and sliced
40g/1½oz dark brown sugar	¼ cup dark brown sugar

Preheat the oven to 190°C/375°F, Gas Mark 5.
Mix together the shortbread, butter, almonds, sugar, egg and cream.
Use one-third of the mixture to cover the bottom of a greased deep pie dish.
Drain the mulberries, reserving 300ml/½ pint (1¼ cups) of the can syrup. Put the syrup in a saucepan with the arrowroot and spices. Heat gently, stirring, until thickened. Remove from the heat and stir in the mulberries.
Arrange half the apple slices in a layer in the pie dish. Sprinkle with half the brown sugar, then cover with half the mulberry mixture. Repeat these layers, then cover with the rest of the shortbread mixture.
Bake for 30 to 40 minutes or until golden brown.   **SERVES 4-6**

Pumpkin pie

Metric/Imperial

shortcrust pastry made with 175g/
  6oz flour and 75g/3oz fat
100g/4oz brown sugar
7.5ml/1½ tsp. ground cinnamon
2.5ml/½ tsp. ground ginger
1.25ml/¼ tsp. ground cloves
¾kg/1½lb canned puréed pumpkin
3 eggs
300ml/½ pint single cream

American

pie pastry made with 1½ cups
  flour and 6 tbs. fat
⅔ cup brown sugar
1½ tsp. ground cinnamon
½ tsp. ground ginger
¼ tsp. ground cloves
1½lb canned puréed pumpkin
3 eggs
1¼ cups light cream

Preheat the oven to 190°C/375°F, Gas Mark 5.
Roll out the dough and use to line a 23cm/9in flan tin (pie pan). Mix together the remaining ingredients until smooth, then pour into the pastry case. Bake for 45 to 50 minutes or until the filling is set, and a knife inserted into the centre comes out clean.
Serve warm or cold.   **SERVES 6**

Pineapple cake

Metric/Imperial	American
250g/8oz white marshmallows	½lb white marshmallows
120ml/4fl oz medium sherry	½ cup medium sherry
8 canned pineapple rings, with 120ml/4fl oz of the can syrup reserved	8 canned pineapple rings, with ½ cup of the can syrup reserved
15g/½oz gelatine	1 envelope unflavored gelatin
60ml/4 tbs. warm water	¼ cup warm water
300ml/½ pint double cream	1¼ cups heavy cream
250g/8oz digestive biscuits, crushed	2 cups crushed graham crackers
30ml/2 tbs. sugar	2 tbs. sugar
75g/3oz unsalted butter, melted	6 tbs. unsalted butter, melted
4 glacé cherries	4 candied cherries

Put the marshmallows, sherry and reserved pineapple can syrup in a saucepan and cook gently until the marshmallows have melted. Remove from the heat. Dissolve the gelatine in the water and stir into the marshmallow mixture. Allow to cool.

Whip the cream and fold into the marshmallow mixture. Chill until half set.

Meanwhile, mix together the crushed biscuits (crackers), sugar and butter. Press into the bottom of a greased 23cm/9in loose-bottomed cake pan. Chill until set.

Arrange four of the pineapple rings on the crumb crust, then spoon over the marshmallow mixture. Smooth the top. Arrange the remaining pineapple rings on top with a cherry in the centre of each. Chill for at least 6 hours or until set.

Turn out and decorate with whipped cream, if you like. **SERVES 6-8**

Gooseberry pie

Metric/Imperial	American
300g/10oz flour	*2½ cups flour*
2.5ml/½ tsp. grated nutmeg	*½ tsp. grated nutmeg*
175g/6oz butter	*¾ cup butter*
75g/3oz sugar	*6 tbs. sugar*
½kg/1lb gooseberries	*1lb gooseberries*

Preheat the oven to 200°C/400°F, Gas Mark 6.

Sift the flour and nutmeg into a mixing bowl. Rub in the butter until the mixture resembles breadcrumbs. Stir in half the sugar. Press the mixture into the bottom of a greased ovenproof serving dish. Cover with the gooseberries and sprinkle over the remaining sugar.

Bake for 40 minutes or until the gooseberries are tender.   **SERVES 6**

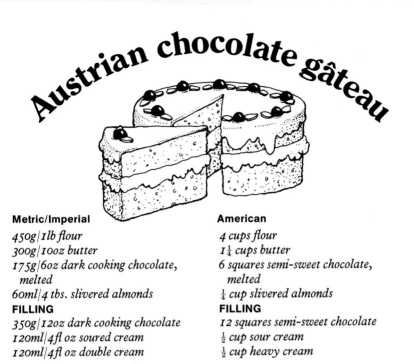

Austrian chocolate gâteau

Metric/Imperial	American
450g/1lb flour	4 cups flour
300g/10oz butter	1¼ cups butter
175g/6oz dark cooking chocolate, melted	6 squares semi-sweet chocolate, melted
60ml/4 tbs. slivered almonds	¼ cup slivered almonds
FILLING	**FILLING**
350g/12oz dark cooking chocolate	12 squares semi-sweet chocolate
120ml/4fl oz soured cream	½ cup sour cream
120ml/4fl oz double cream	½ cup heavy cream

Sift the flour and 2.5ml/½ teaspoon salt into a mixing bowl. Rub in the butter until the mixture resembles breadcrumbs. Add the melted chocolate and knead to a smooth and evenly coloured dough.

Divide the dough into four portions and roll out each between sheets of greaseproof or waxed paper into an 18cm/7in circle. Chill for 1 hour.

Preheat the oven to 170°C/325°F, Gas Mark 3.

Place the dough circles on baking sheets and bake for 15 to 20 minutes or until firm. Allow to cool.

For the filling, melt the chocolate and stir in the sour and double (heavy) creams. Use about one-third of the filling to sandwich together the layers, then cover the top and sides with the remaining filling. Sprinkle the almonds over the top. **SERVES 4-6**

Coconut cake

Metric/Imperial	American
150g/5oz butter	*⅔ cup butter*
60ml/4 tbs. golden syrup	*¼ cup light corn syrup*
115g/4½oz sugar	*½ cup plus 2 tbs. sugar*
2 eggs	*2 eggs*
250g/8oz desiccated coconut	*2 cups shredded coconut*
175g/6oz flour	*1½ cups flour*
7.5ml/1½ tsp. baking powder	*1½ tsp. baking powder*
60ml/4 tbs. milk	*¼ cup milk*

Preheat the oven to 180°C/350°F, Gas Mark 4.

Melt 25g/1oz (2 tablespoons) of the butter with the syrup and 15ml/1 tablespoon of the sugar. Pour this syrup into a greased 20cm/8in round deep cake pan.

Cream the remaining butter and sugar together until pale and fluffy. Beat in the eggs, one at a time. Fold in 175g/6oz (1½ cups) of the coconut. Sift over the flour and baking powder and fold in, followed by the milk.

Spoon the batter into the cake pan and bake for 50 minutes to 1 hour or until a skewer inserted into the centre of the cake comes out clean. Allow to cool in the pan for 5 minutes, then turn out onto a serving plate, upside-down. Sprinkle over the remaining coconut. **SERVES 8**

Plum tart

Metric/Imperial	American
shortcrust pastry made with 175g/6oz flour and 75g/3oz fat	*pie pastry made with 1½ cups flour and 6 tbs. fat*
1kg/2lb plums, halved and stoned	*2lb plums, halved and pitted*
175g/6oz caster sugar	*¾ cup superfine sugar*
5ml/1 tsp. ground cinnamon	*1 tsp. ground cinnamon*
2.5ml/½ tsp. ground allspice	*½ tsp. ground allspice*
50g/2oz flaked almonds, toasted	*½ cup flaked almonds, toasted*

Preheat the oven to 200°C/400°F, Gas Mark 6.

Roll out the dough and use to line a 23cm/9in flan tin (tart pan). Arrange the plums in the pastry case, cut sides down. Mix together the sugar and spices and sprinkle over the plums.

Bake for 35 to 40 minutes or until the pastry is golden and the plums are tender. Sprinkle over the almonds and serve hot or cold.

SERVES 4-6

CAKES

Tipsy cake

Metric/Imperial	American
175g/6oz butter	¾ cup butter
175g/6oz sugar	¾ cup sugar
3 eggs	3 eggs
175g/6oz flour	1½ cups flour
5ml/1 tsp. baking powder	1 tsp. baking powder
50g/2oz dark cooking chocolate, melted	2 squares semi-sweet chocolate, melted
5ml/1 tsp. grated orange rind	1 tsp. grated orange rind
5ml/1 tsp. vanilla essence	1 tsp. vanilla extract
2.5ml/½ tsp. grated lemon rind	½ tsp. grated lemon rind
300ml/½ pint double cream	1¼ cups heavy cream
60ml/4 tbs. apricot jam	¼ cup apricot jam
30ml/2 tbs. flaked almonds	2 tbs. flaked almonds
60ml/4 tbs. sherry	¼ cup sherry
45ml/3 tbs. orange liqueur	3 tbs. orange liqueur

Preheat the oven to 190°C/375°F, Gas Mark 5.
Cream the butter and sugar together until pale and fluffy. Beat in the eggs one at a time, then sift in the flour and baking powder and fold in thoroughly. Divide the batter in half. Add the chocolate and orange rind to one portion and the vanilla and lemon rind to the other. Put alternate spoonsful of the batters in a greased and lined 15cm/6in round deep cake pan. Swirl the batters together slightly to give a marbled effect.
Bake for 45 minutes or until a skewer inserted into the centre of the cake comes out clean. Cool the cake completely, then cut it into two layers. Whip the cream and fold in the jam and almonds. Use half to sandwich the cake together again.
Pour the sherry and liqueur over the top and leave to soak for 15 minutes, then cover the top and sides of the cake with the remaining cream mixture. Serve immediately.

Courgette (zucchini) cake

Metric/Imperial	American
½kg/1lb courgettes, grated	1lb zucchini, grated
250ml/8fl oz vegetable oil	1 cup vegetable oil
350g/12oz sugar	1½ cups sugar
3 eggs, beaten	3 eggs, beaten
300g/10oz flour	2½ cups flour
7.5ml/1½ tsp. baking powder	1½ tsp. baking powder
5ml/1 tsp. bicarbonate of soda	1 tsp. baking soda
7.5ml/1½ tsp. ground cinnamon	1½ tsp. ground cinnamon
5ml/1 tsp. grated nutmeg	1 tsp. grated nutmeg
175g/6oz walnuts, chopped	1½ cups chopped walnuts

Preheat the oven to 180°C/350°F, Gas Mark 4.

Mix together the courgettes (zucchini), oil, sugar and eggs. Sift the flour, baking powder, soda, spices and 5ml/1 teaspoon salt into another bowl. Add the flour mixture to the courgette (zucchini) mixture and combine thoroughly. Stir in the walnuts.

Spoon into a greased and lined 1kg/2lb loaf pan. Bake for 1¼ hours or until a skewer inserted into the centre of the loaf comes out clean. Cool in the pan for 15 minutes before turning out onto a wire rack to cool completely.

Zodiac cake

Metric/Imperial	American
300g/10oz caster sugar	1¼ cups superfine sugar
8 eggs	8 eggs
2.5ml/½ tsp. vanilla essence	½ tsp. vanilla extract
250g/8oz flour	2 cups flour
250g/8oz unsalted butter, melted	1 cup unsalted butter, melted
Buttercream, made with 75g/3oz butter and 350g/12oz icing sugar	Buttercream made with ⅓ cup butter and 3 cups confectioners' sugar
ICING	**ICING**
600g/1½lb sugar	3 cups sugar
450ml/¾ pint water	1 pint water
350g/12oz icing sugar	3 cups confectioners' sugar

Preheat the oven to 190°C/375°F, Gas Mark 5.

Put the sugar, eggs and vanilla in a heatproof bowl over a pan of hot water and beat until the mixture is thick and pale and the beater leaves a trail when lifted. (If using an electric mixer, no heat is needed.) Remove from the heat. Sift in the flour and fold in with the melted butter. Divide the batter between two greased and floured 23cm/9in sandwich (layer) cake pans.

Bake for 20 to 30 minutes or until the cakes spring back when lightly pressed. Cool the cakes completely, then sandwich them together with the buttercream.

For the icing, dissolve the sugar in the water, then boil until the syrup reaches 102°C/215°F. Cool slightly, then beat the syrup gradually into the icing (confectioners') sugar in the top of a double saucepan. Continue stirring over the heat until the icing is of a spreading consistency, then use half of it to cover the cake. Smooth the surface with a dampened knife. Colour the remaining icing and use to mark 12 lines on top of the cake (as shown). Pipe the zodiac signs into the divisions. Allow the icing to set before serving.

Rum fruit cake

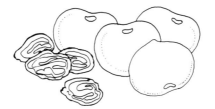

Metric/Imperial	American
250g/8oz raisins	1⅓ cups raisins
250g/8oz currants	1⅓ cups currants
250g/8oz stoned dates, chopped	1⅓ cups chopped pitted dates
75g/3oz glacé cherries	½ cup candied cherries
300ml/½ pint dark rum	1¼ cups dark rum
150ml/¼ pint dry sherry	⅔ cup dry sherry
350g/12oz flour	3 cups flour
5ml/1 tsp. bicarbonate of soda	1 tsp. baking soda
5ml/1 tsp. baking powder	1 tsp. baking powder
5ml/1 tsp. mixed spice	1 tsp. apple pie spice
250g/8oz butter	1 cup butter
250g/8oz sugar	1 cup sugar
4 eggs	4 eggs

Put the fruit in a bowl and pour over the rum and sherry. Soak for at least 24 hours, stirring occasionally.

Preheat the oven to 150°C/300°F, Gas Mark 2.

Sift the flour, soda, baking powder and spice into a mixing bowl. In another bowl, cream the butter and sugar together until the mixture is pale and fluffy. Beat in the eggs one at a time, then fold in the flour mixture. Stir in the fruit mixture.

Spoon into a greased 20cm/8in round deep cake pan. Bake for 2 to 2½ hours or until a skewer inserted into the centre of the cake comes out clean. Cool completely, then wrap in foil and store for 3 weeks before serving.

Rich chocolate cake

Metric/Imperial	American
100g/4oz butter	*½ cup butter*
100g/4oz caster sugar	*½ cup superfine sugar*
3 eggs, separated	*3 eggs, separated*
100g/4oz dark cooking chocolate, melted	*4 squares semi-sweet chocolate, melted*
15ml/1 tbs. coffee liqueur	*1 tbs. coffee liqueur*
15ml/1 tbs. black coffee	*1 tbs. black coffee*
50g/2oz ground almonds	*½ cup ground almonds*
50g/2oz flour, sifted	*½ cup flour, sifted*

Preheat the oven to 180°C/350°F, Gas Mark 4.

Cream the butter and sugar together until the mixture is pale and fluffy. Beat in the egg yolks one at a time, then stir in the chocolate, liqueur and coffee. Fold in the almonds and flour. Beat the egg whites until stiff and fold into the cake batter.

Spoon into a greased and lined 20cm/8in round deep cake pan. Bake for 40 to 50 minutes or until the centre of the cake will spring back when lightly pressed.

Cool in the pan for 10 minutes before turning out to cool completely on a wire rack.

Simnel cake

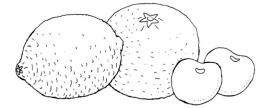

Metric/Imperial	American
175g/6oz flour	1½ cups flour
25g/1oz rice flour	¼ cup rice flour
5ml/1 tsp. baking powder	1 tsp. baking powder
175g/6oz butter	¾ cup butter
175g/6oz caster sugar	¾ cup superfine sugar
3 eggs	3 eggs
175g/6oz sultanas	1 cup seedless white raisins
175g/6oz currants	1 cup currants
100g/4oz glacé cherries, chopped	⅔ cup chopped candied cherries
grated rind of 1 lemon	grated rind of 1 lemon
5ml/1 tsp. grated orange rind	1 tsp. grated orange rind
1kg/2lb marzipan	2lb marzipan

Preheat the oven to 180°C/350°F, Gas Mark 4.
Sift together the flour, rice flour and baking powder. Cream the butter and sugar together until the mixture is pale and fluffy. Beat in the eggs one at a time, then fold in half the flour mixture. Stir the fruit and rind into the remaining flour mixture, then add to the creamed mixture. Mix thoroughly.
Spoon half the cake mixture into a greased and lined 18cm/7in round deep cake pan. Shape one-third of the marzipan into a circle to fit in the pan and place on top of the cake mixture. Cover with the remaining cake mixture.
Bake for 1½ hours, then reduce the temperature to 150°C/300°F, Gas Mark 2 and continue baking for 1 to 1¼ hours or until a skewer inserted into the centre of the cake comes out clean. Cool on a wire rack.
Shape half the remaining marzipan into a circle to fit the top of the cake. Brush the cake with glaze (made by melting and then straining apricot jam) and place the marzipan circle in position. Roll the remaining marzipan into 11 balls, coat with glaze and arrange around the top edge of the cake. Grill (broil) until the tops of the balls are golden brown.

Danish butter cake

Metric/Imperial	American
25g/1oz fresh yeast	1 cake compressed yeast
150ml/¼ pint lukewarm milk	⅔ cup lukewarm milk
450g/1lb flour	4 cups flour
5ml/1 tsp. ground cardamom	1 tsp. ground cardamom
50g/2oz caster sugar	¼ cup superfine sugar
300g/10 oz butter	1¼ cups butter
2 eggs	2 eggs
FILLING	**FILLING**
50g/2oz butter	¼ cup butter
100g/4oz caster sugar	½ cup superfine sugar
5ml/1 tsp. vanilla essence	1 tsp. vanilla extract
5ml/1 tsp. ground cinnamon	1 tsp. ground cinnamon

Cream the yeast with 30ml/2 tablespoons of the milk and leave until frothy. Sift the flour, spice, sugar and 5ml/1 teaspoon salt into a mixing bowl. Rub in 50g/2oz (¼ cup) of the butter. Mix in the yeast mixture, eggs and remaining milk.

Knead the dough until it is smooth and elastic, then roll out to an oblong about 30 x 20cm/12 x 8in. Beat the remaining butter into a rectangle about 23 x 13cm/9 x 5in and place in the centre of the dough. Fold the dough over to enclose the butter, then roll out to an oblong again. Fold in three, turn and roll out again. Repeat this twice more, then chill well.

For the filling, beat the ingredients together well. Shape one-third of the dough into a circle and use to line the bottom of a loose-bottomed 23cm/9in round cake pan (springform pan). Roll out the remaining dough to a 45cm/18in square. Spread with the filling, fold in half and cut into 9 strips. Roll these up like Swiss (jelly) rolls and place in the pan in a circle, cut sides up. Brush with beaten egg and let rise in a warm place for 30 minutes.

Preheat the oven to 200°C/400°F, Gas Mark 6. Brush again with beaten egg and bake for 35 minutes. Serve drizzled with glacé icing, if liked.

Norwegian sponge cake

Metric/Imperial	American
6 eggs	6 eggs
250g/8oz sugar	1 cup sugar
5ml/1 tsp. vanilla essence	1 tsp. vanilla extract
150g/5oz self-raising flour	1¼ cups self-rising flour
FILLING	**FILLING**
450ml/¾ pint double cream	1 pint heavy cream
50g/2oz caster sugar	¼ cup superfine sugar
canned berries, such as mulberries or raspberries, drained	canned berries, such as mulberries or raspberries, drained

Preheat the oven to 180°C/350°F, Gas Mark 4.

Break 4 eggs into a mixing bowl. Separate the remaining 2 eggs and add the yolks to the whole eggs. Reserve the whites. Beat the whole eggs and yolks together, then add the sugar and vanilla and continue beating until pale and thick. Sift over the flour and fold in.

Beat the egg whites until stiff and fold in. Spoon into a greased and lined loose-bottomed 23cm/9in round deep cake pan (springform pan). Bake for 10 minutes, then reduce the temperature to 170°C/325°F, Gas Mark 3 and continue baking for 50 minutes or until a skewer inserted into the centre of the cake comes out clean. Cool in the pan for 5 minutes, then turn out onto a wire rack to cool completely.

For the filling, whip the cream with the sugar until thick. Cut the cake into three layers and use about three-quarters of the cream to sandwich it back together. Use the remaining cream to cover the sides, leaving the top plain, and to pipe an attractive border around the top and bottom edges. Cover the top with the berries and serve.

Strawberry & almond cake

Metric/Imperial	American
75g/3oz butter	6 tbs. butter
75g/3oz caster sugar	6 tbs. superfine sugar
3 eggs	3 eggs
50g/2oz self-raising flour	½ cup self-rising flour
75g/3oz ground almonds	¾ cup ground almonds
FILLING	**FILLING**
350g/12oz strawberries, puréed	¾lb stawberries, puréed
50g/2oz icing sugar	½ cup confectioners' sugar
150ml/¼ pint double cream	⅔ cup heavy cream
7g/¼oz gelatine softened in	1 envelope unflavored gelatin
15ml/1 tbs. hot water	softened in 1 tbs. hot water

Preheat the oven to 190°C/375°F, Gas Mark 5.

Cream the butter and sugar together until pale and fluffy. Beat in the eggs. Sift in the flour, then fold in with the almonds. Spoon into a greased and floured 18cm/7in round deep cake pan. Bake for 30 to 40 minutes or until a skewer inserted into the centre of the cake comes out clean. Cool, then remove from the pan.

For the filling, mix together the strawberry purée and sugar. Whip the cream and fold in with the gelatine. Pour into the washed and dampened cake pan and chill until set.

Cut the cake into two layers. Sandwich together with the strawberry filling. Sprinkle the top with icing (confectioners') sugar and decorate with halved strawberries.

Frosted walnut cake

Metric/Imperial	American
250g/8oz flour	2 cups flour
10ml/2 tsp. baking powder	2 tsp. baking powder
75g/3oz butter	6 tbs. butter
250g/8oz caster sugar	1 cup superfine sugar
2.5ml/½ tsp. vanilla essence	½ tsp. vanilla extract
2 eggs, separated	2 eggs, separated
100g/4oz walnuts, chopped	1 cup chopped walnuts
120ml/4fl oz milk	½ cup milk
FROSTING	**FROSTING**
2 egg whites	2 egg whites
350g/12oz sugar	1½ cups sugar
75ml/5 tbs. cold water	5 tbs. cold water
1.25ml/¼ tsp. cream of tartar	¼ tsp. cream of tartar
2.5ml/½ tsp. vanilla essence	½ tsp. vanilla extract
50g/2oz walnuts, chopped	½ cup chopped walnuts

Preheat the oven to 190°C/375°F, Gas Mark 5.
Sift together the flour, baking powder and 2.5ml/½ teaspoon salt.
Cream the butter and sugar together until pale and fluffy. Beat in the
vanilla and egg yolks with 50g/2oz (½ cup) of the flour mixture. Fold
in the walnuts, then the remaining flour mixture and finally the milk.
Beat the egg whites until stiff and fold into the batter. Divide
between two greased 20cm/8in sandwich (layer) cake pans. Bake for
35 to 40 minutes or until a skewer inserted into the centre comes out
clean. Cool.
For the frosting, beat the egg whites, sugar, water and cream of
tartar together in the top of a double saucepan. Continue beating
over the heat for 7 minutes, then remove from the heat and beat in
the vanilla. Continue beating until the frosting is thick enough to
spread. Fold in the walnuts. Use about one-third of the frosting to
sandwich the cakes and the remainder to cover the top and sides.
Decorate with walnut halves.

Orange cake

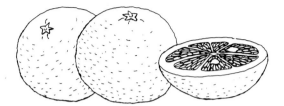

Metric/Imperial	American
300g/10oz flour	*2½ cups flour*
50g/2oz cocoa powder	*½ cup unsweetened cocoa powder*
15ml/1 tbs. baking powder	*1 tbs. baking powder*
grated rind of 4 oranges	*grated rind of 4 oranges*
300g/10oz butter	*1¾ cups butter*
300g/10oz sugar	*1¼ cups sugar*
4 eggs	*4 eggs*
200ml/7fl oz orange juice	*⅞ cup orange juice*
½kg/1lb marzipan	*1lb marzipan*
orange food colouring	*orange food coloring*
350g/12oz dark cooking chocolate, melted	*12 squares semi-sweet chocolate, melted*

Preheat the oven to 180°C/350°F, Gas Mark 4.

Sift together the flour, cocoa, baking powder and orange rind. Cream the butter and sugar together until pale and fluffy. Beat in the eggs one at a time, then fold in the flour mixture. Stir in the orange juice. Spoon the batter into a greased and floured 23cm/9in square deep cake pan. Bake for 1½ hours or until a skewer inserted into the centre of the cake comes out clean. Cool.

Colour the marzipan orange with food colouring.

Remove the cake from the pan and cover the top and sides with the melted chocolate. Allow to cool and set. Roll out the marzipan and use to cover the cake, making a decorative pattern at the edges. Decorate with candied orange slices and angelica.

Madeira cake

Metric/Imperial	American
250g/8oz butter	*1 cup butter*
250g/8oz caster sugar	*1 cup superfine sugar*
5 eggs	*5 eggs*
250g/8oz self-raising flour	*2 cups self-rising flour*
grated rind of 1 lemon	*grated rind of 1 lemon*
juice of ½ lemon	*juice of ½ lemon*
3 strips of candied citron peel	*3 strips of candied citron peel*

Preheat the oven to 180°C/350°F, Gas Mark 4.

Cream the butter and sugar together until pale and fluffy. Beat in the eggs, one at a time, then sift in the flour. Fold in with the lemon rind and juice.

Spoon the batter into a greased and floured 15cm/6in round deep cake pan. Sprinkle a little extra sugar over the top and bake for 30 minutes. Place the citron peel on top and continue baking for 45 to 50 minutes or until a skewer inserted into the centre of the cake comes out clean. Allow to cool before serving.

Poppy seed cake

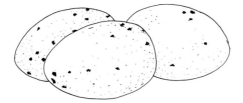

Metric/Imperial	American
175g/6oz butter	¾ cup butter
250g/8oz sugar	1 cup sugar
7.5ml/1½ tsp. vanilla essence	1½ tsp. vanilla extract
50g/2oz poppy seeds	½ cup poppy seeds
150ml/¼ pint milk	⅔ cup milk
30ml/2 tbs. soured cream	2 tbs. sour cream
300g/10oz flour	2½ cups flour
5ml/1 tsp. baking powder	1 tsp. baking powder
3 egg whites	3 egg whites

Preheat the oven to 180°C/350°F, Gas Mark 4.

Cream the butter and sugar together until pale and fluffy. Beat in the vanilla, poppy seeds, half the milk and the sour cream. Sift together the flour, baking powder and 2.5ml/½ teaspoon salt and fold into the creamed mixture. Stir in the remaining milk. Beat the egg whites until stiff and fold into the batter.

Spoon into a greased and floured loose-bottomed 18cm/7in round cake pan (springform pan). Bake for 1¼ to 1½ hours or until a skewer inserted into the centre of the cake comes out clean. Cool on a wire rack.

Strawberry ziggurat

Metric/Imperial	American
7 egg whites	7 egg whites
400g/14oz caster sugar	1¾ cups superfine sugar
600ml/1 pint double cream	2½ cups double cream
60ml/4 tbs. orange liqueur	¼ cup orange liqueur
1kg/2lb strawberries	2lb strawberries

Preheat the oven to 140°C/275°F, Gas Mark 1.

Line three baking sheets with non-stick (parchment) paper. On one draw a 23cm/9in circle, on another a 15cm/6in circle and a 7.5cm/3in circle, and on the third a 19cm/7½in circle and an 11cm/4½in circle.

Beat the egg whites until stiff. And 45ml/3 tablespoons of the sugar and continue beating for 1 minute. Fold in the remaining sugar. Spoon the mixture into a piping bag fitted with a plain nozzle (tube) and pipe within the circles on the paper, filling the circles completely. Bake for 1 hour or until the meringue layers are firm. Cool.

Whip the cream and fold in the liqueur. Peel the meringue layers carefully from the paper. Place the largest circle on a flat serving plate and spread with some of the cream. Cover with strawberries and place the next size meringue circle on top. Continue in this way, ending with the smallest meringue circle. Chill for 30 minutes before serving.

Refrigerator cheesecake

Metric/Imperial	American
14 zwieback or rusks, crushed	*14 zwieback or rusks, crushed*
75g/3oz butter, melted	*6 tbs. butter, melted*
2.5ml/½ tsp. ground allspice	*½ tsp. ground allspice*
3 egg yolks	*3 egg yolks*
75g/3oz caster sugar	*6 tbs. superfine sugar*
20g/¾oz gelatine, softened in	*3 envelopes unflavored gelatin,*
30ml/2 tbs. hot water	*softened in 2 tbs. hot water*
½kg/1lb cream cheese	*2 cups cream cheese*
2.5ml/½ tsp. vanilla essence	*½ tsp. vanilla extract*
10ml/2 tsp. grated lemon rind	*2 tsp. grated lemon rind*
450ml/¾ pint soured cream	*1 pint sour cream*
250g/8oz raspberries	*½lb raspberries*

Mix together the zwieback or rusks, butter and allspice and use to line the bottom of a loose-bottomed 20cm/8in round deep cake pan (springform pan). Chill until set.

Beat the egg yolks and sugar together in a heatproof bowl over hot water. Beat until the mixture is thick and pale, then stir in the gelatine until dissolved. Remove from the heat and gradually beat in the cream cheese. Stir in the vanilla, lemon rind and sour cream.

Spoon the filling into the cake pan and smooth the top. Chill for 1 to 1½ hours or until set. Decorate with the raspberries before serving.

Redcurrant cheesecake

Metric/Imperial	American
250g/8oz digestive biscuits, crushed	2 cups crushed graham crackers
100g/4oz butter, melted	½ cup butter, melted
5ml/1 tsp. ground cinnamon	1 tsp. ground cinnamon
½kg/1lb cream cheese	1lb cream cheese
50g/2oz caster sugar	¼ cup superfine sugar
120ml/4floz single cream	½ cup light cream
625g/1¼lb redcurrants	1¼lb redcurrants
15g/½oz gelatin	2 envelopes unflavored gelatin
30ml/2 tbs. hot water	2 tbs. hot water
450ml/¾ pint double cream	1 pint heavy cream
1 egg white, stiffly beaten	1 egg white, stiffly beaten

Mix together the crushed biscuits (crackers), butter and cinnamon. Press into the bottom of a greased 23cm/9in loose-bottomed cake pan. Chill until set.

Beat the cream cheese and sugar together. Stir in the single (light) cream and ½kg/1lb of the redcurrants. Dissolve the gelatine in the water and add to the redcurrant mixture. Spoon into the pan on top of the crumb crust. Chill until set.

Whip the double (heavy) cream and fold in the egg white.

Remove the cheesecake from the pan. Spoon over the cream mixture and top with the remaining redcurrants.

Italian chocolate cake

Metric/Imperial	American
1 Madeira cake, 23cm/9in long and 7.5cm/3in high	*1 pound cake, 9in long and 3in high*
½kg/1lb ricotta or cottage cheese	*1lb ricotta or cottage cheese*
30ml/2 tbs. double cream	*2 tbs. heavy cream*
50g/2oz sugar	*¼ cup sugar*
30ml/2 tbs. chopped candied peel	*2 tbs. chopped candied peel*
15ml/1 tbs. chopped pistachio nuts	*1 tbs. chopped pistachio nuts*
50g/2oz dark cooking chocolate, grated	*2 squares semi-sweet chocolate, grated*
CHOCOLATE ICING	**CHOCOLATE ICING**
350g/12oz dark cooking chocolate	*12 squares semi-sweet chocolate*
175ml/6fl oz black coffee	*¾ cup black coffee*
250g/8oz unsalted butter	*1 cup unsalted butter*

Cut the cake into four layers. Press the cheese through a strainer and beat until smooth. Beat in the cream and sugar, then fold in the peel, nuts and grated chocolate. Use the cheese mixture to sandwich the cake back together. Wrap the cake in foil and chill for 3 hours.

For the icing (frosting), melt the chocolate with the coffee, then beat in the butter in pieces. Allow to cool until it is thick enough to spread, then use to cover the sides and top of the cake. Chill for 12 hours before serving.

Carrot cake

Metric/Imperial	American
6 eggs, separated	*6 eggs, separated*
250g/8oz sugar	*1 cup sugar*
350g/12oz carrots, cooked and puréed	*¾lb carrots, cooked and puréed*
15ml/1 tbs. grated orange rind	*1 tbs. grated orange rind*
15ml/1 tbs. brandy	*1 tbs. brandy*
350g/12oz ground almonds	*3 cups ground almonds*

Preheat the oven to 170°C/325°F, Gas Mark 3.

Beat the egg yolks and sugar together until pale and thick. Mix in the carrot purée, orange rind, brandy and almonds. Beat the egg whites until stiff and fold in. Spoon into a greased loose-bottomed 23cm/9in round deep cake pan (springform pan).

Bake for 50 minutes or until a skewer inserted into the centre of the cake comes out clean. Cool in the pan for 15 minutes, then turn out onto a wire rack to cool completely.

Christmas gingerbread

Metric/Imperial	American
250g/8oz butter	*1 cup butter*
450ml/¾ pint dark treacle	*1 pint molasses*
250g/8oz sultanas	*1⅓ cups seedless white raisins*
250g/8oz chopped candied peel	*1⅓ cups chopped candied peel*
250g/8oz sugar	*1 cup sugar*
15ml/1 tbs. bicarbonate of soda	*1 tbs. baking soda*
15ml/1 tbs. ground coriander	*1 tbs. ground coriander*
15ml/1 tbs. ground cloves	*1 tbs. ground cloves*
30ml/2 tbs. ground ginger	*2 tbs. ground ginger*
10ml/2 tsp. caraway seeds	*2 tsp. caraway seeds*
550g/1¼lb flour	*5 cups flour*

Preheat the oven to 150°C/300°F, Gas Mark 2.

Heat the butter and treacle (molasses) together until the butter has melted. Mix together the sultanas (raisins), peel, sugar, soda, spices and caraway seeds. Stir in the butter mixture, then sift in the flour and mix thoroughly.

Spoon into a greased and lined 25cm/10in round deep cake pan and smooth the top. Bake for 2¾ to 3 hours or until a skewer inserted into the centre of the gingerbread comes out clean.

Cool in the pan for 5 minutes before turning out onto a wire rack to cool completely.

Chamonix

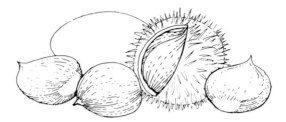

Metric/Imperial	American
4 egg whites	*4 egg whites*
250g/8oz caster sugar	*1 cup superfine sugar*
FILLING	**FILLING**
250ml/8fl oz double cream	*1 cup heavy cream*
60ml/4 tbs. caster sugar	*¼ cup superfine sugar*
1.25ml/¼ tsp. vanilla essence	*¼ tsp. vanilla extract*
30ml/2 tbs. brandy	*2 tbs. brandy*
250g/8oz canned unsweetened chestnut purée	*½lb canned unsweetened chestnut purée*

Preheat the oven to 140°C/275°F, Gas Mark 1.
Beat the egg whites until stiff. Add 20ml/4 teaspoons of the sugar and continue beating for 1 minute. Fold in the remaining sugar. Pipe the meringue in nestlike shells on a baking sheet lined with non-stick (parchment) paper. Each shell should be 5 to 7.5cm/2 to 3in in diameter and 6cm/2½in high with a hollow centre. Bake for 1 hour or until firm. Cool.
For the filling, whip the cream with half the sugar and vanilla until thick. Beat the remaining sugar and brandy into the chestnut purée.
Pipe the chestnut purée mixture around the top of each meringue shell and fill the hollows with the cream mixture. Serve immediately.

SERVES 6

Queen cakes

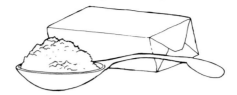

Metric/Imperial	American
75g/3oz currants	*½ cup currants*
175g/6oz flour	*1½ cups flour*
5ml/1 tsp. baking powder	*1 tsp. baking powder*
100g/4oz butter	*½ cup butter*
100g/4oz caster sugar	*½ cup sugar*
2 eggs	*2 eggs*
30ml/2 tbs. milk	*2 tbs. milk*

Preheat the oven to 190°C/375°F, Gas Mark 5.

Divide the currants between 12 greased patty (shallow muffin) tins and arrange them in a ring in the bottoms. Sift together the flour, baking powder and a pinch of salt. Cream the butter with the sugar until pale and fluffy. Beat in the eggs, one at a time, then fold in the flour mixture and milk.

Spoon the batter into the patty (muffin) tins. Bake for 15 to 20 minutes or until the centres of the cakes spring back when lightly pressed with a fingertip. Cool on a wire rack. **MAKES 18**

Fairy cakes

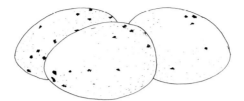

Metric/Imperial	American
100g/4oz butter	*½ cup butter*
100g/4oz sugar	*½ cup sugar*
2 eggs	*2 eggs*
100g/4oz self-raising flour	*1 cup self-rising flour*
2.5ml/½ tsp. vanilla essence	*½ tsp. vanilla extract*
15ml/1 tbs. milk	*1 tbs. milk*
GLACE ICING	**GLACE ICING**
175g/6oz icing sugar	*1½ cups confectioners' sugar*
1.25ml/¼ tsp. lemon flavouring and yellow food colouring, or 15ml/1 tbs. cocoa powder and 1.25ml/¼ tsp. vanilla essence	*¼ tsp. lemon flavoring and yellow food coloring, or 1 tbs. unsweetened cocoa powder and ½ tsp. vanilla extract*
30-45ml/2-3 tbs. warm water	*2-3 tbs. warm water*

Preheat the oven to 190°C/375°F, Gas Mark 5.

Cream the butter and sugar together until pale and fluffy. Beat in the eggs, one at a time, then sift in the flour. Fold in with the vanilla and milk. Divide the batter between 16 paper cases placed on a baking sheet. Bake for 15 to 20 minutes or until golden. Cool on a wire rack. For the icing, sift the sugar into a bowl and beat in the lemon flavouring and food colouring with the warm water, or the cocoa, vanilla and water. The icing should just coat the back of the spoon. Drop enough icing on the top of each cake just to cover and leave until set. **MAKES 16**

Apple muffins

Metric/Imperial	American
250g/8oz flour	*2 cups flour*
10ml/2 tsp. baking powder	*2 tsp. baking powder*
50g/2oz sugar	*¼ cup sugar*
5ml/1 tsp. mixed spice	*1 tsp. apple pie spice*
2 eggs	*2 eggs*
50g/2oz butter, melted	*¼ cup butter, melted*
150ml/¼ pint buttermilk	*¾ cup buttermilk*
15ml/1 tbs. lemon juice	*1 tbs. lemon juice*
2 medium eating apples, peeled, cored and grated	*2 medium eating apples, peeled, cored and grated*

Preheat the oven to 230°C/450°F, Gas Mark 8.

Sift the flour, baking powder, sugar, spice and 2.5ml/½ teaspoon salt into a mixing bowl. In another bowl, beat the eggs together, then beat in the butter, buttermilk and lemon juice. Quickly stir the egg mixture into the flour mixture. Do not overmix. Fold in the apples.

Spoon the batter into a greased 12-cup muffin pan. Bake for 15 to 20 minutes or until a skewer inserted into the centre of a muffin comes out clean. Serve warm or cold. **MAKES 12**

BREADS

Quick bread

Metric/Imperial

15g/½oz fresh yeast
300ml/½ pint lukewarm water
5ml/1 tsp. sugar
350g/12oz flour
100g/4oz wholemeal flour
15ml/1 tbs. cracked wheat

American

½ cake compressed yeast
1½ cups lukewarm water
1 tsp. sugar
3 cups flour
1 cup wholewheat flour
1 tbs. cracked wheat

Cream the yeast with 15ml/1 tablespoon of the water and the sugar and leave in a warm place until frothy. Sift the flours and 5ml/1 teaspoon salt into a mixing bowl. Make a well in the centre and add the yeast mixture and the remaining water. Gradually draw the flours into the liquid and mix until the dough comes away from the sides of the bowl.

Turn the dough out onto a floured surface and knead for 3 minutes. Shape into a loaf and place in a greased ½kg/1lb loaf pan. Cover and leave in a warm place for 1 to 1½ hours or until risen to the top of the pan.

Preheat the oven to 240°C/475°F, Gas Mark 9.

Sprinkle the top of the loaf with the cracked wheat and bake for 15 minutes. Reduce the temperature to 220°C/425°F, Gas Mark 7 and continue baking for 25 to 30 minutes or until the bread sounds hollow when tapped on the bottom. Cool on a wire rack.

MAKES 1 LOAF

Wholemeal (wholewheat) bread

Metric/Imperial	American
100g/4oz strong white flour	*1 cup all-purpose or bread flour*
350g/12oz wholemeal flour	*3 cups wholewheat flour*
300ml/½ pint lukewarm water	*1½ cups lukewarm water*
25g/1oz fresh yeast	*1 cake compressed yeast*
5ml/1 tsp. sugar	*1 tsp. sugar*
25g/1oz butter, cut into pieces	*2 tbs. butter, cut into pieces*

Sift the white flour and 10ml/2 teaspoons salt into a mixing bowl. Stir in the wholemeal (wholewheat) flour. Make a well in the centre and pour in the water. Crumble the yeast on top of the water and sprinkle over the sugar. Dot the pieces of butter around the edge. Leave in a warm place until the yeast is frothy.

Gradually draw the flours into the liquids and mix until the dough comes away from the sides of the bowl. Turn out onto a floured surface and knead until elastic and smooth. Shape into a loaf and place in a greased ½kg/1lb loaf pan. Cover and let rise in a warm place for 20 minutes or until risen to the top of the pan.

Preheat the oven to 200°C/400°F, Gas Mark 6. Bake for 5 minutes, then reduce the temperature to 190°C/375°F, Gas Mark 5 and continue baking for 20 minutes, or until the bread sounds hollow when tapped on the bottom. Cool on a wire rack. **MAKES 1 LOAF**

Wheat germ bread

Metric/Imperial	American
25g/1oz fresh yeast	1 cake compressed yeast
300ml/½ pint lukewarm milk	1½ cups lukewarm milk
5ml/1 tsp. sugar	1 tsp. sugar
450g/1lb barley flour	4 cups barley flour
175g/6oz wholemeal flour	1½ cups wholewheat flour
120ml/8 tbs. wheat germ	¼ cup wheat germ
50g/2oz butter, melted	¼ cup butter, melted
1 egg	1 egg

Cream the yeast with 30ml/2 tablespoons of the milk and the sugar and leave in a warm place until frothy. Put the flours, 30ml/2 tablespoons wheat germ and 5ml/1 teaspoon salt in a mixing bowl. Make a well in the centre and add the yeast mixture, butter, egg and the remaining milk. Gradually draw the flours into the liquids and mix until the dough comes away from the sides of the bowl.

Turn out onto a floured surface and knead until elastic and smooth. Cover and let rise in a warm place for 1 to 1½ hours or until almost doubled in bulk.

Knead for 5 minutes, then shape into a loaf and place in a greased 1kg/2lb loaf pan. Sprinkle over the remaining wheat germ. Let rise again for 30 minutes.

Preheat the oven to 230°C/450°F, Gas Mark 8. Bake for 15 minutes, then reduce the temperature to 220°C/425°F, Gas Mark 7 and continue baking for 25 to 30 minutes, or until the bread sounds hollow when tapped on the bottom. **MAKES 1 LOAF**

Irish soda bread

Metric/Imperial	American
450g/1lb flour	*4 cups flour*
5ml/1 tsp. bicarbonate of soda	*1 tsp. baking soda*
120-250ml/4-8fl oz buttermilk	*½-1 cup buttermilk*

Preheat the oven to 220°C/425°F, Gas Mark 7.

Sift the flour, soda and 5ml/1 teaspoon salt into a mixing bowl. Beat in 120ml/4fl oz (½ cup) buttermilk. The dough should be smooth but firm, so add more buttermilk if necessary.

Turn out onto a floured surface and shape into a round flat loaf, about 4cm/1½in thick and 20cm/8in diameter. Place on a greased baking sheet and cut a deep cross in the top of the loaf.

Bake for 30 to 35 minutes or until the top is golden brown. Cool on the baking sheet and serve warm. **MAKES 1 LOAF**

Lardy cake

Metric/Imperial	American
15g/½oz fresh yeast	*½ cake compressed yeast*
300ml/½ pint lukewarm water	*1½ cups lukewarm water*
5ml/1 tsp. sugar	*1 tsp. sugar*
450g/1lb flour	*4 cups flour*
5ml/1 tsp. vegetable oil	*1 tsp. vegetable oil*
100g/4oz lard, cut into pieces	*½ cup lard, cut into pieces*
50g/2oz sugar	*¼ cup sugar*
2.5ml/½ tsp. ground cinnamon	*½ tsp. ground cinnamon*
2.5ml/½ tsp. grated nutmeg	*½ tsp. grated nutmeg*
2.5ml/½ tsp. ground ginger	*½ tsp. ground ginger*
350g/12oz currants	*2 cups currants*
45ml/3 tbs. sugar dissolved in	*3 tbs. sugar dissolved in 3 tbs.*
45ml/3 tbs. water to glaze	*water to glaze*

Cream the yeast with 15ml/1 tablespoon of the water and sugar and leave in a warm place until frothy. Sift the flour and 5ml/1 teaspoon salt into a mixing bowl. Make a well in the centre and add the yeast mixture, oil and remaining water. Gradually draw the flour into the liquid and mix until the dough comes away from the sides of the bowl.

Turn out onto a floured surface and knead until elastic and smooth. Cover and let rise in a warm place for 1 to 1½ hours or until almost doubled in bulk.

Knead the dough for 10 minutes, then roll it out to an oblong about 5mm/¼in thick. Sprinkle the top two-thirds with half the lard, sugar, spices and currants. Fold into three, turn and roll out again. Repeat the process, then shape into a round and place in a greased 20cm/8in round cake pan. Let rise for 40 to 45 minutes.

Preheat the oven to 200°C/400°F, Gas Mark 6. Bake the cake for 45 minutes, brushing with the glaze ten minutes before the baking time is up. Cool on a wire rack. **MAKES 1 CAKE**

Raisin bread

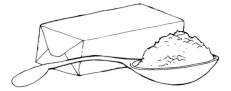

Metric/Imperial	American
20g/¾oz fresh yeast	¾ cake compressed yeast
5ml/1 tsp. sugar	1 tsp. sugar
15ml/1 tbs. lukewarm water	1 tbs. lukewarm water
500ml/16fl oz milk	2½ cups milk
75ml/3fl oz treacle	6 tbs. molasses
175g/6oz butter	¾ cup butter
175g/6oz brown sugar	1 cup brown sugar
350g/12oz Muscatel raisins, soaked in boiling water for 20 minutes and drained	2 cups Muscatel raisins, soaked in boiling water for 20 minutes and drained
450g/1lb wholemeal flour	4 cups wholewheat flour
450g/1lb rye flour	4 cups rye flour

Cream the yeast with the sugar and water and leave in a warm place until frothy. Meanwhile, put the milk and treacle (molasses) in a saucepan and bring to simmering point. Stir in the butter and sugar until dissolved, then remove from the heat. Allow to cool to luke-warm.

Mix together the raisins, flours and 7.5ml/1½ teaspoons salt. Make a well in the centre and add the yeast and milk mixtures. Gradually draw the dry ingredients into the liquid and mix until the dough comes away from the sides of the bowl.

Turn out onto a floured surface and knead until elastic and smooth. Cover and let rise in a warm place for 1½ to 2 hours or until almost doubled in bulk.

Knead vigorously for 4 minutes, then divide in half. Shape each piece into a loaf and place in greased ½kg/1lb loaf pans. Let rise again for 30 to 45 minutes.

Preheat the oven to 240°C/475°F, Gas Mark 9. Bake for 15 minutes, then reduce the temperature to 220°C/425°F, Gas Mark 7 and continue baking for 25 to 30 minutes, or until the loaves sound hollow when tapped on the bottom. **MAKES 2 LOAVES**

German dried fruit bread

Metric/Imperial	American
25g/1oz fresh yeast	*1 cake compressed yeast*
850ml/1 pint 8fl oz lukewarm water	*3½ cups lukewarm water*
5ml/1 tsp. sugar	*1 tsp. sugar*
1⅓kg/3lb flour	*12 cups flour*
2.5ml/½ tsp. ground coriander	*½ tsp. ground coriander*
1.25ml/¼ tsp. ground fennel	*¼ tsp. ground fennel*
pinch of ground cloves	*pinch of ground cloves*
100g/4oz butter, melted	*½ cup butter, melted*
175g/6oz dried fruit (apricots, pears, apples), chopped	*1 cup chopped dried fruit (apricots, pears, apples)*
300g/10oz whole hazelnuts	*2 cups whole hazelnuts*
175g/6oz raisins	*1 cup raisins*
100g/4oz chopped candied peel	*⅔ cup chopped candied peel*

Cream the yeast with 120ml/4fl oz (½ cup) of the water and the sugar and leave in a warm place until frothy. Sift half the flour into a mixing bowl with the spices and 5ml/1 teaspoon salt. Make a well in the centre and add the yeast mixture, remaining water and butter. Gradually draw the flour into the liquid and mix well together.

Sift the remaining flour into another bowl and add the dried fruit, nuts, raisins and peel. Knead this mixture into the dough, then turn out onto a floured surface and knead until the dough is smooth and elastic. Cover and let rise in a warm place for 1 to 1½ hours or until almost doubled in bulk.

Knead the dough for 3 minutes, then divide into three. Shape each piece into a ball and place on greased baking sheets. Let rise again for 30 to 40 minutes.

Preheat the oven to 220°C/425°F, Gas Mark 7. Bake the bread for 15 minutes, then reduce the temperature to 190°C/375°F, Gas Mark 5 and continue baking for 30 minutes, or until the bread sounds hollow when tapped on the bottom. **MAKES 3 LOAVES**

Bremer kuchen

Metric/Imperial	American
50g/2oz fresh yeast	2 cakes compressed yeast
10ml/2 tsp. sugar	2 tsp. sugar
120ml/4fl oz lukewarm water	½ cup lukewarm water
775ml/1 pint 6fl oz milk	3¼ cups milk
100g/4oz butter	½ cup butter
1⅓kg/3lb flour	12 cups flour
100g/4oz sugar	½ cup sugar
2.5ml/½ tsp. ground cardamom	½ tsp. ground cardamom
grated rind of 3 lemons	grated rind of 3 lemons
175g/6oz raisins	1 cup raisins
100g/4oz currants	⅔ cup currants
100g/4oz slivered almonds	1 cup slivered almonds

Cream the yeast with 10ml/2 teaspoons sugar and the water and leave in a warm place until frothy. Meanwhile, heat the milk and butter together until the butter has melted. Allow to cool to lukewarm. Sift the flour, sugar, cardamom and 5ml/1 teaspoon salt into a mixing bowl. Stir in the lemon rind. Make a well in the centre and add the yeast and milk mixtures. Gradually draw the dry ingredients into the liquid and mix until the dough comes away from the sides of the bowl. Turn out onto a floured surface and knead until elastic and smooth. Cover and let rise in a warm place for 1 to 1½ hours or until almost doubled in bulk.

Knead the dough for 2 minutes, then knead in the fruit and half the nuts. Divide the dough in half and shape each piece into a long loaf. Place on greased baking sheets and let them rise again for 30 to 45 minutes.

Preheat the oven to 190°C/375°F, Gas Mark 5. Press the remaining almonds into the tops of the loaves and bake for 1 hour or until the loaves sound hollow when tapped on the bottom. Brush the tops with melted butter or dust with icing (confectioners') sugar and allow to cool. **MAKES 2 LOAVES**

Spice loaf

Metric/Imperial	American
350g/12oz flour	*3 cups flour*
7.5ml/1½ tsp. bicarbonate of soda	*1½ tsp. baking soda*
2.5ml/½ tsp. ground cinnamon	*½ tsp. ground cinnamon*
2.5ml/½ tsp. ground cloves	*½ tsp. ground cloves*
2.5ml/½ tsp. grated nutmeg	*½ tsp. grated nutmeg*
5ml/1 tsp. ground ginger	*1 tsp. ground ginger*
75g/3oz raisins	*½ cup raisins*
60ml/4 tbs. black treacle	*¼ cup molasses*
50g/2oz butter	*¼ cup butter*
3 eggs	*3 eggs*
60ml/4 tbs. milk	*½ cup milk*

Preheat the oven to 170°C/325°F, Gas Mark 3.
Sift the flour, soda, spices and a large pinch of salt into a mixing bowl.
Stir in the raisins. Heat the treacle (molasses) and butter together until the butter has melted, then add to the dry ingredients with the eggs and milk. Mix together to make a soft dough.
Spoon into a greased 1kg/2lb loaf pan and bake for 1¼ hours or until a skewer inserted into the centre of the loaf comes out clean. Cool on a wire rack. **MAKES 1 LOAF**

Banana bread

Metric/Imperial

175g/6oz flour
50g/2oz rice flour
7.5ml/1½ tsp. baking powder
2.5ml/½ tsp. ground ginger
pinch of ground allspice
100g/4oz soft brown sugar
30ml/2 tbs. ground almonds
100g/4oz butter, melted
3 eggs
grated rind of 1 lemon
4 bananas, mashed

American

1½ cups flour
½ cup rice flour
1½ tsp. baking powder
½ tsp. ground ginger
pinch of ground allspice
⅔ cup dark brown sugar
2 tbs. ground almonds
½ cup butter, melted
3 eggs
grated rind of 1 lemon
4 bananas, mashed

Preheat the oven to 180°C/350°F, Gas Mark 4.
Sift the flours, baking powder, spices and sugar into a mixing bowl.
Stir in the ground almonds. Mix together the butter, eggs and lemon
rind and stir into the dry ingredients. Beat in the bananas.
Spoon into a greased ½kg/1lb loaf pan. Bake for 1 hour or until a
skewer inserted into the centre of the bread comes out clean.
Cool in the pan for 5 minutes before turning out onto a wire rack to
cool completely. **MAKES 1 LOAF**

Doughnuts

Metric/Imperial	American
250g/8oz flour	2 cups flour
10ml/2 tsp. baking powder	2 tsp. baking powder
100g/4oz sugar	½ cup sugar
1.25ml/¼ tsp. grated nutmeg	¼ tsp. grated nutmeg
40g/1½oz butter, melted	3 tbs. butter, melted
1 egg, beaten	1 egg, beaten
75ml/3fl oz milk	6 tbs. milk
oil for deep frying	oil for deep frying

Sift the flour, baking powder, half the sugar, the nutmeg and 2.5ml/½ teaspoon salt into a mixing bowl. Beat in the butter and egg, then half the milk. Gradually beat in the remaining milk to make a smooth but firm dough. Chill for 15 minutes.

Roll out the dough to about 1cm/½in thick. Cut into 7.5cm/3in circles and cut out the centres to make rings. Leave for 10 minutes, then deep fry in oil heated to 190°C/375°F, for about 5 minutes or until golden brown. Drain the doughnuts on paper towels and sprinkle with the remaining sugar.

Note: the doughnuts may be shaped into balls, if you prefer.

MAKES 10-12

Herb bread crisp

Metric/Imperial	American
75g/3oz butter	*6 tbs. butter*
5ml/1 tsp. lemon juice	*1 tsp. lemon juice*
2.5ml/½ tsp. dried chervil	*½ tsp. dried chervil*
2.5ml/½ tsp. dried tarragon	*½ tsp. dried tarragon*
1.25ml/¼ tsp. dried thyme	*¼ tsp. dried thyme*
2.5ml/½ tsp. chopped chives	*½ tsp. chopped chives*
2.5ml/½ tsp. chopped parsley	*½ tsp. chopped parsley*
1 garlic clove, crushed	*1 garlic clove, crushed*
6 slices of bread	*6 slices of bread*

Preheat the oven to 180°C/350°F, Gas Mark 4.
Mix together the butter, lemon juice, herbs and garlic. Spread this mixture on the bread slices and cut each slice in half diagonally. Place on a baking sheet and bake for 20 minutes or until the bread is golden brown and crisp. Serve hot. **SERVES 4-6**

BISCUITS (COOKIES)

Pecan bars

Metric/Imperial	American
100g/4oz butter	*½ cup butter*
250g/8oz sugar	*1 cup sugar*
1 egg	*1 egg*
175g/6oz flour	*1½ cups flour*
20ml/4 tsp. coffee essence	*4 tsp. strong black coffee*
250g/8oz pecans, chopped	*2 cups chopped pecans*
3 egg whites	*3 egg whites*

Preheat the oven to 180°C/350°F, Gas Mark 4.

Cream the butter and one-quarter of the sugar together until pale and fluffy. Beat in the egg. Sift in the flour, then fold in. Mix in the coffee essence (strong black coffee). Spoon into a greased 18 x 27cm/7 x 11in baking pan and smooth the top. Bake for 15 minutes.

Meanwhile, mix together the pecans, egg whites and remaining sugar in a saucepan. Heat gently, stirring to dissolve the sugar, then continue cooking for 6 to 8 minutes or until the mixture leaves the sides of the pan. Spread the pecan mixture over the biscuit (cookie) base in the baking pan. Return to the oven and continue baking for 15 minutes.

Cool, then cut into bars.   **MAKES ABOUT 28**

Marshmallow squares

Metric/Imperial	American
175g/6oz butter	*¾ cup butter*
75g/3oz sugar	*6 tbs. sugar*
2.5ml/½ tsp. vanilla essence	*½ tsp. vanilla extract*
175g/6oz flour	*1½ cups flour*
24 large marshmallows	*24 large marshmallows*
75ml/3fl oz milk	*6 tbs. milk*
75g/3oz almonds, chopped	*¾ cup chopped almonds*
75g/3oz glacé cherries, chopped	*½ cup chopped candied cherries*

Preheat the oven to 170°C/325°F, Gas Mark 3.

Cream the butter and sugar together until pale and fluffy. Beat in the vanilla, then sift in the flour and fold in. If the mixture is too dry, add a little water. Spoon into a 20cm/8in square cake pan. Bake for 20 to 25 minutes or until golden brown. Cool.

Melt the marshmallows in the milk gently. Remove from the heat and fold in the almonds and cherries. Spoon into the cake pan over the biscuit (cookie) base and smooth the top. Leave to cool and set before cutting into squares. **MAKES ABOUT 32**

Mallow brownies

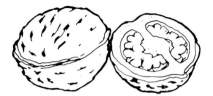

Metric/Imperial	American
75g/3oz flour	*¾ cup flour*
5ml/1 tsp. baking powder	*1 tsp. baking powder*
425g/15oz soft brown sugar	*2½ cups dark brown sugar*
2 egg yolks	*2 egg yolks*
10ml/2 tsp. vanilla essence	*2 tsp. vanilla extract*
150g/5oz butter, melted	*⅔ cup butter, melted*
75g/3oz walnuts, chopped	*¾ cup chopped walnuts*
20 large marshmallows	*20 large marshmallows*
75ml/3fl oz single cream	*6 tbs. light cream*

Preheat the oven to 180°C/350°F, Gas Mark 4.

Sift together the flour, baking powder and 1.25ml/¼ teaspoon salt. Mix together 175g/6oz (1 cup) of the sugar, the egg yolks and half the vanilla. Beat in 75g/3oz (6 tablespoons) of the butter, then fold in the flour mixture. Stir in the walnuts.

Spoon the mixture into a greased and floured 20cm/8in square cake pan. Bake for 30 minutes. Cool.

Melt the marshmallows gently, then pour over the top of the cake.

Put the remaining sugar and butter, the cream and 1.25ml/¼ teaspoon salt in a saucepan and bring to the boil. Boil until the mixture registers 120°C/240°F on a sugar thermometer, or until a little dropped into cold water forms a soft ball. Remove from the heat and cool for 4 minutes, then beat in the remaining vanilla. Continue beating until thick and creamy. Pour over the marshmallow topping and allow to cool completely before cutting into squares. **MAKES 16**

Melting moments

Metric/Imperial	American
100g/4oz butter	*½ cup butter*
100g/4oz vegetable fat	*½ cup shortening*
175g/6oz sugar	*¾ cup sugar*
1 egg	*1 egg*
300g/10oz flour	*2½ cups flour*
5ml/1 tsp. baking powder	*1 tsp. baking powder*
60ml/4 tbs. rolled oats	*¼ cup rolled oats*

Cream the butter, fat (shortening) and sugar together until pale and fluffy. Beat in the egg, then sift in the flour and baking powder and fold in.

Divide the dough into 18 portions and roll each into a ball. Coat the balls in the rolled oats and place, well spaced apart, on baking sheets. Slightly flatten each ball with the prongs of a fork. Chill for 30 minutes.

Preheat the oven to 180°C/350°F, Gas Mark 4. Bake for 20 to 25 minutes or until golden brown. Cool on a wire rack. **MAKES 18**

Shortbread

Metric/Imperial	American
250g/8oz flour	*2 cups flour*
100g/4oz rice flour	*1 cup rice flour*
100g/4oz plus 15ml/1 tbs. caster sugar	*½ cup plus 1 tbs. superfine sugar*
250g/8oz butter	*1 cup butter*

Sift the flour and rice flour into a mixing bowl. Stir in 100g/4oz (½ cup) of the sugar. Rub in the butter until the mixture resembles breadcrumbs. Knead gently to form a smooth dough. Divide the dough in half and shape each piece into a circle about 1cm/½in thick and 15cm/6in in diameter. Place the circles on a baking sheet and prick the tops. Chill for 20 minutes.

Preheat the oven to 180°C/350°F, Gas Mark 4.

Bake the shortbread for 10 minutes, then reduce the temperature to 150°C/300°F, Gas Mark 2 and continue baking for 30 to 40 minutes or until crisp and lightly browned.

Mark the circles into wedges. Allow to cool slightly, then sprinkle over the remaining sugar. Cool on a wire rack.   **MAKES 2**

Nutty chocolate chip cookies

Metric/Imperial	American
100g/4oz butter	½ cup butter
50g/2oz soft brown sugar	⅓ cup dark brown sugar
250g/8oz flour	2 cups flour
30ml/2 tbs. golden syrup	2 tbs. light corn syrup
75g/3oz almonds, chopped	¾ cup chopped almonds
60ml/4 tbs. chocolate dots	¼ cup chocolate chips

Preheat the oven to 180°C/350°F, Gas Mark 4.

Cream the butter and sugar together until fluffy. Sift in the flour and fold in, then mix in the syrup, almonds and chocolate dots (chips).

Form the mixture into walnut-sized balls and place them, well spaced apart, on greased baking sheets. Slightly flatten each ball with the prongs of a fork.

Bake for 15 to 20 minutes or until golden brown. Cool on a wire rack.   **MAKES 24**

Ginger & cream wafers

Metric/Imperial	American
100g/4oz butter	*½ cup butter*
50g/2oz caster sugar	*¼ cup superfine sugar*
50g/2oz light brown sugar	*⅓ cup light brown sugar*
30ml/2 tbs. black treacle	*2 tbs. molasses*
15ml/1 tbs. clear honey	*1 tbs. clear honey*
1 egg	*1 egg*
350g/12oz flour	*3 cups flour*
7.5ml/1½ tsp. ground ginger	*1½ tsp. ground ginger*
FILLING	**FILLING**
300ml/½ pint double cream	*1¼ cups heavy cream*
5ml/1 tsp. grated lemon rind	*1 tsp. grated lemon rind*
15ml/1 tbs. sugar	*1 tbs. sugar*

Cream the butter and sugars together until fluffy. Stir in the treacle (molasses) and honey, then beat in the egg. Sift over the flour and ginger and fold in. Mix well to a dough, then chill for 30 minutes.

Preheat the oven to 180°C/350°F, Gas Mark 4.

Roll out the dough very thinly and cut into 6cm/2½in circles. Place the circles on greased baking sheets and bake for 10 to 12 minutes or until firm. Cool on a wire rack.

For the filling, whip the cream with the lemon rind and sugar until thick. Use to sandwich together pairs of wafers. **MAKES 36**

Peppermint clouds

Metric/Imperial	American
250g/8oz caster sugar	*1 cup superfine sugar*
4 eggs	*4 eggs*
6 drops peppermint essence	*6 drops peppermint extract*
175g/6oz flour	*1½ cups flour*

Preheat the oven to 180°C/350°F, Gas Mark 4.
Spread the sugar out on a baking sheet and bake for 5 minutes.
Remove from the oven and increase the temperature to 200°C/400°F,
Gas Mark 6.
Pour the sugar into a mixing bowl and add the eggs. Beat together
until pale. Stir in the peppermint, then sift over the flour and fold in.
Drop large spoonsful of the mixture onto greased baking sheets, well
spaced apart. Bake for 15 to 20 minutes or until light golden brown.
Cool on a wire rack.   **MAKES ABOUT 36**

Hazelnut macaroons

Metric/Imperial	American
3 egg whites	*3 egg whites*
250g/8oz sugar	*1 cup sugar*
175g/6oz ground hazelnuts	*1½ cups ground hazelnuts*
5ml/1 tsp. vanilla essence	*1 tsp. vanilla extract*
5ml/1 tsp. grated lemon rind	*1 tsp. grated lemon rind*

Beat the egg whites until frothy. Gradually beat in the sugar and continue beating until the mixture is stiff. Fold in the hazelnuts, vanilla and lemon rind. Drop heaped spoonsful of the mixture onto a baking sheet lined with non-stick (parchment) paper, leaving about 2.5cm/1in space around each. Leave for 1½ hours.
Preheat the oven to 180°C/350°F, Gas Mark 4. Bake for 15 minutes or until firm. Cool on the baking sheet. **MAKES 20**

Oatmeal cookies

Metric/Imperial	American
75g/3oz butter	6 tbs. butter
250g/8oz plus 45ml/3 tbs. soft brown sugar	1⅓ cups plus 3 tbs. dark brown sugar
2 eggs	2 eggs
1 egg yolk	1 egg yolk
5ml/1 tsp. vanilla essence	1 tsp. vanilla extract
175g/6oz flour	1½ cups flour
2.5ml/½ tsp. baking powder	½ tsp. baking powder
175g/6oz oatmeal, soaked in 60ml/4 tbs. milk	1½ cups oatmeal, soaked in ¼ cup milk

Preheat the oven to 180°C/350°F, Gas Mark 4.
Cream the butter and 250g/8oz (1⅓ cups) of the sugar together until fluffy. Beat in the eggs, egg yolk and vanilla. Sift over the flour, baking powder and 2.5ml/½ teaspoon salt and fold in. Fold in the oatmeal.
Drop spoonsful of the mixture onto greased baking sheets, well spaced apart. Sprinkle over the remaining sugar. Bake for 10 to 12 minutes or until golden brown. Cool on a wire rack. **MAKES ABOUT 25**

Chocolate fudge

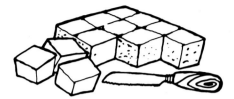

Metric/Imperial	American
450g/1lb sugar	*2 cups sugar*
150ml/¼ pint milk	*⅔ cup milk*
50g/2oz dark cooking chocolate	*2 squares semi-sweet chocolate*
50g/2oz butter	*¼ cup butter*

Put the sugar, milk and chocolate in a saucepan and heat gently until the sugar has dissolved and the chocolate melted. Bring to the boil and boil until the mixture registers 120°C/240°F on a sugar thermometer, or until a little dropped into cold water forms a soft ball. Remove from the heat and leave for 5 minutes.

Beat in the butter in small pieces. Pour the fudge into a greased 20cm/8in square cake pan and allow to cool before marking into squares. Cool completely. **MAKES ABOUT 48**

INDEX

PICTURE CREDITS